Ratio Legis

Verena Klappstein • Maciej Dybowski
Editors

Ratio Legis

Philosophical and Theoretical Perspectives

Springer

Editors
Verena Klappstein
Faculty of Law, Department for German and European Private Law, Civil Procedural Law, and Legal Theory of Prof. Dr. Thomas Riehm
University of Passau
Passau, Germany

Maciej Dybowski
Department of Legal Theory and Philosophy
Adam Mickiewicz University in Poznań
Poznań, Poland

ISBN 978-3-030-08951-1 ISBN 978-3-319-74271-7 (eBook)
https://doi.org/10.1007/978-3-319-74271-7

Printed on acid-free paper

This Springer imprint is published by the registered company Springer International Publishing AG part of Springer Nature.
The registered company address is: Gewerbestrasse 11, 6330 Cham, Switzerland

Introduction

During the XXVIII World Congress of the IVR in Lisbon, 16–21 July 2017, with the theme 'Peace Based on Human Rights', a special workshop was held with the title **'Is There a *Ratio Legis* and if So, How Many Are There? – The Most Powerful Method of Legal Reasoning Uncovered'**. If you are German speaking, you will know that the title is inspired by *Richard David Precht's* well-known book *Wer bin ich und wenn ja wie viele* (Who am I, and if so, how many). In fact, *ratio legis* is such a kaleidoscope of different meanings and aspects of possible research topics, such as reason and rationality, legal interpretation and argumentation, as well as legistics and legislation.

Within the method of legal interpretation and legal reasoning, both being the most important of intellectual tools deployed by lawyers, *ratio legis* seems to be an extremely powerful argument. Declaring the *ratio legis* of a statute can lead to a U-turn argumentation throughout the lifespan of the statute itself—in parliament, in practice during court sessions, when it is tested against the constitution. Though the argument from *ratio legis* is used widely, much about it remains to be examined. On the general philosophical plan, there are many overlapping areas, which concern different approaches to human rationality and to the problems of practical reasoning. Particular problems with *ratio legis* arise in the field of different accounts of legal philosophy and theory, especially as far as methods of intellectual work of lawyers, with legal interpretation and argumentation in the first place, are concerned. These problems can be further subdivided into particular aspects of activities undertaken by lawyers and officials who use the *ratio legis* in their work and underlying theories.

Setting off from scepticism regarding the actual content of the term *ratio legis* and a connected 'argument from *ratio legis*', *Adam Dyrda* is interested in the use of such an argument as a 'legislative' action within the boundaries of practical legal discourse. The list of platitudes about *ratio legis* leads *Dyrda* to noting the unrestricted use of the term, which renders impossible a descriptive theoretical account of the concept in legal discourse. The author concludes that it is much easier to construe *ratio legis* as a normative argument, as long as any hope for revealing some general concept of *ratio legis* is abandoned. *Dyrda* observes that every instance of labelling (whereby it is claimed that 'The *ratio legis* of this legislative act is X') is in need of further justification.

Marzena Kordela's account of *ratio legis* as a binding legal value offers a perspective on the axiological assumptions ascribed to the rational legislator whose preferences are characterised by her as definite, hierarchically ordered and formed into a relatively stable system. The author categorises rational legislator's values as legally binding values or extra-legal reference values or values of a universal character that nonetheless belong to a given legal culture. Adopting this analytical framework leads *Kordela*, first, to qualifying *ratio legis* as a value, and moreover a legally binding one, and, second, to developing ordering criteria for such *rationes* that can be used when law is being applied. Among such criteria, she elaborates the degree of a purpose's generalisation and the legal power of a purpose, corresponding to the hierarchy of normative sources in a given legal system.

Maciej Dybowski's article explores the relationship between *ratio legis* and practical reasoning, adopting as a point of departure the claim that conflicting accounts of *ratio legis* are predominantly concerned with legal interpretation, at the expense of practical reasoning. The author establishes connection between such accounts and one-sided semantics. *Dybowski* identifies three types of one-sided semantics and examines how they translate into respective accounts of legal interpretation and *ratio legis*. This is followed by an alternative account based on *Brandom's* inferential pragmatism, and a merger of semantics and practical reasoning in legal theory is developed. In the final part of the chapter, the author tests the usefulness of inferential pragmatism in legal theory with regard to the problem of *ratio legis* and extends an inferentialist account provided by *Canale* and *Tuzet* by a model of agent's actions and reasons and an analysis of their impact on the reasoning of interpreters and decision-makers.

While remaining within the methodological framework of the same 'derivational' conception of legal interpretation, *Michał Krotoszyński* points out an ontological gap between the rational lawmaker, as an ideal type, and actual legislators. This observation leads him to clarifying the use of legislative history involving *ratio legis* in the above-mentioned paradigm of legal interpretation and to setting the conditions under which legislative history can be deployed. *Krotoszyński* thus provides a useful check for admissible reliance on legislative history where he includes public availability, antecedent accessibility of all legislative materials to the members of the legislative body and a sufficient degree of straightforwardness.

Verena Klappstein explores the problem of *ratio legis* from a perspective of the influence exercised in the moral philosophy of *Imanuel Kant* on modern European legal systems. She investigates the question whether Kant's concept of purpose could have any impact on the modern discourse of *ratio legis*, broadly understood as legal consequence and purpose of a legal rule. The author proceeds by explaining different aspects of purpose in connection with, respectively, hypothetical, categorical and legal categorical imperative. She also offers an account of classes of duties. *Klappstein's* article provides an analytic *Kantian* framework, which can serve to clarify our discussion and understanding of purposes, and as such it can be adapted to *ratio legis*.

In his chapter, *Nonconsequential Conception of Neutrality*, *Wojciech Ciszewski* deals with the question of what it means for a state to be neutral. The consequential conception of state neutrality requires that political actions equally influence different conceptions of the good held by citizens in a given society. The non-consequential conception, which points to some understanding of the rationale (or *ratio legis*) of an action, depends on some aspect of a political action, other than the effects that it causes. *Ciszewski* broadens our understanding of *ratio legis* by offering a classification of non-consequential conceptions of neutrality, understood as a general standard that forbids state officials from recognising and promoting certain conceptions of the good. The justificatory neutrality points to the best available justification of an action, the intentional neutrality indicates the motive behind political agency and the expressive neutrality focuses on how the observers perceive an action. The lesson for establishing the content of state neutrality, which he draws from the above classification, is that such content should be applicable to individual cases, action guiding and intuitively plausible. Seen from this perspective, probably any *ratio legis* can be scrutinised by an anti-perfectionist (and non-consequentialist) with regard to these criteria, in order to test its content.

Teresa Chirkowska-Smolak and *Marek Smolak* discuss the problem of imitative *ratio legis*, which they define as the purpose of the legislator who does not intend for his activity to produce effects other than mere conviction among the addressees that certain social problems have been ostensibly solved. Adopting as their point of departure the thesis that such ostensibility is inadmissible, at least in the rule of law tradition, the authors discuss three types of reasons in support of such a belief, which can be found in the philosophy of law. However, as they reveal, all of these reasons are based on certain assumptions concerning the existence of some kind of a conventional-normative community of judges based on mutually shared moral judgements and rationality. *Chirkowska-Smolak* and *Smolak* explain why judges' moral reasoning cannot be characterised as rational and provide an extensive support for this from the field of experimental moral psychology. Following *Ron den Otter*, the authors argue for inadmissibility of imitative *ratio legis* from the perspective based on public reasons. The arguments that they find plausible for refusing the ostensibility refer to reasons that could not be rationally questioned or challenged by any reasonable sceptic, in which the latter would bear witness to his or her own responsibility for the community of citizens.

Konstanze von Schütz examines the notion of *ratio legis* as encountered in the context of legal interpretation. She observes critically that prevalent approaches conceive of *ratio legis* as belonging to externally determined purposes that posited legal norms seek to achieve. *Schütz* believes that under such approaches, law is ultimately seen as deprived of any rationality at all and offers an alternative idea of immanently rational law, inspired by the formalist theory of *Ernest J. Weinrib*. Her account of this 'Formalist' conception of law, focusing on legal forms, coherence, law's immanent rationality and immanent intelligibility, provides the necessary basis from which she further develops the idea of an immanent *ratio legis*, paying particular attention to legal interpretation.

Mikołaj Hermann's chapter discusses the influence of *ratio legis* on the result of the interpretation process and seeks to determine the relation between the purposive (teleological) and linguistic or systemic rules of interpretation. His approach is rooted in the so-called derivational conception of legal interpretation based on a distinction between a legal provision and a legal norm. Following the tradition of Poznań school of legal theory, *Hermann* associates *ratio legis* with the lawmaker's purpose of establishing a specific regulation. Such a purpose can be understood instrumentally—as the configuration of social relations that should be achieved through such a regulation—or axiologically—as the value that a given regulation serves to protect or actualise. The author shows how the purposive rules affect the result of an interpretation in each of its phases, which sheds the light on the non-linear character of the process of interpretation. In particular, *Hermann* analyses the impact of *ratio legis* on the settlement of the competition of legal provision, as well as the possible impact on the interpretive results obtained through the linguistic interpretation.

The following articles might shed some—colourful—light at the kaleidoscopic term of *ratio legis*; however, many more of the different aspects still need to be further explored.

Passau, Germany Verena Klappstein
Poznań, Poland Maciej Dybowski

Contents

Part I What Is *Ratio Legis*?

The Real *Ratio Legis* and Where to Find It 3
Adam Dyrda

***Ratio Legis* as a Binding Legal Value** 19
Marzena Kordela

Articulating *Ratio Legis* and Practical Reasoning 29
Maciej Dybowski

Legislative History, Ratio Legis, and the Concept of the Rational Legislator 57
Michał Krotoszyński

Part II What Can *Ratio Legis* Be?

The Concept of Purpose in *Kant's* Metaphysical Elements of Justice . . . 77
Verena Klappstein

Nonconsequential Conception of Neutrality 119
Wojciech Ciszewski

Is There an Imitative *Ratio Legis*, and if so, How Many Are There? Psychological Perspective 137
Teresa Chirkowska-Smolak and Marek Smolak

Part III What Practical Implications Can *Ratio Legis* Have?

Immanent *Ratio Legis*? Legal Forms and Statutory Interpretation 161
Konstanze von Schütz

How Can *Ratio Legis* Help a Lawyer to Interpret a Legal Text? Employing the Purpose of a Regulation for Legal Interpretation 187
Mikołaj Hermann

Part I
What Is *Ratio Legis*?

The Real *Ratio Legis* and Where to Find It

A Few Pragmatic Considerations

Adam Dyrda

Abstract The term *ratio legis* is an important term of legal practice. Thus, reflection over the general conceptual content of *ratio legis* may be a window through which practitioners could see the relevance of philosophizing about terms and arguments applied generally in legal practice. However, the primary question with regard to *ratio legis* is not conceptual but existential: is there any *real ratio legis* that can be discovered and described? The positive answer opens the door for further investigation over the term's *real* conceptual content. I will argue, however, that the answer to this question cannot be positive and every qualification of something as the "law's reason" is a creative activity. If it is so, then every instance of such a labeling (in which one says, "The *ratio legis* of this legislative act is X") is in need of further justification. The example of *ratio legis* shows that legal theorizing is profoundly a normative study of how we *should*, rather than of how we *do*, use legal terms (concepts).

1 When Practitioners Should Think About Concepts and Why

Legal practitioners have a strong proclivity to discriminate between practical legal matters and philosophical, unpractical speculation about law that is irrelevant to the resolution of the case at hand. There is a general intuition that law need not be infused with philosophical speculation, and even legal-theoretical reflections, not to mention ordinary court discourse, should be as "aphilosophical" as possible.[1] Although it is, I think, obvious for any legal philosopher (or just any philosopher)

This chapter was written as a result of a research project No. 2016/21/D/HS5/03839, financed by the Polish National Science Centre.

[1]See Wróblewski (1966).

A. Dyrda (✉)
Jagiellonian University, Department of Legal Theory, Krakow, Poland
e-mail: adam.dyrda@uj.edu.pl

V. Klappstein, M. Dybowski (eds.), *Ratio Legis*,
https://doi.org/10.1007/978-3-319-74271-7_1

that we cannot dispense with substantial philosophical assumptions while talking about any object (whether we talk about abstract objects like classes, physical objects like electrons, social objects like groups, or institutional objects like "Supreme Court"), many practitioners in law think that they need not indulge in philosophical thinking while resolving the case.

There are at least a couple of arguments that support this kind of attitude. To my mind, the most important argument is that even if one recognizes the general importance of philosophical questions, one can plausibly claim that there is no place for asking and answering them in situations where one has to decide *practically* what to do (or what one should do). People who embrace such a position are usually aware that there are many philosophical theories of law (as well as different legal institutions), but—as they say—in a stabilized legal system of—let it be so—a liberal democracy, in a majority of cases different legal theories (positivistic, nonpositivistic, etc.) usually lead to the same results or have the same practical implications. This means that philosophy serves practical needs only in situations of crisis but not in ordinary, "easy" cases. From this point of view, the famous Dworkininan *dictum* that "jurisprudence is a general part of adjudication, [the] silent prologue to any decision at law"[2] is accepted but with certain limitations: first, there are easy cases that are philosophically (jurisprudentially) underdetermined in the sense that it does not really matter whether the judge is a positivist or a nonpositivist because in either circumstance, he or she will decide the case in the same manner; second, Dworkin's later idea of making every easy case a hard one is itself hardly practical. Why should one engage in philosophical speculation if there is no real need to do it? Why should one scrutinize the assumptions about law that are tacitly agreed by the participants of the dispute if there is general agreement about their validity?

The described view seems to be convincing. As far as I can see, one can understand the "philosophical circumstances" of legal discourse in a majority of cases as "incompletely theorized."[3] That is why the same cases usually serve as a basis for philosophizing about law in general.[4] Different legal philosophers draw different conclusions about what the law is and how it (should) function, referring to the same or at least comparable "evidence." The point is that from incompletely theorized (or philosophized) circumstances of legal action (manifested in practical resolution of legal cases), many equally good, systematic accounts of law (and related concepts) can be inferred. Moreover, that account does justice to the division of labor: philosophers analyze and develop the main concepts, and practitioners use these concepts in practice. If, however, there is a great disagreement among legal philosophers and, simultaneously, a great agreement among practitioners of law, that means that differing philosophical opinions do not really matter practically.

[2]See Dworkin (1986), p. 90.

[3]See Sunstein (1995).

[4]Cf. Scheppele (1990) and Leiter (2007).

There is, however, one consideration that puts the account described above at risk (and it is irrelevant whether we think about concepts from the domain of law or any other domain), for one can never know whether the ostensible agreement among the practitioners is a real agreement about the concept (but not about the particular philosophical conception) or whether it is merely an agreement in terms (or in the use of a term), when in fact everyone ascribes a very different meaning to it. In the second situation, it would be unlikely to think that all practitioners refer to the same concept, unless we think of such a concept as operating on the highest possible level of philosophical abstraction. And such abstract entities are much too philosophical for practitioners to accept. Because there would be no common meaning ascribed to the term used, practitioners will in fact be talking past one another.

On the other hand, the first possibility relies on the assumption that the discrimination between concepts and conceptions is plausible and can be categorically drawn. There are different versions of such discrimination, with roots in philosophical enterprises of classical pragmatists and later Wittgenstein, which have been influentially developed by analytical (J. Rawls, W.B. Gallie), behavioral, or, more recently, cognitivistic accounts in the philosophy of language. Without digging into details, it may generally be said that all we get from such accounts is a hope for giving better or worse descriptions of the significant resemblances of contents of propositional attitudes or mental contents that can be described as instances of the same "concept"[5] (what is actually a descriptive matter). However, once we describe some propositional content as falling under a certain concept (where "propositional content" and "concept" do not necessarily have a platonic sense of being abstract and mind independent), we can always ask two normative questions, which are connected with the so-called Hume's predicament[6]: (1) how should we generalize our observations or particular descriptions in order to get a universal statement about the criteria of adequate conceptual use (applicable to further circumstances), and (2) why should we use this rather than that description of conceptual content? It is because it seems obvious that what is and what ought to be done are two different things, although we cannot help answering descriptive questions without giving reasons (justification) for choosing rather than giving (descriptive) answers. It seems, then, that we cannot describe anything, even on the most general level, without assuming some method of description that is in fact a method of labeling some language uses, namely deciding whether they fall under the same term (label)

---

[5]See Johnston and Leslie (2012).

[6]"Hume's predicament" is an idea of D. Hume that the stock of our instinctive beliefs about the world is in fact rationally indefensible, because every scientific reconstruction (system) that we try to present cannot be rationally defended, simply because the construction of the system by the human mind relies not on the observation and experiment, but rather—to a great extent—on different types of inferences (mainly "causal" in character). In consequence, we can never be sure whether the "systematic" knowledge about a certain supposed object is any knowledge at all (because, inter alia, even the existence of such an object cannot be rationally acceptable). In our case, we ask whether certain concepts exist and what their contents are. But how can we *rationally* do so? (For a further discussion of Hume's predicament, see for example Aune 1991, p. 177).

that is supposed to refer to the concept in question. And we can always ask why we should use this method and whether there are no better methods available.

All of the considerations above support the view that philosophical reflection is simply a study of how we *use* and how we *should use* language in different types of argumentative practice.[7] Even if we can describe some linguistic practice and determine the scope or content of concepts used in certain types of practice (let it be even on a general, incompletely theorized level), we are always left with a twofold question about justification: (1) the question of justification of the given description and (2) the question of justification of any further use of the term as referring to the same concept.

Usually, in practical discourse, answers to these types of normative questions come for free. Such normative assumptions are treated as fundamental in our culturally determined webs of belief. As a great holistic pragmatist, M. White, once wrote:

> Philosophers and ordinary human beings always begin their thinking by accepting a set of sentences, statements, or beliefs that are terminal in the sense of being pinned down at that moment, statements to which we are prepared to stake a great deal at that moment without considering their "consequences", logical or psychological. These statements are not only accepted by us, but we feel that we are justified in accepting them. Our total stock of accepted statements at any given time consist of pinned-down statements and others that are accepted partly because they stand in certain relations to the pinned down.[8]

According to this view, we must pay a substantial deference to—in W. James's famous phrase—"the older stock of truths" in order to make any further argument in particular discourse reasonable, assuming that all participants of the discourse rely tacitly on the same or similar pinned-down beliefs. In such a situation, among participants there would be the fundamental agreement in belief (i.e., regarding the content of the pinned-down beliefs) accompanied by the agreement in attitude (regarding their feeling that "[they] are justified in accepting them"). The general fact about the discourse would be the following: nobody would ever ask any question about the real justification for the terminal beliefs because everybody will be convinced that these beliefs are well justified. For the very same reason, any argument built on the negation of pinned-down beliefs would be invited by practitioners with irritation (and would serve as a "recalcitrant experience," to use W.V.O. Quine's famous phrase). As James indicated, "an *outree* explanation, violating all our preconceptions, would never pass for a true account for novelty. We should scratch around industriously till we find something less eccentric."[9] The relevance of this point can be easily extended to every use of argument in argumentative practice: if the argument does not assume at least to some extent our pinned-down preconceptions (regarding the content of certain basic concepts), it will usually be dismissed by practitioners as inadequate, irrelevant, or stupid and not merely false.

---

[7]See White (2002), p. 3.

[8]See White (1963), pp. 279–280.

[9]See James (1907), p. 192; cf. White (1963), pp. 277–278.

Such a dismissal shows primarily that practitioners do not feel any need to think more thoroughly about the justification of their own language practices (in such a situation, the eccentric argument does not force any further reflection). If, however, the existence of the common preconception determines the possibility of such a recalcitrant experience regarding the "wrong" use of the argument, then by the logic of transposition, the lack of such recalcitrant experience with regard to some arguments is supposed to imply that there is no such preconception shared by the practitioners. In such circumstances, the rules of the language game played by some groups of people would allow for some types of arguments to be posited without any consensual basis; there would be no shared criteria of wrongness or eccentricity pertaining to them (the general rule would be "there are no rules!"). Note that for identifying such arguments, we do not have to presuppose any particular philosophical conception of semantic criteria or rules; the fact whether there are such rules or criteria is irrelevant in the case at hand because our observation is that with respect to certain arguments (or, more precisely, terms used in argument) in which we are interested, there are no specified conditions of their use. Full stop.

Now, if—as pragmatists like James or White think—people sometimes feel that they are justified in their preconceptions, one might extend this assumption to cover also the situation described above where there is no substantial preconception of something about which people nonetheless regularly speak. The question is, to put it in the simplest terms, whether people can feel that they are justified in thinking that certain arguments (relying on the use of certain terms) are valid, even though they may easily infer (from the fact that there is no possibility of any recalcitrant experience with regard to the use of that particular type of argument) that these arguments are empty, all being just art for art's sake.

In the following pages, I want to pose a question as to whether the term *ratio legis* and the connected argument form *ratio legis* are not such empty phrases in the sense that there are no conceptual restrictions regarding their actual content. If this is so, that would mean that the argument form *ratio legis* (henceforth ARL) is merely a functional instrument, a rhetorical device in legal practical discourse rather than a substantial argument revealing any fact about law or the lawmaker. However, as I indicated earlier, such a consequence is of minor importance because it itself relies on some normative assumptions regarding the description of an actual use of the term and connected argument (such a negative description is still a description). What I mean by this is that such a skeptical conclusion about the general content of ARL does not preclude one from posing normative questions about how the term *ratio legis* (and thus the whole argument) should be used.

If there is no substantial preconception of *ratio legis* in legal discourse, lawyers may use ARL as a persuasive argument indicating certain reason (*ratio*) of law (*legis*) arbitrarily—depending on their interests, i.e., on considerations of what reason, if any, is for them expedient in the particular case, from the perspective of the client, other parties, the court, the abstract idea of law, or whatever or whomever else. Because almost every fact can be cited as roughly understood "reason," the skeptical problem regarding *ratio legis* is a serious one. If my description is plausible, then there is no *real ratio legis*. Nonetheless, a recognition of such a situation not only does not preclude asking normative questions about how lawyers should use ARL, but it even strengthens the demand for doing so. Perceived in this way, the problem of understanding what *ratio legis* is is actually of great philosophical importance: any use of ARL is from my perspective a performatory, legislative action within the boundaries of practical legal discourse. Dubbing something as the "law's reason" is a creative activity. If this is so, every instance of such a labeling (in which one says, "The *ratio legis* of this legislative act is X") is in need of further justification because there is no general feeling of being justified in thinking about *ratio legis* in this way or another.

I think that these types of considerations regarding such terms as *ratio legis* are much more philosophically illuminating than considerations about the "nature" or the "concept" of law, which are typical of contemporary analytical post-Hartian general jurisprudence. Lawyers rarely use arguments from the nature of law in practice because they are afraid to open a philosophical Pandora's box. In contrast, the ARL seems to be a very popular argument in legal practice (as other contributions to this volume clearly show). Thus, reflection over the general content of *ratio legis* may be a window through which practitioners could see the relevance of philosophizing about applied terms and arguments in general—the window they cannot do without looking through.

2 Different Uses of "the Argument from *Ratio Legis*"

A popular method of conceptual analysis consists, in its first step, of collecting the platitudes about the concept to which a certain term refers.[10] Such platitudes are usually understood as generally acceptable sentences in which the term in question is used. Collected platitudes are then organized in a process of reflective thinking into a big conjunction that is supposed to serve as a theory (of a concept). However, the result of this reflective thinking is not obvious. Some more analytically oriented philosophers assume that the conjunction of selected platitudes fixes (or determines) the content of the concept in question, and other more pragmatically oriented philosophers claim that the conjunction of platitudes only partially and temporarily determines the content of the concept.[11] In this second interpretation, there is no way to gain certainty about conceptual content, and the whole enterprise of the first group of philosophers is—to use J. Dewey's phrase—a "useless quest for certainty." From the perspective of pragmatists, even a logically coherent set of platitudes does not

[10]T. Gizbert-Studnicki describes the whole enterprise in the following way: "The subject matter of legal philosophy is not law as a part of mind-independent reality but rather the folk theory of law: how law is comprehended and perceived by members of society. Such folk theory is not explicitly formulated anywhere. Rather, it is indirectly manifested in certain popular beliefs and convictions in which responses to possible cases are based. Such popular beliefs (...) constitute the point of departure for legal theory." (Gizbert-Studnicki 2016, p. 142).

[11]See for example Johnston and Leslie (2012) (and literature indicated there).

determine, but merely underdetermines, the concept in question. For reasons that I cannot discuss here, I prefer the second option. There are different platitudes about *ratio legis* that underdetermine different possible conceptions of *ratio legis*. In practical discourse, we can find such uses of *ratio legis*, where it is characterized, as, inter alia:

(a) real intention of a lawgiver or judge (reasons provided or implied);
(b) considerations that caused a lawgiver to enact certain legislative acts or a judge to impose a certain sentence;
(c) subjective aim of a statute (or the sentence);
(d) (re)constructed intention of a lawgiver or judge (reasons lawgiver or judge should have);
(e) type of constructed legal argument ascribing an intention or a reason to a lawgiver (or judge);
(f) objective aim of a statute (or sentence);
(g) particular aim of a statute or sentence (relevant in certain circumstances);
(h) all aims of a statute or sentence;
(i) justification (external, justificatory reasons) for certain legislative or judicial acts.

Clearly, saying that *ratio legis* is anything from the list above would not produce any recalcitrant experience for a practical legal practitioner [apart from those who are also more philosophically oriented and have their own more sophisticated conceptions of what *ratio legis* is, but even in that case, such a conception could be understood as some account developing at least one description from the (a)–(i) list]. In that sense, all these characteristics are platitudinous. Of course, such a list can be supplemented with other platitudes, so the list cannot be treated as exhaustive, and there is no big difference between platitudes referring to the ordinary term "reason" and a qualified term "law's reason" (the qualification "law's" or "lawgiver's" is supposed to make that "reason" domain specific, but it is itself not clear in what sense). The point is that lawyers define *ratio legis* as a fact about a lawgiver's (respectively judicial) motivation, reasons, objective reasons, or aims for the legislative product, but all of these things are different types of facts or reasons. Some of them may be called descriptive, in the sense that they make certain descriptions of what some legislative bodies or people thought or did (keeping in mind that legislative bodies "think" in a different sense than do particular persons, e.g., judges). Some may be called normative because they would describe what a legislator *ought to think* or on what reason a legislator should act. What I mean is that there is no clear discrimination between cause, motivation, purpose, and reason in practical discourse. ARL may be used, then, both as a descriptive argument (about what really caused some legal act, whether legislative or judicial) and as a normative argument (about what ought to be taken as a reason) for that act. Similar considerations pertain to thinking about *ratio legis* as an aim or purpose of a legal act.

Now, one may think that the mere fact that we have such a list shows that there is at least some common understanding of what *ratio legis* is within legal discourse. However, such a conclusion would be wrong because we can label everything as a reason for action that was taken by somebody who took part in some legal process. Consider the following sentences:

"The *ratio legis* of this crisis legislation is the hurricane Irma."
"The *ratio legis* of this tax statute is the fact that the government is in desperate need of money."
"The *ratio legis* of this act is God's will" (while pointing to a list of the Ten Commandments).
"The *ratio legis* of this act is a flourishing of humanity" (while pointing to a list of the Ten Commandments).
"The *ratio legis* of this legislative act is the lawgiver's intention."
"The *ratio legis* of this legislative act is not the lawgiver's intention, because *ratio legis* is not always equal to what some might call '*mens legislatoris*.'"
"The *ratio legis* of the rule that we don't allow our cat to enter our bedroom is that he pisses on our bed."
"The *ratio legis* of the provisions of the criminal code is to prevent crimes."
"The *ratio legis* of the provisions of the criminal code is to punish crimes."
"The *ratio legis* of the provisions of the criminal code is to restore justice."
"The *ratio legis* of that particular provision is that stealing is wrong."
"The *ratio legis* of that particular provision is that one ought not steal."
"The *ratio legis* of that particular provision is that private property ought to be protected."

From these and other examples, presumably infinite in number, I cannot see whether there is any restriction regarding what can plausibly be cited as motivation, aim, reason, or justification of a legislative or judicial act. There is no general rule that would restrict the use of the term *ratio legis*. ARL may be understood, depending on the context and will of its user, as a descriptive argument—either factual (e.g., about the real intention of a lawgiver, *mens legislatoris*, or a lawgiver's will, *voluntas legislatoris*, or, more generally, real causes, which we could call *causa legis*) or counterfactual (as a more objectively perceived principle being a foundation for the law, *anima legis, medulla legis*, or even a more general purpose of all law, *voluntas legis*). ARL may also be understood normatively as an answer (at least a partial one) to the question, "how ought the legislator/judge justify her/his decision?" All we can say is that the term *ratio legis* is used differently in different contexts.

The other important problem is that a commonly accepted set of sentences about what *ratio legis* is is inherently inconsistent. Now, one might say that this is the main reason for developing some philosophical theory of *ratio legis* that will somehow eliminate these inconsistencies. But "logic chopping" and philosophical analysis are precisely what the practitioner wants to avoid. Moreover, if one can develop different competing theories of *ratio legis* on the basis of the same, consistent set of platitudes, the fact that we start from the inconsistent set gives even more options for theoretical development. From this it seems that if the point of departure for analysis is just a set of ordinary and inherently inconsistent platitudes about *ratio legis*, then each theoretical decision to stick to some of them and eliminate others is arbitrary. We cannot justify our decision by the fact that it better fits some shared preconception of *ratio legis* because there is no such preconception. There is, in other words, no fact of the matter that could ever help us decide which way of defining *ratio legis* is more accurate. W. James would probably say that it is just another example of the situation where the theorist is faced with the problem of deciding between two theories and in which he or she cannot be advised to accept that which corresponds to facts in a way that will be helpful. Any ordinary, platitudinous way of using the term *ratio legis* can be developed into a theory. But that means simply that each such use can be followed by questions: "But what exactly do you mean by that?" and "Why should I accept your use rather than mine?" etc.

All of this is not to deny that ARL is sometimes a reasonable argument. This implies only that there is no general truth about *ratio legis* that can be revealed and presented in some kind of descriptive study. Any descriptive study of *ratio legis* boils down to the study of all particular *rationes legis*, i.e., sentences starting with the labeling operator "The *ratio legis* of . . . is. . .." These particular uses may be treated as a basis for developing different theories of the concept of *ratio legis*, not the other way around (because these uses are not grounded in any preestablished and shared theory). However, such theories would necessarily be parochial and context dependent, so the scope of their application would be limited. And there certainly would be no other justification for their application than a normative one.

Lawyers simply think that law cannot be made without reason, but this is not necessarily true, apart from the fact that the meaning of "reason" is itself unclear. In fact, it seems to me that legal uses of the *ratio-legis* operator are often as unclear as uses of the term "reason" in ordinary discourse. Both demand philosophical clarification, which is in fact an engagement in constructive, quasi-legislative practice of defining a term in question for particular theoretical or practical purposes. I think, however, that such an enterprise can be reasonable (in a more substantial sense) only if it aims at producing some justification for its theoretical developments. In a more instrumental sense of reasonability, it suffices to say that any use of the *ratio-legis* operator in a sentence is an expressive device, applied to make an impression that there is something "rational" in legal matters that we discuss.

In the remaining part of the paper, I will try to present some in my view promising paths for the theoretical development of the concept of *ratio legis* in legal discourse. However, this and other similar inquiries resemble conceptual engineering rather than description. Thus, all such postulates should be individually addressed and contextually evaluated before putting them into practice.

3 Some Possible Clarifications and Qualifications

The list of (subjectively) suggested paths of clarification and qualification is as follows:

A. It seems plausible to discriminate between *the ratio legis* and *a ratio legis*. When one speaks about *the ratio legis*, one may interpret it as a statement about the exclusive cause, reason, or intention of a lawgiver or the aim of a legislative act. On the contrary, when one speaks about *a ratio legis*, one may interpret it as a statement about just one reason, intention of a lawgiver, or aim of a legislative act—which does not exclude the possibility that there are other (possibly even more important *rationes legis*). *Ratio* is here examined analogously to "a cause" and "the cause" in the methodology of historical sciences, where "a cause" is merely a so-called contributive cause and "the cause" is usually understood as "the whole cause."

B. One should distinguish between the descriptive and normative uses of the term *ratio legis* (and ARR). Statements about *ratio legis* may be used as descriptive statements in a bigger deductive-explanatory argument[12] given by a lawgiver, lawyer, judge, et al. in answer to the question, "What caused the lawgiver to enact L?" In that descriptive sense, the ARL is an answer to that factual question, presented by assuming some covering-law model of explanation (of how some cause C caused some legal action L in context Z). In contrast, in the normative use of ARL, statements about *ratio legis* are understood as normative statements that are part of the normative-deductive argument with the conclusion that "something ought to be done." In this sense, an ARL is more persuasively used in legal interpretation because rather than describing what happened, it prescribes some kind of—presumably justified—action (in this sense, among different ARL arguments, we may discriminate between so-called golden rule arguments, which establish what absurd consequences law ought to help avoid, and so-called mischief rule arguments, which aim to determine what "mischief and defect" the statute ought to remedy). The establishment of *ratio legis* via normative ARL is supposed to justify legal action and not merely to describe its causes by means of some generalized causal rule (covering law, as in descriptive ARL).

C. The important thing to note is that in a sentence "The *ratio legis* is X," the variable X can be substituted either by a descriptive clause that something is/was the case or a normative clause that it is right or ought to be done (other evaluative terms can be used as well). However, such a distinction between descriptive and normative forms does not determine the way—either descriptive or normative—in which ARL is used. For one thing, if one assumes moral realism (or other forms of cognitivism), all ARLs with normative grammatical form will have a descriptive function (because they would be describing some normative facts). On the other hand, one may use ARLs that have a descriptive grammatical form normatively (when it is not a description of fact but a postulate of its use for some further circumstances).

D. Although it may be plausible to discriminate between implicit and explicit *ratio legis* on the basis of conviction that both descriptive and normative uses of ARL may by expressed explicitly by a lawgiver ("the reasons for enacting X are A, B, C...") or may be implicit in secondary sources of law (committee reports, treatises, law review articles, corresponding statutes, or even interviews

[12]See White (1965), p. 66.

or media reports), such a discrimination yields the following problem. Explicitly presented *ratio legis* may be in conflict with those *rationes legis* that are implicit (i.e., logically deducible from secondary sources). Moreover, to process with such an implicit deduction, one must usually assume some type of rationality of a lawgiver, who is usually a collective body, and this is something that cannot be done without deep philosophical (ontological) commitments. Thus, speaking of implicit *ratio legis* seems to be a dangerous way of referring to obscure metaphysical entities, in fact precipitating more confusion than clarification. At best, such a reference can be perceived as an ascription of reasons in a counterfactual mode ("If a lawgiver were a rational being (s)he would say that 'The *ratio legis* of the legislative act X is Y'").

E. One might try to discriminate between *ratio legis* and *ratio juris*. In one of the legal dictionaries we find the following definitions. *Ratio iuris* is defined as "the reasonableness (rationality) of a legal provision, the logic of law. The Roman jurists stress the *ratio iuris* as a means of interpretation of the law (*ratio suadet, efficit* and the like)." And *ratio legis* is defined as "the reason (ground) of a written law (a statute), the spirit to be drawn from the law itself (not from external elements), the purpose, the motive which inspired the promulgation of a specific law, as, e.g. *Ratio legis Falcidiae*..."*)*.[13] However, such a definitional and historical discrimination is of no practical use whatsoever and should itself be clarified and developed (reasons are equated with purposes and motives, and rationality of law with means of legal interpretation and logic of law). So, in my opinion, instead of relying on such historical distinctions, it might be more interesting to develop the concepts of *ratio legis* and *ratio juris* in such a direction that the first would be related to the descriptive ARL mentioned above and the second to the normative ARL. However, following this path would force us to discriminate between ARL *largo sensu* (covering both descriptive and normative uses of ARL) and ARL *sensu stricto* (covering only *ratio legis* in its normative, justificatory use).

F. The descriptive idea of ARL discussed in point B is connected with some interesting philosophical problems that must be taken into account by every lawyer thinking of using ARL argument in a descriptive way. The first problem is that lawgivers may be disposed toward reasons for a particular legal action, but nonetheless the action may occur not for these reasons. If we suppose that what we want to do by use of the descriptive ARL is to describe the actual reasons that the lawgiver had before he or she acted in a particular way, we have to establish a connection between the action and the reason. In other words, it seems implausible to refer to reasons that are supposed to explain actions if there is no obvious causal connection between the two. D. Davidson argues that we might think of intentional action as "action for a reason," where reason

[13]See Berger (1991), p. 667.

causes action "in the right way."[14] I cannot see how such a connection can be established without further (possibly futile) empirical inquiry. Lawyers simply do not engage in such inquiries and instead assume that reasons must have caused the action. But this has much more to do with an idealization or an ascription than a real description. At this point, lawyers usually refer to the concept of a "rational legislator," a famous menace of legal theorists. In this way, the descriptive argument tacitly transforms into a normative argument. So it seems to me that it would be more fruitful to dispense with the idea of descriptive ARL altogether.

G. Even if some lawyers would be able to engage in serious empirical inquiry about reasons that really caused the lawgiver to enact a certain legislative act, there remain philosophical problems related to the mere idea of causation.[15] Recall the simple regularity conception of cause (proposed by J.S. Mill), in which the proper cause is conceived as the whole cause, namely, the conjunction of all necessary and sufficient conditions for something to occur. But ordinary people usually do not use the word "cause" as indicating "the whole cause" in that sense. Sometimes they mean one of the following: (1) a necessary cause (x is a necessary cause of y, then the presence of y necessarily implies the prior occurrence of x; the presence of x, however, does not imply that y will occur), (2) a sufficient cause (x is a sufficient cause of y, then the presence of x necessarily implies the subsequent occurrence of y; however, another cause z may alternatively cause y, so the presence of y does not imply the prior occurrence of x), or just (3) a contributory cause (a factor that is a contributory cause is one among several cooccurrent causes). The distinction between *a ratio legis* and *the ratio legis*—if taken in its descriptive form—becomes more complicated because now it seems that *the ratio legis*, being an exclusive cause, can be understood as the whole cause, and *a ratio legis* can be understood as indicating individually one of causes 1–3. But how can we know which one? The other possibility is to understand *the ratio legis* as a distinctive cause of a legal act (but then we need to propose some criteria for its distinctive character).

H. Finally, with respect to the descriptive use of ARL, if one wants to think of a lawgiver's reason as a real cause of his or her action, one has to be aware of the role that the term "cause" plays in historical explanations (the type of which a search for *causa legis* certainly would be). There are at least two ways of

[14]Davidson's description of "intentional action" is as follows: "A φs for a reason→(for some property F, (i) A has some pro-attitude toward actions which are F, (ii) A believes that her φing is F, and (iii) this belief and desire caused A 'in the right way' to φ)." It follows that the idea of causation is fundamental to understand the idea of reasonable action. It does not mean, of course, that the idea of reason can be reduced to the idea of a cause, but for Davidson the first idea is much more obscure (for further details, see Davidson 1971, pp. 43–61).

[15]Note that speaking about causes is inevitable if we want to present a descriptive use of ARL. Even if an agent (legislator) acts on reasons, a historian (here, lawyer) who tries to describe the action does it in a causal mode. The lawyer's descriptive reasoning is causal even if the agent's own reasoning is not. This point was illustrated by White (1965), pp. 186–194.

understanding this. According to J.S. Mill, unless we speak about the whole cause, our explanatory statement "X because Y" is arbitrary (because we choose Y arbitrarily). In that case, the ARL that would not specify the whole *ratio* would be arbitrary. However, we can also understand particular causal statements differently. For example, C. Hempel proposes to understand causal statements in historical thinking as merely sketches of explanation that assume certain laws that remain hidden. In a somewhat similar vein, M.G. White argues that typical causal statements about contributory causes simply imply that there exists a full-fledged deductive argument of the covering-law form.[16] Perceived in this way, the descriptive ARL will be either merely a sketch of an argument that would have to be further developed or an indication that there are lawgivers' reasons that somehow caused a legislative act. To my mind, the latter way of understanding the role of descriptive ARL is probably the most adequate; what follows from the lawyer's use of descriptive ARL in the circumstances of a legal case is merely the indication that there exists a full-fledged argument about reasons that the lawgiver had. What is problematic is that due to some factual limitation, the presentation of such an argument sometimes cannot be given (and then we are back with the consequence described in point F).

I. What follows from points F–H is that the descriptive use of ARL demands a clarification that often cannot be given, and even if such a clarification could be given, it will deem a lawyer's talk about the reasons for the laws or legislators too demanding. Thus, lawyers who use ARL in that way, without having in mind the obvious obstacles (some of which I mentioned above), might rather simply create or ascribe the reasons that they think they describe. My conclusion at this point is that lawyers who are not ready to commit themselves to deep, hard, and time-consuming empirical investigations about what really caused what, and in what sense, should rather withdraw an ambition to use ARL descriptively or, at least, give up a manner of speech that suggests the descriptive use of that argument.

J. Independently of what has been said above, the discrimination between descriptive ARL and normative ARL rests on a basic assumption that one can cite one and the same thing both as a cause and as a reason for something else. At best, when one thinks that the lawgiver acted for reasons, these two ways of using the ARL can be manifested in one explanation of the legislator's action that will also be its justification. Nonetheless, these two modes or forms of argument should be kept separate (for the reasons indicated in earlier points, especially point F). Not every explanation of an act is its justification and vice versa.

K. It is quite usual for critics of the courts' decisions to argue that although the judgments of the courts (or, analogously, legislative acts) are right or reasonable—in the sense that the merit of the judgments is acceptable—these judgments are badly justified. Now, it is not entirely clear what that argument is

---

[16]For a more detailed discussion on casual interpretation, see White (1965), pp. 105–181.

supposed to imply. We may wonder whether it means that the court had right reasons but did not act on them (in that case that would be a kind of descriptive argument pertaining to causes or motives, usually identified implicitly) or that the court gave explicit reasons justifying the judgment but that the reasons were (then) or are (now) not supposed to be the best available reasons (there are better reasons for such a judgment that should be cited as its justification). The first understanding brings us back to the problems of the descriptive ARL mentioned above. The second understanding of the criticism, however, seems to be quite reasonable, if only a lawyer can provide an account of those better reasons. However, presentation of such an account would be an engagement in normative, justificatory enterprise about what the lawmaker/judge ought to do or should have done. Nonetheless, I think that such an engagement is easier to accomplish because it depends on a lawyer's argumentative skills and his or her reasonableness and not on problematic philosophical assumptions about the proper meaning of "cause" and—what is most important—empirical investigations that are usually impossible for a lawyer to undertake.

4 General Conclusion

I conclude that it is much easier to construe ARL as a normative rather than a descriptive type of argument. However, such a construal demands from a lawyer a high level of argumentative skill. I am even prone to say that such expertise can only be achieved by a lawyer who is also a philosopher, fully aware of normative assumptions and implications of the particular use of *ratio legis*.

Moreover, I think that such a lawyer need not construe any general theory of *ratio legis* (although it is, of course, not forbidden). However, such a construal may become useless, and as such it could not help assess many practical uses of ARL that rely on platitudes or ordinary intuitions about reasons that lawyers and laypersons share. The philosophically oriented lawyer should, however, try to carefully analyze the use of the *ratio-legis* operator in particular circumstances, without any hope for revealing some general concept of what *ratio legis* is and where to find it. At best, the philosophically oriented lawyer may differentiate between different uses of ARL following the path indicated above. If one tries to make any theory of *ratio legis*, he or she should be aware of its parochial and normative character. At this point, a lawyer *qua* philosopher becomes a rational quasi-legislator who tries to present a useful definition of a term, as a postulate to clarify the important term in practical discourse.

Were one to not rationally and with full awareness engage in such a quasi-legislative activity, one should abandon the use of the term *ratio legis* while construing a legal argument because it brings more obscurity than clarity.

Of course, all of the considerations above rely on the claim that there is no coherent preconception of the *ratio legis* in legal practice. But one may demonstrate that claim to be false. However, *ei incumbit probatio qui dicit non qui negat*. This pragmatic rule of the burden of proof justifies the whole skeptical enterprise I have conducted above. I will gladly invite every conclusive argument, for that matter.

In the end, I should stress that there is one thing that remains certain. The term *ratio legis* is an important term of legal practice, so any problems of its conceptualization and clarification should open legal practitioners' eyes and minds to the requisite philosophical scrutiny. There are, of course, many other phenomena in legal practice that invite philosophical investigation, but to practical and aphilosophically oriented lawyers, contemplation about possible uses of *ratio legis* seems to be a good start.

References

Aune B (1991) Knowledge of the external world. Routledge, London
Berger A (1991) [1953] Encyclopedic dictionary of Roman law. Transactions of the American Philosophical Society; New Series. 43:2. The American Philosophical Society, Philadelphia
Davidson D (1971) Agency. In: Essays on actions and events, chapter 3. Oxford University Press, Oxford, pp 43–61
Dworkin R (1986) Law's empire. Harvard University Press, Cambridge
Gizbert-Studnicki T (2016) Social sources thesis and metaphilosophy. In: Banaś P, Dyrda A, Gizbert-Studnicki T (eds) Metaphilosophy of law. Hart, Oxford, pp 121–146
James W (1907) Pragmatism. Longmans, Green, New York
Johnston M, Leslie S-J (2012) Concepts, analysis, generics and the Canberra plan. Philos Perspect 26:113–171
Leiter B (2007) Explaining theoretical disagreement. Univ Chic Law Rev 76:1215–1250
Scheppele KL (1990) Facing facts in legal interpretation. Representations 30:49–54
Sunstein CR (1995) Incompletely theorized agreements. Harv Law Rev 108(7):1733–1772
White M (1963) Towards the reunion in philosophy. Atheneum, New York
White M (1965) Foundations of historical knowledge. Harper & Row, New York
White M (2002) A philosophy of culture: the scope of holistic pragmatism. Princeton University Press, Princeton
Wróblewski J (1966) Postawa filozoficzna i afilozoficzna we współczesnej teorii prawa. Studia Prawnicze 13:60–89

Adam Dyrda is as an assistant professor in the Department of Legal Theory, Jagiellonian University, Cracow. He obtained PhD in Legal Theory in 2012. He is the author of two books: "Convention as Foundation of Law. Controversies Within Contemporary Legal Positivism" [in Polish: Konwencja u podstaw prawa. Kontrowersje współczesnego pozytywizmu prawniczego] (2013) and "Theoretical Disagreements in Law. The Perspective of Holistic Pragmatism" [in Polish: Spory teoretyczne w prawoznawstwie. Perspektywa holistycznego pragmatyzmu]. He published articles on various topics connected with legal positivism, pragmatism, and cultural theory.

Ratio Legis as a Binding Legal Value

Marzena Kordela

Abstract The assumption of the legislator's rationality, which is accepted in the legal sciences, predetermines, that also in the sphere of axiology rational actions are ascribed to them. As a rational axiologist, the legislator professes definite values, ordering them in a hierarchy and making this system relatively stable. The values ascribed to the legislator consist of three categories: legal values (legally binding values), reference values, and values of a universal character. In the perspective of a legislator's axiological system, *ratio legis* may be qualified as a value, and also as a legally binding value.

1 The Assumption of Axiological Rationality of the Legislator

The underlying assumption, either clearly stated or implied, in both legal science and the application of law, is that of the **rational legislator**.

The legislator as a rational subject is consistently governed in their activity by two types of pattern that are characterised formally:

1. a non-contradictory **knowledge** system,
2. a coherent class of **values**, built preferentially and sufficiently stable.

Thus, in accordance with the general principle of rationality, if a legislator accepts some given knowledge and has given preferences, they undertake such an action from among those available (in light of this knowledge) that unfailingly leads to the state of affairs that is the most strongly preferred.[1]

[1]Nowak (1973), p. 39.

M. Kordela (✉)
Adam Mickiewicz University, Faculty of Law and Administration, Poznań, Poland
e-mail: kordela@amu.edu.pl

V. Klappstein, M. Dybowski (eds.), *Ratio Legis*,
https://doi.org/10.1007/978-3-319-74271-7_2

One detail in the general principle of rationality is the principle of the axiological rationality of the legislator.[2] In 1966, Zygmunt Ziembiński, in a monograph on the formal aspects of law, clearly emphasised that 'to the legislator, legal norms have axiological justification, therefore what must be attempted is to recreate the **legislator's values** (emphasis mine – M.K.) and to ascribe such meanings to legal provisions being interpreted that would express orders that are maximally compliant with those values'.[3]

The legislator, however, being a rational axiologist, not only creates a given set of values but is also able to pinpoint the relations occurring between them.

A primary correlation that builds the very groundwork of the legislator's axiological system is a preferential relation.

This relation results from compounding the relation of asymmetry and transitivity.[4]

An asymmetry of preference relation occurs when the legislator has a preference for state of affairs V_1 to V_2, which means that they do not prefer state of affairs V_2 to V_1, whereas **transitivity** means that if the legislator has a preference for state of affairs V_1 to V_2 and V_2 to V_3, thereby they prefer V_1 to V_3.

It is highly characteristic for a legal system that a change in the relation of preference, and not a change in the content of values as such, most frequently determines revolutionary change, as understood by Hans Kelsen. The introduction in 1989 of the principle of the rule of law into the Polish legal system, while most normative acts fundamental for the previous formation remained unchanged, was sufficient for an authoritarian system to be transformed into a democratic one. In a situation of a profound social transformation, the power of the analyticity of the construction of a legal order proves to be beneficial for its actual duration.

A legislator's axiological system, thus characterised, is created by values that are defined in the doctrine of law as 'ascribed to the legislator', or 'accepted by the legislator'[5] or that are simply the 'legislator's values'.[6]

[2]Formulated along with such principles as, e.g., the principles of linguistic, epistemic or praxeological rationality. Cf. Z. Ziembiński (1980), pp. 272–273.

[3]Ziembiński (1966), p. 220. Similarly: Ziembiński (1972), p. 107; Ziembiński (2001), p. 167.

[4]Nowak (1973), pp. 39–40; cf. Nowak (1968), pp. 131–136; Nowak (1974a), p. 111; Ziembiński (1980), pp. 271–274; Wronkowska (1990), p. 122; Nowak (1974b), p. 13.

[5]Ziembiński (1990), p. 162.

[6]*Ibidem*, pp. 173, 174, 175.

2 Axiological System of the Legislator

Every legislator's axiological system is composed of three subsystems.

2.1 Legal Values (Legally Binding Values)

The **first** subsystem comprises values that are legally binding, that is, values that become legally binding by virtue of the act of enactment, in analogy to the enactment of legal norms and their validity resulting from it.

By acquiring the status of being legally valid, these values constitute a certain type of values that is different from moral, customary, religious or any other values.

Moreover, it is of no importance whether a given legal value was previously defined as a moral or customary value or whether it was created in its entirety, both in its content and form (in the sphere of validity). Legislative *fiat* has a decisive character.

Ultimately then, what the interpreter of a legal text deals with is not their own creation but something that is given.

The values encoded in the provisions of a binding normative act result from the process of evaluation conducted by the legislator themself and not by the interpreter. Their final shape fixed in legal terms is of an objective character that can be read either in an intersubjectively communicable and controllable manner, or at least assuming rational argumentation 'for' and 'against' a given position. This happens because decoding legal values is carried out in a way that is analogous to decoding norms, with allowances made for their specificity. This characteristic of values formulated in legislative activity predetermines them to become a legitimate research object in analytical theories of law—and not exclusively natural law theories.

The first and most characteristic feature of the specificity of value decoding is that unlike norms, which nearly always require a complex and complicated reconstruction from several legal provisions, values may be directly revealed by the legislator.

Not every legislator makes use of the legislative technique of directly expressing values (usually by naming them) in the text of a normative act; however, such a method of constructing law axiology has several representatives in our culture.

Article 1 Sect. 1 of the Spanish Constitution of 1978 clearly states:

> Spain is hereby established as a social and democratic state, subject to the rule of law, which advocates freedom, justice, equality and political pluralism as the **highest values of its legal system** (emphasis mine – M.K.)'.[7]

[7] Cf: "Comparison of these two methods of regulating 'justice' (in the Spanish Constitution and Constitution of the Republic of Poland – M.K.) enables the observation that, at least formally, constitutionalisation may be achieved both by accepting a formula of justice as value and justice as principle". Łabno (2003), p. 179.

The same applies to the Constitution of the Republic of Croatia of 1990. Article 3 states:

> Freedom, equality, national equality and gender equality, peace, social justice, respect for human rights, inviolability of ownership, conservation of nature and the environment, the rule of law and a democratic multiparty system are the **highest values of the constitutional order** (emphasis mine – M.K.) of the Republic of Croatia and the ground for interpretation of the Constitution.

Article 3 Sect. 3 of the Constitution of Romania of 1991 states:

> Romania is a democratic and social state, subject to the rule of law, in which human dignity, citizens' rights and freedoms, the free development of human personality, justice and political pluralism are **supreme values** (emphasis mine – M.K.) and are guaranteed.

Despite the lack of explicit positivisation of values, it is clear not only in the Polish doctrine of law that the effect of a legislative decision has a 'value creating' function.[8] Values, in the strict meaning, legal (legally binding), are decoded by means of accepted methods of interpretation, e.g. by accepting that a norm with the character of legal principle expresses (protects or even commands[9]) the realisation of predefined values.[10]

The underlying source of fundamental constitutional values is the principle of the rule of law. Put as 'a collective principle'[11] in the normative sphere, it has the function of a 'collective value' in the axiological one. The rule of law as a value not only implies a number of detailed values but also arranges them into an entity with the evident features of a system. The collection of all the values of the rule of law is primarily divided into formal and material values. The former incorporates values protected by the legal principles defined as primary: first of all, legal certainty, legal security, the predictability of the action of a public authority, the autonomy of law, legalism, proper legislation, non-retroactivity, the principle of hierarchy of normative acts, the primacy of the law, the right to a fair trial, citizens' trust in the state and its law-making function, and the protection of acquired rights and transactions in progress. The formal values of the rule of law are supplemented with material values: human dignity, personal autonomy, fundamental rights (with particular emphasis on the role of the right to privacy), equality and material justice. Each of these values acquires the normative shape of a legal principle.

A similar procedure for the recreation of legal values may be applied to the civil code. On the basis of explicitly formulated principles, the following values may be defined as legally binding:

[8] Cf.e.g. phrase by Leszczyński (2001), p. 31.

[9] Kordela (2014a), p. 102.

[10] Cf. e.g. "Speaking about the principles of civil code we first and foremost think of a certain category of legal norms that stand out because of their importance and special role they play in this branch of law. They point to **values** (emphasis mine – M.K.) that norms of civil code should realise above all". Radwański (1979), pp. 21–22; Radwański (1993), p. 26; Radwański (2005), p. 17.

[11] Garlicki (2011), p. 59.

1. recognition and protection of the personality of each individual in equal measure,
2. complete and equal protection of property,
3. prohibition of the abuse of subjective rights,
4. personal autonomy,
5. protection of confidence.[12]

2.2 *Reference Values*

The second subsystem of the legislator's values is made up of those values that, albeit extra-legal, must be applied by a court in accordance with the legislator's command formulated in the reference provisions.

A regulation contains a **general reference provision** if, on its basis, a court acquires the competence to be guided by the individual evaluations of a given situation (**general reference provisions type I**) or non-legal principles that are axiologically justified in general values (**general provisions type II**), such as principles of social coexistence or the principle of equity.

They do not have the character of values that are legally binding; however, the fact that the courts are obliged to apply them makes them 'inbuilt' into the legal order.[13]

These are values such as the following:

1. social interest,
2. public interest,
3. principles of equity,
4. requirements of good faith,
5. social noxiousness of an act (as a negative value),
6. principles of social justice, as well as
7. important reasons,
8. justified reasons,
9. established habits.[14]

2.3 *Universal Values*

The final class of values ascribed to the legislator are values defined as 'fundamental values deemed as an element of legal culture of a country'.[15]

---

[12]Radwański (2005), pp. 17–19 (also: Radwański 1993, pp. 26–27; Radwański 1979, pp. 23–24).
[13]Legal order defined as "an actually working legal system". Lang (2008), p. 13.
[14]Leszczyński (2001), p. 21.
[15]Ziembiński (1990), p. 92.

This category is connected with '**universal values**' and '**universal human values**', as referred to in the preamble to the Constitution of the Republic of Poland.

The ascertainment of those values as being binding stems from the empirical observation that 'people accept certain values as elementary or universal and demand that they are realised'.[16]

Systems of legal values, reference values and universal values are arranged in a ring-like fashion: first there is an axiological core in the form of legal values, then reference values surround the primary set and the 'outermost' layer of the legislator's axiological system is made up of universal values.

3 Axiological Law Interpretation

The legislator as a subject exclusively creating norms of conduct and not propositions in a logical sense, or axiological statements, must 'inbuild' the values that they profess into the content of provisions from which they will be then recreated.

Tentatively, the rules of axiological interpretation may be formulated as follows:

1. If the decoded legal norm formulates a command to pursue a defined conduct (or to realise a defined state of affairs), then this conduct (this state of affairs) has the character of positive value in the legislator's axiological system.
2. If the decoded legal norm formulates a prohibition of a defined conduct (or realisation of a defined state of affairs), then this conduct (this state of affairs) has the character of a negative value.
3. If the text of a normative act contains phrases such as 'right to...', 'right of...', 'freedom to ...', 'freedom of...', then complementation of these phrases plays the function of names of the legislator's positive values.
4. A legal norm with the unquestionable status of a legal principle in a given system, named 'principle of x' (e.g., the principle of the rule of law, principle of sovereignty, principle of legal certainty), in the part designated 'x', contains the name of a protected value (respectively, the rule of law, sovereignty, legal certainty).
5. A legal norm with the status of a programme norm (political directive) and displaying in its structure the purpose of a state policy predetermines the fact that the state of affairs included in the purpose becomes a positive value (in the form of, e.g., protection of the environment; protection of consumers, tenants and users; adequate access to public health care).[17]
6. If a defined purpose can be ascribed to a norm, institution, normative act or the entire legal system (*ratio legis*, *ratio iuris*), then this purpose has the character of a positive value.

[16]Woleński and Hartman (2008), p. 23.

[17]Cf: Kordela (2001), pp. 43–46; Kordela (2014b), pp. 28–48.

4 *Ratio Legis* as a Value

Regardless of the fact that, as a result of interpretation, a defined purpose (*ratio legis*) will be expressed as a purpose of a single norm or a group of norms and regardless of the fact of to whom this purpose is ascribed—a historical or the current legislator—the state of affairs deemed as required will always acquire the status of value,[18] and this value will be a legal value (a legally binding value) in the strict sense of this phrase.[19]

5 *Rationes Legis* System

The fact of ascribing the status of value to *ratio legis* (valuable object) is not synonymous with excluding from deliberations, on its fundamental reference points, what is to be the subject of legal protection (thus what should be preserved in its given form) and a definite state of affairs that should arise as a consequence of the realisation of a given norm or group of norms. In both these cases, the purpose of law may be interpreted as a state of affairs—current or potential—and so be included in the order of facts. Its description will be contained in an entire spectrum of definiteness: from purposes that are precisely set and that can be translated into a predetermined, practically enclosed group of actions and acts of forbearance unfailingly leading to an anticipated result, through to purposes that assume alternative methods (e.g., the reduction of unemployment by means of adequate taxation or educational policies), all the way to purposes of the most general character and attributed to law as a complete entity—peace, justice, safety, common good. At this last level, a clear reference to values can be observed; however, the element of factuality is preserved by the assumption that the existence and functioning of the legal system as a whole will meet the assumed values–purposes provided that a state of social, political and economic relations appears (a determined state of affairs appears) that can be interpreted as fulfilment (within a given time period) of those values.

The multiplicity of functions realised by a normative order, such as law, also predetermines the multiplicity of its purposes. The assumption of the systematicity of law, which underlies the multiplicity of norms, can also be applied to the multiplicity of the values of the legislator. Nevertheless, not only do legislator-ascribed values assume the form of an axiological system, but the systematicity also 'renews' itself on all the levels below. Besides the most general division into three subsystems, the values protected by individual branches of law are, for instance, sets of values with the distinctive features of a system, where the role of fundamental values is executed by those values that express the principles of law

[18]Cf.: Barak (2002), p. 71.

[19]See: Dworkin (1986), p. 60.

(e.g., the value of objective truth in criminal proceedings); values that can be recreated from normative acts, mostly of a complex character (e.g., the bill that regulates the system of the courts of general jurisdiction); or values that make up a given legal institution, for instance the institution of property, family or appeal examination. The assumption that the legislator is a rational subject also in the sphere of self-created purposes entails the necessary acceptance of the conditions of minimal systematicity in this sphere: non-contradictoriness and hierarchy. Thus, all *rationes legis* should undergo ordering from the most to the less important, and their mutual relations must not be conflicting.

A starting criterion of purpose preference, which is also one of the most crucial, is the degree of its generalisation. The purposes of the entire legal system, followed by its individual parts (groups of norms) and, finally, individual norms in a model setting remain in a relation 'from the general to the specific' and thus not only build a clear hierarchy, but also incompatibility between them is analytically eliminated.

Another criterion, and not less important, is the legal power of a purpose. Constitutional purposes will always prevail over statutory purposes, and in turn those will prevail over the purposes of executive acts. The ascertainment of incompatibility between them must involve a reaction that will restore coherence within a given section of the law system. As a standard, three types of action to repair the system are indicated. The first one is a reinterpretation of those legal provisions from which the incompatible purposes have been recreated; it should be conducted in such a way as to avoid this incompatibility, by adequately narrowing the scope of one or even both purposes. The second action consists of an analogous application of a collision rule of a hierarchical type: a more powerful purpose suppresses a less powerful purpose (*lex superior derogat legi inferiori*). An ultimate method for doing away with the conflict is the legislator's intervention, which, when executed at the level of the formulation of a normative act and not as a result of corrective interpretation, will ensure a convergence of purposes.

The necessity to make the purposes coherent at the level of the recreation of the legal system (from mere provisions to legal norms as proper elements of the law system), when they are interpreted as definite states of affairs, does not raise doubts from the standpoint of praxeology requirements: the addressee of legal norms may not be present in two different places at the same time, or one batch of a raw material may serve to manufacture only one item if this item must be made of the entire batch. However, in the process of qualifying law purposes as values, the immanently colliding nature of values (therefore a natural feature and not a culpable feature of the legislator's axiological system) predetermines that, firstly, frequently it is only while a law is being applied and not at the stage of constructing the system that such an incompatibility may manifest itself, and, secondly, it requires a special reaction. When purposes–values collide, a distinctive mechanism comes into play—the procedure of their balancing. This procedure encompasses two levels. Firstly, in the definite individual circumstances of a given case, a greater importance is ascribed to one of the purposes, and only this one will be realised (whereas the purpose with lesser importance will remain legally binding to be realised in the other circumstances that give it dominance),[20] or proportions are negotiated so that both are realised. The second level is to ascertain which already precisely designated state of affairs will play the role of a dominant value (or values that have been suitably agreed).[21] Thus, by placing law purpose in an axiological order and so granting subjects that apply law the competence to 'transfer'[22] values to definite states of affairs, a rational legislator increases the likelihood that even in a world that has been dramatically altered when compared with that at the moment of making legislative decisions, the adequacy of the ideas of law and their realisation will be preserved.

References

Alexy R (2002) A theory of constitutional rights (trans. J. Rivers). Oxford University Press

Barak A (2002) Foreword: a judge on judging: the role of a Supreme Court in a democracy. Harv Law Rev 116(16):19–162

Dworkin R (1986) Law's empire. Fontana Press

Garlicki L (2011) Polskie prawo konstytucyjne. Zarys wykładu (Polish constitutional law. An outline of lecture), 5th edn. Liber, Warszawa

Kordela M (2001) Zarys typologii uzasadnień aksjologicznych w orzecznictwie Trybunału Konstytucyjnego (An outline of axiological justifications in judicature of constitutional tribunal). Oficyna Wydawnicza Branta, Bydgoszcz-Poznań

Kordela M (2014a) Zasady prawa. Studium teoretycznoprawne (Principles of law. A study in legal theory), 2nd edn. Wydawnictwo Naukowe UAM, Poznań

Kordela M (2014b) Wstęp metodologiczny do wykładni aksjologicznej (Methodological introduction to axiological interpretation). In: Czapska J, Dudek M, Stępień M (eds) Wielowymiarowość prawa (Multidimensional character of law). Wydawnictwo Adam Marszałek, Toruń, pp 28–48

Łabno A (2003) Sprawiedliwość jako najwyższa wartość porządku prawnego. Rozważania na tle art. 1 ust. 1 Konstytucji Hiszpanii z 1978 r. (Justice as the supreme value of legal order. Thoughts on Article 1 of Section 1 of the Spanish Constitution of 1978). In: Bogucka I, Tobor Z (eds) Prawo a wartości. Księga jubileuszowa Profesora Józefa Nowackiego (Law and values. A jubilee book of Professor Józef Nowacki). Kantor Wydawniczy Zakamycze, Zakamycze, pp 177–185

Lang W (2008) System prawa i porządek prawny (A law system and legal order). In: Bogucki O, Czepita S (eds) System prawny a porządek prawny (A legal system and legal order). Wydawnictwo Naukowe Uniwersytetu Szczecińskiego, Szczecin, pp 9–27

Leszczyński L (2001) Stosowanie generalnych klauzul odsyłających (Application of general clauses of reference). Kantor Wydawniczy Zakamycze, Kraków

Nowak L (1968) Normodawca – racjonalny aksjolog. Teoria racjonalnego preferowania (Normmaker – rational axiologist. A theory of rational preference). In: Nowak L (edn) Próba metodologicznej charakterystyki prawoznawstwa (An attempt at methodological characterisation of jurisprudence). Wydawnictwo Naukowe UAM, Poznań, pp 131–136

Nowak L (1973) Interpretacja prawnicza. Studium z metodologii prawoznawstwa (Law interpretation. A study in methodology of jurisprudence). Warszawa

Nowak L (1974a) The methodological status of the rationality assumption. Studia Metodologiczne 11:111–126. Poznań

---

[20]Alexy (2002), pp. 52–54.

[21]*Ibidem*, p. 56.

[22]Kordela (2014a), pp. 102, 313.

Nowak L (1974b) U podstaw marksistowskiej aksjologii (Basis of Marxist axiology). Państwowe Wydawnictwo Naukowe, Warszawa

Radwański Z (1979) Prawo cywilne – część ogólna (Civil law – general). PWN, Warszawa

Radwański Z (1993) Prawo cywilne – część ogólna (Civil law – general). C.H. Beck, PWN, Warszawa

Radwański Z (2005) Prawo cywilne – część ogólna (Civil law – general), 8th edn. C.H. Beck, PWN, Warszawa

Woleński J, Hartman J (2008) Wiedza o etyce (A branch of ethics). Wydawnictwo Szkolne PWN ParkEdukacja, Warszawa

Wronkowska S (1990) Prawodawca racjonalny jako wzór dla prawodawcy faktycznego(A rational legislator as a model for actual legislator). In: Wronkowska S, Zieliński M (eds) Szkice z teorii prawa i szczegółowych nauk prawnych (Sketches in legal theory and specific legal sciences). Wydawnictwo Naukowe UAM, Poznań, pp 117–134

Ziembiński Z (1966) Logiczne podstawy prawoznawstwa (Logical foundations of jurisprudence). Wydawnictwo Prawnicze, Warszawa

Ziembiński Z (1972) Teoria prawa (Legal theory), 1st edn. Państwowe Wydawnictwo Naukowe, Warszawa-Poznań

Ziembiński Z (1980) Problemy podstawowe prawoznawstwa (Fundamental issues in jurisprudence). Państwowe Wydawnictwo Naukowe, Warszawa

Ziembiński Z (1990) Wstęp do aksjologii dla prawników (Introduction to axiology for jurists). Wydawnictwo Prawnicze, Warszawa

Ziembiński Z (2001) Wykładnia prawa i wnioskowania prawnicze (Law interpretation and legal inferences). In: Wronkowska S, Ziembiński S (eds) Zarys teorii prawa (An outline of legal theory). Przedsiębiorstwo Wydawnicze Ars boni et aequi, Warszawa, pp 147–179

Marzena Kordela is a professor at the Adam Mickiewicz University, Poznań, Poland, Faculty of Law and Administration, Chair of the Theory and Philosophy of Law. Her main research areas are legal theory, legal principles, axiology of law, legal methodology, axiological interpretation, formal aspects of legal systems. The paper is a version of the speech of the same title given during the XXVIII World Congress of IVR—'Peace Based on Human Rights', 16–21 July 2017, University of Lisbon, Portugal, in the Special Workshop 'Is There a *Ratio Legis* and if So, How Many Are They? – The Most Powerful Method of Legal Reasoning Uncovered'.

Articulating *Ratio Legis* and Practical Reasoning

Maciej Dybowski

Abstract Many irreconcilable accounts of *ratio legis* in legal science, often concerned with legal interpretation, suffer from being disconnected from practical reasoning. Different theories of legal interpretation which result in one-sided views of *ratio legis* are by-products of one-sided semantics. The first part of the chapter diagnoses this problem by providing a model of three types of one-sided semantics—upstream, midstream and downstream—and explaining how they translate into respective accounts of legal interpretation and *ratio legis*. The second part of the chapter presents an alternative to one-sided semantics in legal theory. The alternative account which combines semantics and practical reasoning in legal theory is based on Brandom's inferential pragmatism. The usefulness of inferential pragmatism in legal theory with regard to the problem of *ratio legis* is tested and followed by extending an inferentialist account of *ratio legis* provided by Canale and Tuzet. A model of agent's actions and reasons, and their impact on the reasoning of interpreters and decision-makers is the essential part of this extension.

The problem with *ratio legis* is that, especially in statutory law tradition, there are too many irreconcilable accounts of it in legal science. This chapter is based on a claim that such accounts are disconnected from practical reasoning, and most of the discussion is predominantly concerned with legal interpretation, at the expense of practical reasoning. The various and incompatible one-sided views of *ratio legis* are by-products of one-sided semantics that, in one way or another, are adopted by theories of legal interpretation. The first part of the chapter identifies three types of one-sided semantics—upstream, midstream and downstream—and shows how they translate into respective accounts of legal interpretation and *ratio legis*. The diagnostic part of the chapter is followed by an account based on inferential pragmatism

M. Dybowski (✉)
Adam Mickiewicz University, Poznań, Poland
e-mail: dybowski@amu.edu.pl

V. Klappstein, M. Dybowski (eds.), *Ratio Legis*,
https://doi.org/10.1007/978-3-319-74271-7_3

considered as alternative to one-sided semantics in legal theory. Drawing on Brandom's ideas, an approach that combines semantics and practical reasoning in legal theory is developed. The final part of the chapter tests the usefulness of inferential pragmatism in legal theory with regard to the problem of *ratio legis*. An inferentialist account of *ratio legis* provided by Canale and Tuzet is extended by a model of agent's actions and reasons, and their impact on the reasoning of interpreters and decision-makers.

1 *Ratio Legis* and Legal Interpretation

1.1 Narrow Focus of **Ratio Legis** *Debates. The Case of Polish Jurisprudence*

The discussion of *ratio legis*, at least in modern jurisprudence, has been connected with interpretation of legal texts. Savigny says in his famous *System of the Modern Roman Law* that the process of interpretation—'recognizing the contents of the written law'—is a 'necessary one by the very destination of the written law; since every written law is to enter into life, which is at first only possible through intellectual conception of it' (Savigny 1867, p. 169). For him, *ratio legis* has two temporal dimensions: it either belongs to the past, as something in which the law is grounded, or it belongs to the future, as the *telos* or the effect expected from the law.

Polish legal theory in the twentieth century can illustrate the claim that *ratio legis* is typically associated with legal interpretation, especially with a teleological one, where the objectives or purposes are viewed as something belonging to, but distinct from, the functional context of interpretation.[1] If this association is accepted, it raises many interconnected questions about *telos*: is *telos* identical with *ratio legis*? What is it anyway? What is it the *telos* or *ratio* of, and how can one have epistemic access to it? Polish legal theorists of the second half of the twentieth century have shared the view that the purpose of law is identical with *ratio legis*.[2] Consequently, an interpreter who uses teleological interpretation must assume that whatever is interpreted by him—whether it is a legal norm or a set of norms or a piece of legislation—must have a discernible purpose (*telos*, *ratio*). Such an assumption is risk-free only as long as no conflicts occur between the results of linguistic interpretation and the results of teleological interpretation. If some other methods than teleological modes or techniques of interpretation reaffirm what has been identified as the purpose, the interpreter may enjoy interpretive success justified by reliance on any or all directives deployed. However, it becomes more problematic when the interpreter has to choose

[1] See Gizbert-Studnicki (1985), p. 52; Smolak (2010), p. 152. The courts in Poland usually apply the terms "functional interpretation" and "teleological interpretation" interchangeably.

[2] See Wróblewski (1959), pp. 355–356; Nowak (1973), p. 104; Peczenik (1989), p. 406; Morawski (2002), p. 211; Zieliński (2002), p. 301.

between different results of interpretation and give preference to one at the expense of the other. Polish theory of legal interpretation and jurisprudence of higher courts has a general tendency to set limits to the use of teleological interpretation; for example, it is claimed that this kind of interpretation should only be used if the linguistic directives yield no clear result or such result otherwise requires to be modified. This limitation is based on practitioners' and theorists' worries about legal certainty.

Setting the limits for the use of teleological interpretation, justified as it may be, still leaves the puzzle of *telos* unsolved. Even if it is accepted that the *telos* is associated with a legal regulation, the interpretation theorists disagree on the nature of the purpose. Is it consciously and actually set by someone, e.g. by the legislator? Is the *telos* just declared by someone, and if so, can it be different from the purpose actually set, or can there be no such purpose to begin with? Can the *telos* be ascribed to someone on the grounds of attributed rationality and also regardless of the actual intent or declaration?

In the Polish legal scholarship, one may also encounter the view that *ratio legis* is about the content of legal norms and that content can be identified with the reasons for recognising such norms as justified, rational, valuable, etc.[3] Under this view, *ratio legis* is conceived of more broadly than just *telos* since the conduct prescribed by legal norms may be seen as valuable in itself.[4] Under this broader account, the purpose of legal rule can figure among many different factors that justify that rule.

This brief overview of contemporary Polish jurisprudential debates concerning *ratio legis* reveals the exclusive focus of legal theorists on the interpretation of legal texts and little, if any, interest in practical reasoning. Nevertheless, the connection between law and practical reasoning is rather straightforward. The function of law is utterly practical: it is concerned with actions that are prescribed to those who are subject to it. Therefore, reducing theoretical concern to the semantic dimension, which is of paramount importance to the theorists of legal interpretation, is missing half of the picture of the practice of law.

1.2 Types of One-Sided Semantics and Their Impact on Theoretical Accounts of Ratio Legis

The critical diagnostic claim advanced in this chapter to explain the difficulties that legal theories face in their account of *ratio legis* is that these various and incompatible views of *ratio legis* are by-products of one-sided semantics. A predominance of theoretical concern with legal interpretation results in a multitude of theories of interpretation, and each of these theories is bound to adopt some semantics. Most accounts of semantics are one-sided, as will be shown, and it is acceptable for them

[3]See Lang (1986), pp. 27–28.

[4]See Borowicz (2009), pp. 54–56.

to be so. However, there should be no bewilderment in the fact that such one-sided semantics produce incoherent solutions of problems in legal theory, having a bearing on legal interpretation and, consequently, on their treatment of *ratio legis*.

This part of the chapter identifies three types of one-sided semantics—upstream, midstream and downstream—inspired by a distinction between theories of meaning, based on their missing the inferential connection between the circumstances and the consequences of concept application (Brandom 1994, pp. 116–125). This distinction can be better understood in terms of temporal dimensions. On the one hand, there are those sematic theories that are focused on how concepts acquire their content *prior* to being used, and on the other hand, there are theories concerned with the way the meaning is generated *during* the usage or as a result of it (that is, *after* the acts of usage). In each of the three following sections, I will briefly analyse (1) a given semantic view, (2) its bearing on theory of legal interpretation and (3) its bearing on the account of *ratio legis*.

1.2.1 Upstream Semantics

The first type of one-sided semantics is the view that concepts have their determinate content fixed *before* they are used. Among the factors that are believed to determine the meaning, there might be such diverse ones as natural features of the world (*semantic foundationalism*) or social facts (*semantic conventionalism*). It may be called *upstream semantics* because regardless of the view concerning the nature of meaning, it is focused on antecedents of the semantic content. Semantic foundationalism is the view that language conforms to the language-independent world and that it is ultimately the mind-independent reality that sets the meaning of linguistic expressions, at least the meaning of primary units of content, in terms of which other elements of language can be analysed.[5] According to semantic foundationalism, in order to be able to use a concept, we must have some immediate acquaintance with its object being a feature of the world (e.g., the feature of being red). Some concepts, like 'law', cannot be identified with features of the world or with some sensory content, but semantic reductionists claim that it is enough to show that there are some primary mind-independent concepts, and other concepts can be derived from them. However, it is not the traceability of legal concepts to the features of the world that I am interested in but the underlying view that there is something foundational about the semantic content and that we can access it. It might be unexpected to list semantic foundationalism and conventionalism under the same heading, at least for someone who associates the latter with the core conventionalist assumption that if any reference scheme is adequate, then many are adequate, and,

[5]This approach can be attributed to Locke. In *An Essay Concerning Human Understanding*, Locke claims that words correspond to ideas which are caused to arise in us by corresponding objects in the world, to which the ideas correspond. With some modifications, this approached can also be found in Russell's doctrine of acquaintance presented in his second Monist Lecture in 1918. See Russell (1956).

consequently, the choice of one reference scheme over another is merely a matter of convention (see Field 1975); in other words, under conventionalist view, a linguistic community fixes the extension of a word like 'law'. However, once the choice of reference scheme is made, a convention can be seen as setting the meaning *just like* some selection of natural features. Therefore, from the perspective adopted in the present chapter, it does not make a difference whether someone treats the fixing of the semantic content as a conventionally adopted reference scheme or as a self-imposing set of traceable natural features, as long as any of these is regarded as foundational with regard to the meaning of linguistic units.

The bearing of upstream semantics on legal interpretation can best be illustrated by the view in which interpretation involves epistemic access to the original, fixed meaning of a statutory or constitutional provision (*originalism*). Originalists are in agreement with legal foundationalists in holding that there is some normative core from which all legal decisions can be deduced. Typically, the problem of original meaning is discussed as concerning the nature of legislative *intent* and the *sources* from which interpreters can draw. Apart from the text and context, the main evidence for legislative intent is legislative history, as manifested, e.g., in preparatory works. It turns out that originalists develop significantly different postures towards what constitutes the original meaning. On the one hand, they may prefer to privilege the express aim or intention of the legislator, but on the other hand, the *textualists* may favour reliance on textual meaning when it enters into conflict with the intent.[6] Legislative intent might be understood as (1) the actual mental state of legislators, (2) an embodiment of the objective notion of a rational legislator and (3) a construct based on conventions about what materials count.[7] Since (2) is discussed at length in my treatment of the second type of one-sided semantics and (3) is a meta-level view about how to discern which expressions of the original intent are to be considered, it is the actual mental state of legislators that deserves most attention as the possible meaning-determining factor.

Greenawalt identifies the mental state version of legislative intent as the 'legislator's understanding about what the statute does, his opinion about how courts *should* interpret its language' (2002, p. 284). This approach to group intent seems to exemplify a common ground between semantic foundationalists and conventionalists. On the one hand, there is a theoretically elaborate mental state assigned to the legislator as worldly fact of a kind, but on the other hand, the content of thus conceived legislative intent is something shared or agreed upon, which is close enough to convention. According to M.S. Moore, conventionalist semantics comes in three varieties, which are reflected in the problems faced by conventionalist legal interpretation.[8] The first, shallow conventionalism, claims that conventions accurately generalise how most native speakers use the word. Indeterminacy in novel

[6]See Scalia (1996), pp. 18–23.

[7]For introducing this distinction, see Greenawalt (2002), p. 283.

[8]The characteristics of conventionalisms and their implications for legal interpretation are based on Moore (2016), pp. 130–135.

cases is solved by legal interpreters belonging to that option by reliance on closure rules, such as 'strict construction'.[9] The second variety, rich conventionalism, recognises semantic conventions as extension-determiners (definitions and paradigmatic exemplars). This view in legal interpretation would hold that 'if one has enough rules in the corpus of the legal text, all cases will be covered one way or another' (Moore 2016, p. 134), and so it gives rise to the tendency to increase the numbers of standards and their diversity, as suggested, e.g., by Dworkin. Rather than being effective, this focus on standards generates risk of regress to infinity due to the constant need for elaboration of new standards, especially the principles. The third kind is deep conventionalism, which accommodates the second one but claims that the conventions that give meaning to concepts are deeper and more agreed upon, as opposed to conventions on which people can meaningfully disagree. Any legal theorist, however, knows that the concept of law, just like most other legal concepts, remains essentially contested. The general problems with any conventionalist semantics are that people cannot meaningfully disagree because the terms they use do not have the same meaning and that people run out of conventions sooner than they run out of meaning.

We might be able to draw further conclusions for the problem of *ratio legis*, which stem from Moore's account of semantic conventionalism. Shallow conventionalism, with its reliance on closure rules, which are rare and vague anyway, would imply some kind of mechanical solution and eventually render legal reasoning involving *ratio legis* unnecessary. Under rich conventionalism, the tendency is to increase the numbers of standards and their diversity, which relocates *ratio legis* to the issue of ever more appropriate standards that rich conventionalists believe to be in the law. The third kind, deep conventionalism with its claim that the conventions that give meaning to concepts are deeper and more agreed upon, would have to face the challenge of justifying its reliance on the deep structure from which its proponents want to draw in order to determine *ratio legis*. If originalists who favour legislative intent wanted to associate *ratio legis* with legislative group intent, they would have to address the same objections as rich and deep conventionalists. The originalists who prefer textualism could find themselves in a situation resembling that of shallow conventionalists by self-imposed limitation to textual expressions of original *ratio legis* and in the absence of such indicators would have to admit that there might be no *ratio legis*. If they persisted on the search for *ratio legis*, they would have to re-examine their textual assumptions: either by adopting rich conventionalism about the text and searching for other textual legal sources or by falling into deep conventionalism (e.g., committing to the ideal text of rational legislator) and being led astray from the original text. In sum, upstream semantics with regard to *ratio legis* results in some form of *sematic over-determinacy*, which delegates the content of *ratio* to closure rules or to other legal standards or to deep structures of legal thinking.

---

[9]For example, such a rule in criminal law would provide that if something is not strictly prohibited, it is permitted.

1.2.2 Midstream Semantics

The second type of one-sided semantics, *semantic interpretivism*, provides a model of meaning focused on transformational rules.[10] More precisely, it is based on the idea that interpretive semantic rules treat syntactic structures as their input. Lexicalism is a form of semantic interpretivism since it assumes that 'if transformations themselves do not refer to semantic structures, then they must be supplemented by interpretive rules that relate semantic structure to syntactic structure' (Newmeyer 1986, p. 140). Interpretivism in the narrow sense claims that interpretive rules apply to both superficial and deep syntactic structures and that it is the deep structures that determine semantic representation.[11] Under semantic interpretivism, the meaning of a word like 'law' would be a result of applying appropriate transformational rules. It may be called *midstream semantics* because, under this view, fixing the content of linguistic expressions depends primarily on the transformational rules that serve as an intermediary between antecedents and final results.

The bearing of semantic interpretivism on legal interpretation can be illustrated by one of the most prominent models of legal interpretation in Polish legal theory: the so-called 'derivational' theory. The theory is based on the conceptual distinction between a legal provision and a legal norm, understood as a linguistic expression syntactically made of (1) an order or a prohibition of (2) conduct for (3) the given addressee under (4) given circumstances.[12] According to this theory, legal norms are *derived* from legal provisions in the process of legal interpretation. The process is seen as being made of three phases. After arranging the legal provisions and reconstructing a 'norm-shaped expression', an interpreter proceeds to the final, 'perceptual' phase, where *single* meaning is to be assigned to words and expressions used in a norm-shaped expression. The assigning of meaning in the derivational theory is directed by a number of linguistic[13] and extra-linguistic (systemic and functional) interpretive rules that achieve precisely what I describe as semantic interpretivism, namely, derivation from the deep structures of what is encoded in legal texts, to the surface syntactic representation of a sentence, which is accomplished by reordering, inserting or deleting elements that are inconsistent with the syntactic model of a legal norm. The notion of deep structure of legal science is deeply embedded in the derivational model of legal interpretation, through the conception of a rational legislator, which was meant to explain the superficial

[10]In order to highlight the focus on interpretive rules, I reverse the traditional label of "interpretive semantics" associated with the so-called *Extended Standard Theory*, developed by Chomsky (1972), which evolved out of *Standard Theory*, proposed in Chomsky (1965).

[11]This is outlined in theories of Katz and Postal (1964), and of Chomsky (1965).

[12]The distinction was introduced in Ziembiński (1960). The derivational theory of legal interpretation was developed in Zieliński (1972, 2002). Recent expansions of the theory: Bogucki (2016).

[13]The linguistic interpretive rules are related to the rules of the language in which the legal text was written. Primacy is assigned to the rules based on the legal definitions.

structure of legal dogmatics, including the solution of validity problems and legal interpretation.[14] That conception—originally descriptive, but normative under the model of derivational account of interpretation—includes the assumptions concerning the legislator that legal practitioners are claimed to share. These assumptions reveal all aspects of formal and material rationality, including a rational legislator's knowledge of language and preferences, and these aspects of rationality form the basis for interpretive rules. Thus conceived, the rational legislator is an ideal type of the deep structure of law in a given legal culture. All things considered, the derivational theory of legal interpretation seems to exemplify semantic interpretivism since the deep syntactic and semantic structures determine the semantic representation (in the form of a legal norm) via transformations that result from the application of interpretive rules.

However, the grounding of interpretive rules in the derivational theory of legal interpretation remains debatable in a number of ways: first, internally, on the grounds of the theory itself. These rules are ultimately grounded in the legal culture,[15] which establishes the deep structure repository of the assumptions on which they are based. But these assumptions, focused on the figure of a rational legislator, are unverifiable.[16] Moreover, the interpreting lawyer who is supposed to share them is also treated in an idealised manner as a representative of that culture. Second, the grounding of interpretive rules in the derivational theory of legal interpretation remains debatable externally, due to the uncertainty of interpretive rules as such. It seems to be assumed by the derivational theory of interpretation that appropriateness or correctness of an interpretive practice is always a result of some rules antecedent in relation to that practice, potentially explicit and binding. This assumption can be characterised as regulism, and it can be refuted by metalinguistic arguments developed by Wittgenstein[17] and Sellars.[18]

Determinacy of *ratio legis* and/or *telos*, under the derivational theory of legal interpretation, is assured by functional interpretive rules. Such rules are intended to

[14]See Nowak (1973), pp. 11 and 29–34.

[15]My claim concerns the "ultimate" grounding, even though Zieliński (1998) prioritises characteristic features of a legal text as the major factor which determines the status and contents of interpretive rules in derivational conception of legal interpretation. It has to be pointed out, however, that these textual features are also subject to cultural recognition and acceptance.

[16]Nowak (1973), p. 173 admits it, by stating that lawyers never verify their assumptions concerning the rational legislator.

[17]Wittgenstein has famously noted that one can adopt a pragmatist approach to rules, or that "there is a way of grasping a rule which is not an interpretation, but which is exhibited in what we call 'obeying the rule' and 'going against it' in actual cases" (Wittgenstein 2005, § 201).

[18]According to Sellars 'correct' cannot mean 'correct according to a rule' (Sellars 1963, p. 321). He refutes the thesis that learning to use a language L is learning to obey the rules of L. He notes that a rule which prescribes an action A is a sentence in a language which contains a linguistic expression E for A. Hence, a rule prescribing the use of a linguistic expression E is a sentence in metalanguage containing E. Consequently, learning to use the rules for L presupposes the ability to use the metalanguage containing the rules for L. Using the metalanguage would similarly have to involve the ability to use a metametalanguage, and so forth.

produce the interpretation that is best justified from the axiological point of view, assigned to the ideal of a rational legislator. This result is achieved in two steps: the interpreter must, first, take all relevant values under consideration (global assessment) and, second, choose the legal norm that has the highest degree of consistency with such an evaluation (see Bogucki 2016, p. 262). It is in the above-mentioned steps that the issue of *ratio legis* arises since the axiological considerations of the interpreter are supposed to lead to establishing the value implemented by a norm selected as final result. The purpose or purposes of a legal norm are treated as fundamental within the global assessment because 'unless there had been the need for implementation of these values, the interpreted norm would not have been enacted' (Bogucki 2016, p. 264). However, due to the requirement of strict adherence to the legal text in the process of functional interpretation, the reconstruction of *ratio legis* may again be subject to the linguistic interpretive rules,[19] and if these procedures render no conclusion, the interpreter should rely on subsidiary materials (case law, legal doctrine, preparatory works),[20] once again applying linguistic rules to them. Having relied on these rules, the interpreter may still be unable to discern the purpose of legal norm, in which case the derivational theorists advise recourse to interpretive presumptions (such as *in dubio pro libertate*) or to the hierarchy of legal norms (including principles) and then again to the subsidiary materials, ultimately ending in the presumption *in dubio pro fines*.[21]

All in all, the procedure seems to run in a circular way, ultimately with the application of linguistic interpretive rules considered as decisive in each turn. The focus on transformational rules in this method of legal interpretation, paradoxically, leads to a situation in which the interpreter is fluctuating between over-determinacy and under-determinacy with *ratio legis*. Over-determinacy is due to the recurrent demand for reliance on linguistic interpretive rules, whereas under-determinacy is connected with the insistence to trust in the deep (or deeper) structure from which interpretive assumptions are drawn, thereby leaving room for substituting the assessment of values with personal preference.

1.2.3 Downstream Semantics

Semantic instrumentalism is the name used for many different positions in linguistics, social sciences and philosophy of science.[22] It is assumed for the present purpose that semantic instrumentalism considers meaning to be largely a *voluntary* matter and can be accompanied by the view that linguistic units play the role of

[19]See Bogucki (2016), p. 266.

[20]See Bogucki (2016), pp. 270–272.

[21]See Bogucki (2016), pp. 272–278.

[22]On the one hand, it holds that there are no substantive conditions of having singular thoughts as such thoughts can be generated at will by manipulating the direct reference. See Jeshion (2010). On the other, it claims that the theoretical terms of scientific theories (e.g. electron or tax-payer) should not be taken as referring to unobservable entities, but as constructs serving as tools for systematizing relations between phenomena. See Ladyman (2002), p. 155.

linguistic devices for *cognitive reorientation*. That last technical term refers to objects referred to and to action. Object reorientation takes place when re-evaluation of need and need requirements occur, and it produces new object identification confirmed by social consensus, and action reorientation stems from the selection of new objects and commitments made to attain them.[23] Semantic instrumentalism may accompany an epistemological view called doxastic voluntarism, which is a claim that 'an agent can form beliefs voluntarily' (Shah 2002, p. 436)[24] or that an agent's belief is 'sometimes under direct voluntary control' (Audi 2001, p. 93). This approach may be called *downstream semantics* because its major concern is with the *consequences* produced by users' moves in the language games.

The bearing of semantic instrumentalism on legal interpretation can be seen in a larger context of legal methodology, which embraces *consequentialism* both in legislation and in adjudication, by referring to sciences other than the legal ones, e.g. to economics, via economic analysis of law, or to ecology, via environmental impact assessment and technology impact assessment.[25] It must be noted that the consequences under consideration are not the consequences attached to certain states of affairs by law, which are unproblematic, but rather the *actual* consequences.[26] The distinction is often blurred by introducing to legal thinking such standards as 'policies', which refer to particular goals. The most prominent representation of consequentialism and instrumentalism in legal interpretation is provided by *legal pragmatism* with its emphasis on implications of interpretive solutions and 'the primacy of consequences in interpretation' (Posner 1995, p. 252). However, the reference to consequences in Posner's pragmatism is misleading, considering his acceptance of logical incoherence. This kind of instrumental pragmatism 'openly reduces assertion to an instrument of want-satisfaction or other drives' (Finnis 2002, p. 32). Legal pragmatists would certainly be comfortable with the semantics that restrains conceptual content in virtue of re-evaluation of need and need requirements, as such requirements may point out to new object identification in a specific context, and generate the meaning of legal concept best corresponding to contingent and context-specific needs.[27] The legal justification problem that arises under this approach can be mitigated only to some extent, depending on the interpreter's view concerning the balance between legal values and specific needs of the case that is decided in a given social or economic context. It should perhaps be noted that the greater is the importance attached to the perceived needs (and the smaller is the importance assigned to law or legal values), the more likely it is for the instrumental pragmatist approach to be obtained.

Semantic intrumentalism in legal interpretation is predominantly concerned with the *effects* of an interpretive decision, and this concern informs its approach to *ratio*

[23]See DeWitt (2000), p. 31.

[24]See also critical examination of this view in Shah (2002).

[25]See Mathis (2011), p. 3.

[26]About the distinction between legal and actual consequences, see Lübbe-Wolff (1981), p. 25.

[27]See Tamanaha (1996), p. 315.

legis. Under this view, *ratio legis* cannot be identified with anything that belongs to the past, whether in a precedential or statute-related way. A model instrumentalist interpreter could only situate *ratio legis* in the range of factual implications of his or her decision, presumably based on some empirical sociological or economic data. Admittedly, this approach offers instrumentalist decision-makers a broader set of available reasons and greater flexibility with regard to *ratio legis*. As it was mentioned above, instrumentalisation in legal interpretation is a matter of degree, changing with the extent of faithfulness to the purposes read into the legal text. In the Polish theory of legal interpretation, Ziembiński (1987, p. 25), far from making any pragmatist declarations, remarked that general knowledge, as well as knowledge of particular aspects of analysed situations, is one of the prerequisites when making statements concerning aims and functions of law. However, as long as the choice of the meaning of interpreted legal provisions pertaining to the determination of *ratio legis* is a consequence of *antecedently* established purposes written into the legal text, it remains within a broad scope of semantic foundationalism, rather than the kind of instrumentalism discussed here.[28] The degree of instrumentalisation is certainly higher in the institutional approach to law, where the point of departure for legal interpretation is not so much the legal text itself but rather the role of such texts and their fragments in creating legal institutions.[29] Under the institutional approach, institutional facts in law have to be interpreted as such before their *ratio legis* is considered, but still this approach cannot be identified with radical instrumentalism. In sum, a sharp separation line between instrumentalist and non-instrumentalist positions in theory of legal interpretation with regard to *ratio legis* runs, in my opinion, between those who consider *ratio legis* as instrumental to extra-legal consequences and those who consider it to be somehow attached to law as such. The former approach renders the *ratio legis* severely under-determined.

Table 1 summarises the discussion in the first part of this chapter, showing the impact of different types of one-sided semantics, which underpin the views on legal interpretation, on theoretical accounts of *ratio legis*.

2 Inferential Pragmatism in Legal Theory

One may, although one should not, be satisfied with one-sided semantics in legal theory. Semantic problems are but a part of inquiry in legal disciplines, and most problems that legal theory deals with require a broader and more integrated account of legal phenomena. As shown in the preceding section, a narrow semantic approach certainly proves unsatisfactory as far as an adequate account of *ratio legis* is

[28]It is characteristic of the approach to teleological interpretation in the Polish theory of legal interpretation by Gizbert-Studnicki (1985).

[29]For the paradigmatic account of institutional approach, see MacCormick and Weinberger (1986). In the Polish theory of law this approach is represented in Smolak (1998, 2012).

Table 1 Impact of different types of one-sided semantics on theoretical accounts of *ratio legis*

One-sided semantics type	Semantic view	Legal interpretation view	Bearing on articulation of *ratio legis*	Bearing on determinacy of *ratio legis*
Upstream	Semantic foundationalism	Originalism	Elimination by closure rules or	Meaning over-determinacy
	Semantic conventionalism	Textualism	Relocation to other standards or	
		Conventionalism	Relocation to deep structure	
Midstream	Semantic interpretivism	Derivational/rational legislator conception	Reliance on linguistic interpretive rules or	Meaning over-determinacy
	Lexicalism			
			Reliance on deep structure assumptions	Meaning under-determinacy
Downstream	Semantic instrumentalism	Instrumentalism	Relocation to factual implications	Meaning under-determinacy
		Consequentialism		
		Legal pragmatism		

concerned. The second and third parts of this chapter offer a somewhat different picture of it based on the assumption that the problems of meaning can be connected with those of action and more precisely with practical reasoning. Instead of assuming that situating *ratio legis* in the province of interpretation can lead to solution, we could assume that we might be able to provide an account that does not neglect the interpretation but instead puts it in proper place with regard to action prescribed by law. Integrated approaches to specific academic disciplines, legal science included, can be found in philosophy.[30]

2.1 *Inferential Pragmatism. An Overview*

Inferential pragmatism that can be considered as a good alternative to one-sided semantics in legal theory is an explanatory strategy that, in understanding conceptual content, gives precedence to what is implicit in the practice or activity of applying concepts; moreover, it recognises the practice of making inferences that is constitutive for grasping the content (see Brandom 2000, pp. 4 and 49). Accordingly, the meaning of a linguistic unit is fixed by the set of materially correct inferences in which it is used (see Sellars 1953). Conditions for correct material inferences have a

[30]Another way to look at the integration problem is naturalisation of legal science, which is not discussed in this chapter. Suffice it to say that I reject it philosophically, as unfounded reductionism, and historically, as a story of failure.

normative dimension that can be accounted for in the normative vocabulary of deontic statuses: commitment and entitlement. All these ideas are briefly elaborated below in order to explain why they seem to be fit for addressing the problem of *ratio legis* against the background of one-sided semantics in legal interpretation.

According to Brandom, 'expressions come to mean what they mean by being used as they are in practice, and intentional states (. . .) have the contents they do in virtue of the role they play in the behavioural economy of those to whom they are attributed. Content is understood in terms of proprieties of inferences, and those are understood in terms of the norm-instituting attitudes of taking or treating moves as appropriate or inappropriate in practice' (Brandom 1994, p. 134). Consequently, if one wants to understand what concepts are, one needs a pragmatic theory of that practice, an explanatory strategy starting with what people *do* rather than with what they *mean*.[31] Brandom's account of discursive practices in natural language focuses, in my opinion, on two dimensions: inferential and normative.

The inferential dimension of using concepts has to do with the practice of treating some inferences as materially correct. In the inferentialist picture of any discursive practice, *both our beliefs and our actions have specific propositional content*: they are about something, and it can be put in the form of a sentence. Moreover, their meaning can be fully grasped and articulated only in their inferential relations: '[f]or a response reliably differentially elicited by [for example] red things to qualify as the application of a concept, it must have a significance of a move in the game of giving and asking for reasons. It must be available as a premise for drawing further conclusions, and be liable to challenge by inferences from premises with incompatible consequences. Grasping the concept "red" requires practical mastery of its inferential role, as well as its non-inferential role as an appropriate response to certain sorts of stimuli' (Brandom 2009, p. 184). This approach to semantics underlines the essential rationality of humans as sapient rather than merely as sentient creatures.

Our beliefs and actions also have a normative dimension as far as they can be ascribed to agents and believers either correctly or incorrectly. The moves in the game of applying concepts must follow the criteria of appropriateness.[32] Conditions

---

[31] Alternative, and traditional, account of expressions' meaning would ascribe primacy to semantics. This may be the case in artificial languages, but not in natural ones. For more criticism against the traditional account of semantics, see Brandom (1994). In his more recent work, Brandom elaborates the skills and practices that are sufficient or necessary to ascribe meaning by providing a methodological framework of analysis expanded by pragmatic meta-vocabularies; see Brandom (2008). A less technical depiction of discursive practice can be found in Brandom (2000).

[32] This proposition follows directly from Kant's account of concepts understood as rules, the application of which can be subject to normative assessment as either correct or incorrect. Brandom does not share later Wittgenstein's ultimate scepticism about such assessment, stemming from the possibility of infinite number of different language games. On the contrary, he believes that there are certain core practices, such as asserting which make a general pragmatist account of language possible. Justification or the attribution of responsibility for Wittgenstein could be just another language game, whereas for Brandom it is implicit in natural language discursive practice.

for correct material inferences can be accounted for in the normative vocabulary of deontic statuses: commitment and entitlement.[33] By using concepts, participants of discursive practice adopt discursive commitments for specific conceptual contents. Such commitments result in the entitlements of other participants to verify them and—on the part of those who undertake them—to justify them (see Brandom 1994, p. 172). In standard cases, commitments are inherited from premises because being committed to premises in material inferences leads to being committed to conclusions. Being committed to certain contents may exclude commitments to other contents. Public acts of speech or actions are treated as assertions by those who can assess their inferential significance in the light of their own discursive commitments. Assertions can be supplemented by other acts of speech such as deferral, disavowal, query or challenge. Such discursive moves are normative precisely because they produce the normative statuses of those who participate in discursive practice, not because of some antecedent rules. Keeping track of one's own and others' deontic statuses—that is, commitments and entitlements—is what Brandom calls 'deontic score-keeping'.

Inferential pragmatism is particularly useful to any account that intends to make sense of both our thoughts and actions (i.e., our cognitive and practical commitments). The theoretical account of law that could remedy the one-sidedness of semantic approaches would also have to make sense of our thoughts and actions. It would have to develop, with regard to law, Brandom's claim that 'there are two species of discursive commitment: the cognitive and the practical. (...) practical commitments are like doxastic commitments in being essentially inferentially articulated' (Brandom 1994, p. 233).

Before such an account is offered, however, we need to have a look at Brandom's treatment of action, which is based on five ideas.[34] First, he maintains that our *doxastic commitments* (beliefs) can be inferred not only from our explicit claims but also *from* our *intentional actions*. Second, actions are *intentional* due to some *specification* or description (e.g., alerting the burglar may not be an intentional action of someone who intentionally turns on the lights). Third, a privileged way of specifying an action as an intentional one is featuring it as the *conclusion* of a fragment of practical reasoning. Fourth, in order to examine the sense in which practical reasons are *reasons*, Brandom expresses intentions in *normative vocabulary*, i.e., as practical discursive commitments: commitments to act. Under this scheme, beliefs would correspond to doxastic commitments. Both types of commitments would stand in inferential relations among themselves and with those belonging to the other type. The fourth idea serves double purpose: to advance Brandom's belief model of intending, that is, modelling practical commitments on doxastic ones, and to offer the picture of practical reasoning as relating beliefs as premises to

[33]In legal theory, deontic statuses are conceived of more narrowly than in Brandom's philosophical work. E.g. a deontic status of an action is typically considered as something expressed in statements about whether it is according to the law. See Bulygin (2015), p. 307.

[34]See Brandom (2000), pp. 82–84 and 93–96.

intentions as conclusions. Fifth, in order to examine the sense in which practical reasons are *causes*, he introduces an analogy between acknowledgment of practical commitments ending in states of affairs brought about by intentional action and acknowledgment of doxastic commitments ending in states of affairs brought about by perception. That last idea allows Brandom to model actions as discursive exit transitions on perceptions as discursive entry transitions. Just like perception can be accounted for as an input for acknowledging a commitment, that input being based on the capacity to respond differentially to the presence of things of certain colour, so can action be seen as an output of acknowledging a commitment with a given content. In the former case, perception may cause an appropriate acknowledgment of a commitment, and in the latter it is the acknowledgment of a commitment that causes action.

Brandomian account of action is essentially a pragmatist one since it focuses on what agents do when they engage in practical reasoning. The above-mentioned set of interconnected ideas concerning action allows Brandom to conclude that there is a difference between intentions and reasons: *intentions are to reasons as commitments are to entitlements*. Reasons, for their part, may play different roles in practical reasoning, depending on the kind of normative vocabulary that must be used to characterise the deontic status of an agent. To sum up, Brandom's treatment of action allows us to distinguish between three types or dimensions of acting, which will be used in the subsequent account of *ratio legis*:

1. Acting *intentionally*: an agent acts intentionally when his or her acknowledgement of a practical commitment can be inferred by deontic scorekeepers from the context of his or her action or from speech acts.
2. Acting *with* reasons: an agent acts with reasons when he or she is entitled to his or her practical commitment, which can be made intelligible both to the agent and to others by producing a suitable part of practical reasoning to explain what reasons one had for doing so and so (even though in particular cases one acted intentionally but without reasons).
3. Acting *for* reasons: an agent acts for reasons when his or her acknowledgment of practical commitment is elicited by proper reasoning, and particular reasons function as causes for acting.

2.2 The Value of Inferential Pragmatism in Legal Theory

The above-sketched philosophical framework gives explanatory precedence to pragmatics before semantics and grants intentional action equal footing with belief, thereby combining semantics with practical reasoning. It is thereby suitable to complete the task of explaining the relationship between interpretation (i.e., largely semantic problems) and action, with regard to *ratio legis*. Completion of this task, however, requires some preliminaries to demonstrate the framework's adequacy for theorising about law.

Law fits into this broadly inferentialist picture of semantics, provided that when legal practitioners use legal concepts (when they engage in legal discursive practice (LDP)), they remain within given autonomous discursive practice (ADP) in a natural language. It must be assumed that such practitioners have discursive skills and abilities that extend in some respect beyond those of any participant of ADP. Legislatures, administrative bodies, courts, solicitors, counsels, prosecutors and so on are all institutional users in the sense that their discursive moves in that practice count only in so far as they take place when such users act in their official, status-related, capacity. It must also be assumed that practitioners are reasonable in LDP, just as they are in ADP. LDP is built on the ability to use legal concepts in order to form beliefs and/or actions that can be treated by other participants of that LPD as having determinate content. One can easily, but unconvincingly, associate law exclusively with LDP since it is inconceivable without linguistic utterances, legal rules or norms having pride of place among them. However, the central case of human action is acting on *reasons* and not on linguistic utterances that may articulate them. We would not have developed our ability to prescribe and assess our own conduct and the conduct of other people, unless we were *first* able to treat at least some of our behaviour as prompted by reasons.

Apart from common features of ADP and LDP, we must also introduce some distinctions. First, it is tempting for legal theorists to focus on normative vocabulary used by Brandom. However, deontic statuses in ADP must not be confused with deontic statuses in LDP (commitment to legal content), and those LDP statuses must not be confounded with specifically legal deontic statuses (commitment to legal action). In the socio-legal world as we know it, there have to be social structures of specifically legal authority and legal responsibility. It is by reference to these structures that we assign deontic statuses with regard to legal concepts and legal actions. One could be discursively committed to a certain legal meaning of a linguistic expression (e.g., as a legal historian of an ancient legal system) and thereby 'picture' assuming one's deontic status, within that LDP, but this is not identical with one's treating it as a legal reason for action.

Second, and more importantly for the account of *ratio legis*, we are now able to connect the problems of deploying concepts (by forming beliefs) with those of action. Regardless of philosophical background, it is accepted that practical reasoning is about what one ought to do: it is about action. Among other things, philosophers seem to differ on the epistemic grounds for action. In the classical tradition, the major problem in this regard is that of knowing the good and how it is related to the right action.[35] Modern tradition often replaces knowing the good in practical

[35]In the classical tradition a division of syllogisms into theoretical and practical comes from Aristotle who said that practical inference leads up to or ends in action. The major premise indicates something good or something that ought to be done. See *De Motu Animalium* 701a, 12–14 and *Nichomachean Ethics* 1147a 6–7, 28–30. A concise formulation of the task of practical reasoning was provided by Aquinas: "Practical reason judges and pronounces sentence on matters of action." *Ratio practica iudicat et sententiat de agendis*, *STh*, 1–2, q. 74, a. 7 co. Rhonheimer develops this line of thought: "The judgments of practical reason have as their object good as regards acting from

reasoning with wanting something[36] or focuses on purposive behaviour and action in general.[37] Briefly, received views of practical reasoning focus either on premises (reasons or other possible grounds for action) or on conclusions (action). This last remark seems to mimic the problems we have exposed with regard to one-sided semantic accounts. Brandom's account of practical reasoning may be able to escape that risk since it is based on the fundamental idea that 'giving and asking for reasons for *actions* is possible only in the context of practices of giving and asking for reasons generally – that is, of practices of making and defending *claims* or *judgments*' (Brandom 2000, p. 81).

The question remains whether this approach to practical reasoning applies to *legal reasoning*. To the extent that legal reasoning is about what one ought to do, it falls within the scope of practical reasoning.[38] Again, this is also where the consensus reaches its limits. An accurate account of specifically legal reasons for action remains the bone of contention among legal scholars, and these disagreements are reflected in different accounts of *ratio legis*. Disentangling particular ways of understanding *ratio legis* in legal scholarship is even more difficult, considering the fact that the assumptions on which they rest often remain indirect or unacknowledged. Drawing on Brandom's account of ADP, it can be claimed with regard to law that acquiring and ascribing deontic statuses in LDP presuppose a more primitive ability to engage in legal practical reasoning, to give and ask for specifically legal reasons. This ability to distinguish between legal and non-legal reasons for action can only develop in a given natural language and in a particular socio-legal setting.

This brings us to the question of nature of *legal reasons*, which are related to the *institutional* status of an agent. Brandom identifies three types of practical reasons, exemplified by preferences or desires, social statuses and unconditional duties. What follows are three types of practical inferences: instrumental, institutional and unconditional. Each of these can be expressed in the form of a rule or norm. Yet, according to Brandom, a proposition expressing that norm does not prescribe conduct in the first place but rather explicitly endorses material proprieties of practical reasons.[39] In other words, normative or evaluative vocabulary is to practice as conditionals are to

---

the aspect of its truth. Like the speculative intellect, the practical intellect knows truth. Known good, therefore, is 'practical truth'." Rhonheimer (2008), p. 169 (notes omitted).

[36]This theme is famously developed by G.E.M. Anscombe: "The mark of the practical reasoning is that the thing wanted is *at a distance* from the immediate action, and the immediate action is calculated as the way of getting or doing or securing the thing wanted." Anscombe (1957), p. 79.

[37]According to G.H. von Wright, Hegel in his *Logic* "construed purposive action as an inference, leading from the subjective setting of an end through insight into the objective connections of natural facts to the objectivation of the end in action". Von Wright (1978), p. 47.

[38]See Warner (2005), p. 259.

[39]See Brandom (2000), p. 89.

theory. While *instrumental* inferences are based on preferences acknowledged or attributed to the agent,[40] *unconditional* inferences, in Brandom's account, are characterised by agent-neutral moral reasons.[41] In the case of *institutional* inferences, however, premises are articulated by recognising a particular institutional status of an agent—that status serving as main premise.[42] Alternative institutional inferences are usually not available because it is from a given social status that particular practical conclusions follow.[43] Moreover, the 'goodness' of institutional inferences is licensed not by the norm implicit in such inferences but 'by others associated with the same social institutional status' (ibid.). I endorse the idea that legal reasoning can be assimilated to the institutional pattern of reasoning, with obvious benefits: (1) it saves the realm of law from being confused with instrumental or unconditional reasoning, without leaving it totally disconnected with either; (2) it affirms the connection of law with social world through institutional legal statuses, being essentially social constructs; (3) it grounds law's claims to both rationality and objectivity.

In legal theory, particular attention is paid to explicitly normative statements that prescribe conduct (legal rules or norms, depending on convention), and so theories of legal interpretation have developed methods of elaborating more or less unambiguous prescriptive statements from legal texts. What is usually lost from sight, however, is the fact that the ability to generate such prescriptions—whether by

[40] A given preference or desire is only a *prima facie* reason for a given action, because different preferences may compete, and many alternative actions can be chosen as conclusions of instrumental inferences. E.g. if one's desire is to stay dry when the rain sets in, one *shall* open an umbrella, find shelter under a tree, etc.

[41] This account seems to be closely modelled on Kantian categorical imperative, although a Kantian would probably assimilate all three types of reasoning to that pattern. An agent performing unconditional inference has reasons for action which are expressed in a different rational 'ought' than the prudential or institutional one. E.g. if it is *wrong* to harm anyone to no purpose, and repeating the gossip would harm someone to no purpose, one shall not repeat the gossip (see Brandom 2000, pp. 84–85).

[42] Institutional legal statuses are usually very similar to what Jeremy Waldron calls a condition-status in law: it arises out of conditions into which anyone might fall in virtue of some facts (e.g. being a minor or a bankrupt) or choices (e.g. marriage or being an alien) (see Waldron 2009, p. 242). E.g., if one occupies a status of employer, according to the Polish Labour Code, this should be treated as a sufficient reason for providing safe working conditions for the employees. If one is a professional soldier, one has a status-related reason for not being a member of the board of a commercial company. If one has the status of a refugee in Poland, one has a reason for applying for residence card. The most general institutional legal status would probably be identical with being under jurisdiction (of a state). Statuses as specifically good reasons would obtain for *anyone* enjoying the same status, which is typical of law.

[43] For instance, if one has the status of a bank clerk, and one is going to work, one is *required* to wear a tie. A deontic scorekeeper would consider it a good institutional inference not only for an individual agent, but also for any other agent who occupies the same status. Thus, the status-based premise should be considered as objective (whether based on further factual or normative premises), because—if the scorekeeper is committed to the other agent's occupying that status—such a commitment would correspond to a good reason for action for that agent (see Brandom 2000, p. 91).

legislators or by law-applying agents—presupposes the ability to deploy their content in practical reasoning. To be precise, much of contemporary legal theory is about language,[44] pragmatics included,[45] and about practical reasoning.[46] Yet seldom are these problems connected. Inferential pragmatism, in my view, offers a connection to law by setting an order of explanation that proceeds not from words (refined in LDP into prescriptive legal statements) to actions but from practices of finding specifically legal reasons for actions to statements that codify such practices by licensing certain inferences as distinctly legal. The content of legal concepts is ultimately established within the overall aim of law's practice, i.e., prescribing the right conduct by providing *reasons* for acting.

A feature of law as discursive practice, different from universal ADP, is applying and forming reasons, which are *explicit* rather than implicit. This explicitness is due to rational justification being required and pertinent to judicial decisions (see Brandom 2014, p. 20). Another property of institutional moves in LDP is the existence of *special rules for ascribing meaning*, particularly through applying legal definitions and decisions of other institutional bodies, with regard to identifying conceptual content through the decisions of courts or legal doctrine. While using legal concepts, 'judges are responsible *for* the law, and (...) judges are responsible *to* the law' (Brandom 2014, p. 32).

Decision-makers' responsibility *for* the law has to do with the fact that there is much to that law (more in common law than in civil law) that is the cumulative result of judicial decisions to apply or not to apply the concepts in particular cases. In selecting the prior uses of such concepts and conceptualising current facts, the judge both further determines (in the sense of sharpening) the content of the legal concepts involved and provides precedents and rationales to which future judges are at least potentially responsible. In this way, the deciding judge exercises authority over both the content of the legal concepts being applied and, thereby, the decisions of future judges (Brandom 2014, p. 32).

Decision-makers are also responsible *to* the conceptual contents inherited from prior users, including their justifications, precedents and considerations. This is because 'the justification of a judge's decision can appeal only to the authority of prior decisions, and so to the conceptual content those decisions have conferred on or discovered in the legal term in question' (Brandom 2014, p. 32).[47]

---

[44]In a sense Dworkin rightly argued that Hart suffered from a 'semantic sting', because he thought that lawyers follow certain linguistic criteria for evaluating propositions of law (see Dworkin 1986, p. 45). Jerzy Wróblewski might also have 'suffered' from it, since his interest in language led him to developing a 'semantic conception of a legal norm' (see Wróblewski 1983).

[45]Much work in the pragmatics of legal language continues to focus on Gricean and post-Gricean pragmatics (see e.g. Soames 2008, Solum 2013, and Marmor 2014).

[46]Interestingly, Hart's successors, J. Finnis and J. Raz, each in his respective way of either New School of Natural Law or Legal Positivism, seem to be focused on practical reasoning at the expense of language (see notably Finnis 1990, 2011 and Raz 2009).

[47]This statement may require some qualification, especially in civil law systems, where 'prior decisions' should be understood, e.g. in case of newly enacted statutes, as legislator's decisions.

3 Relevance of Inferential Pragmatism in Legal Theory to *Ratio Legis*

3.1 Inferentialist Account of Ratio Legis *by Canale and Tuzet*

All standard accounts of *ratio legis*, according to Canale and Tuzet (2010, p. 198), address it as an intentional entity or as part of an argumentative scheme. Based on Brandom's inferential semantics, Canale and Tuzet offer another account of *ratio legis*, whereby the claims about the *ratio* are treated as moves in a dialectical exchange of reasons among legal practitioners, and such claims are considered as speech acts. Such acts are characterised by these authors in terms of deontic statuses (commitments and entitlements), following the Brandomian deontic scorekeeping model presented above. Canale and Tuzet propose a pragmatic analysis focused on different argumentative uses of *ratio legis*, their justification and constraints. On that account, if a legal practitioner (e.g., a judge) identifies in a propositional form *p* certain content with a particular *ratio legis*, he or she undertakes commitment with regard to that content and to both premises and consequences of *p*. If the judge 'accomplishes these duties or commitments, she will be entitled to *p* in the argumentation (. . .) and *p* will be considered to be the *ratio* of the rule in that context' (Canale and Tuzet 2010, p. 200).

Argumentative claims that produce deontic statuses of commitments and entitlements of the speakers can be further analysed as relations of commitment-preserving, entitlement-preserving and incompatibility types (see Brandom 2008).

In a commitment-preserving relation, if speaker S is committed to *p*, then S is committed to *q*. According to Canale and Tuzet (2010, pp. 204–205), this kind of inferential relation applied to *ratio legis* would hold if there is an explicitly stated purpose of certain rule or provision that a legal practitioner may be committed to. If this is the case, then such a practitioner would argue within constraints posed by the wording of that explicit statement, and in consequence, he would have to be committed to the *ratio* identified with the literal content of *p*.

In an entitlement-preserving relation, if speaker S is entitled to *p*, then S is *prima facie* entitled to *q*. It must be remembered that according to Brandom, someone is entitled to *p* in virtue of someone else's commitment to that *p*. In other words, one's entitlement consists of having a right to ask for reasons justifying a claim to which someone else is committed. The status of entitlement when dealing with *ratio legis* could result from other practitioners' claims about the legal system (e.g., legislative history, legal scholarship or previous courts' decisions that the purpose of legal provision P is R). If one is entitled to such a claim, then one is *prima facie* entitled to the claim that R is the *ratio legis* (see Canale and Tuzet 2010, pp. 205–206).

In an incompatibility relation, if speaker S is committed to *p*, then S is not entitled to *q*. Canale and Tuzet observe that when consequentialist arguments are used to determine the *ratio legis*, a legal practitioner who is committed to a claim about predictable (desirable or undesirable) consequences of applying a certain legal provision is not entitled to a given claim about the *ratio*. 'The fact that the consequences of a certain interpretation [of a legal provision – MD] are considered desirable or undesirable is the "evaluative ground" for determining the *ratio* of the interpreted statute, once assumed that this interpretation is a necessary condition of the expected social consequences' (Canale and Tuzet 2010, p. 206).

Canale's and Tuzet's pragmatic analyses provide interesting conclusions about how *ratio legis* is justified in the legal argumentative practice: they demonstrate that the burden of argumentation involving *ratio legis* does not rest with the *ratio* as such, but instead it necessarily depends on some other arguments that are made manifest in different types of inferential relations. Correspondingly, commitment-preserving relations seem to show the reliance on linguistic arguments. In case of entitlement-preserving relations, the argumentative dependence is on arguments that either psychologically or genetically refer to implicit intention, but such systemic arguments as legal system's coherence may also be involved. Finally, incompatibility relations reveal legal practitioners' seeking support from evaluative arguments, including principles.

3.2 **Ratio Legis:** ***Reasons and Actions. Towards an Integrated Account***

The inferentialist account of *ratio legis* by Canale and Tuzet provides a good example of employing Brandomian ideas in the theory of legal interpretation (even though they are formulated in argumentative terms), particularly by using the normative vocabulary of deontic statuses to describe the decision-makers' moves in LDP. This account, however, is only half-sufficient, given the broader inferentialist picture of legal practice adopted in the present chapter. Canale and Tuzet provide useful inferentialist tools for meta-analysis of practices of legal interpreters, but they do not take into consideration the action-related dimension of law. Meanwhile, the core tenet of the present approach to *ratio legis* is based on the claim that acquiring and ascribing deontic statuses in LDP presupposes, and thus makes explicit, an ability of agents to engage in legal practical reasoning, to give and ask for specifically legal reasons. What follows is the requirement for an adequate account of *ratio legis* to keep the balance between doxastic statuses related to conceptual content and practical ones related to action.

In that last respect, Canale's and Tuzet's description of deontic statuses acquired by legal interpreters (judges) must be complemented. Both a commitment-preserving relation that holds if the interpreter has epistemic access to an explicitly stated purpose of certain rule or provision and an entitlement-preserving relation resulting from other practitioners' claims about the legal system (e.g., legislative history, legal scholarship or previous courts' decisions) explain what happens when *upstream* semantics is adopted. An incompatibility relation describes a paradigmatic situation of a semantic instrumentalist, and any of the inferential relations characterised by Canale and Tuzet can be the case when interpretive semantics is applied. Each of these relations may occur in interpretivist semantics. This treatment of *ratio legis* can be defended as far as legal interpretation is done *in abstracto*, apart from actual cases, but whenever agents enter into fore, it should include their practical deontic statuses as well.

The space of reasons, also in law, extends both upstream and downstream, and the decision-makers' responsibility has a double dimension—to the law and for the law, and so the account of *ratio legis* has to include them. Complementing the account of Canale and Tuzet can extend in both directions, that is, to the legislator and to the agent, understood as an addressee of legal norms, which is the extension attempted here.

Following Brandom's treatment of action, we can distinguish between three types or dimensions of legal actions, which will be used in the account of *ratio legis*.

Intentional legal action takes place when an agent's acknowledgement of a practical commitment can be inferred by deontic scorekeepers (decision-makers) from the context of his or her action or from speech acts. The same action may acquire one or multiple legal specifications, regardless of many other specifications. Since the agent whose commitment is ascribed by external deontic scorekeepers depends on the ascription, his or her situation with regard to *ratio legis*, and consequently the situation of those who take his or her action to have such and such conceptual content, is trivial, at least in case of commitment-preserving or entitlement-preserving relations. Depending on the deontic status of the scorekeeper, the agent, along with the commitment ascribed to him or her, inherits the scorekeeper's relation with regard to *ratio legis*: whether it is commitment preserving or entitlement preserving. A non-trivial situation may occur if the scorekeeper (who happens to be a consequentialist) is in an incompatibility relation, that is, when he is committed to a claim about predictable (desirable or undesirable) consequences of applying a certain legal provision, but he is not entitled to a given claim about the *ratio*. If the commitment, which such a deontic scorekeeper ascribes to the agent in whose case the incompatibility relation obtains, differs from the one he himself adopted, this may prompt the scorekeeper to revise his own commitment. Taking this fact under consideration may lead to strengthening or weakening the original commitment on the part of the scorekeeper and perhaps to even rectifying the incompatibility. This may ultimately be a mitigating factor for semantic instrumentalism in legal interpretation by providing a counterbalance to consequentialism.

Action *with* legal reasons can be identified when an agent is entitled to his or her practical commitment, which can be made intelligible both to the agent and to others by producing a suitable part of practical legal reasoning to explain what reasons one had for doing so and so (even though in particular cases one acted intentionally but without reasons). In the practice of law, especially in civil law, such an entitlement on the agent's part is due to the corresponding duty of the legislator to provide an agent with legal reasons for action, and an agent's practical commitment has a reservoir of reasons, typically contained in the legislation, elaborated by turning them into agent's legal reasons for action. For the purpose of the present discussion, in order to make more useful the distinction between acting with reasons and acting for reasons, I assume that acting with legal reasons has to do with an agent's ability to produce a minimal legal reasoning for action, and that includes the sufficient characteristics of the legal status that can be treated as a reason for action. This does not include the purpose of a rule, as might be the case in acting for legal reasons. If decision-makers, in virtue of their own *commitment-preserving* relation, are committed to *ratio legis* based on their previous commitment to the content of an explicitly stated purpose of certain rule or provision, they may be faced either with *compatible* practical commitment of the agent whose entitlement would correspond to their own or with *incompatibility* occurring when the commitment generated by the agent's practical legal reasoning does not match their own. In standard cases, provided that doxastic commitments take precedence before practical ones, a particular piece of the agent's reasoning may have to be defeated by the force of better reasons produced by the reasoning of decision-makers. If, on the other hand, decision-makers are in an *entitlement-preserving* relation because they inherit other legal practitioners' commitments to claims about the legal system (e.g., legislative history, legal scholarship or previous courts' decisions that the purpose of legal provision is so and so), their *entitlement* may be further *inherited* by the agent whose own piece of practical reasoning results in similar need for reasons. The decision-makers' entitlement, however, may turn out to be *incompatible* with the agent's practical *commitment*. The principle of primacy of doxastic commitments before practical ones may again defeat the agent's commitment, but decision-makers might be taken by the force of better reasons to re-examine and reclaim their entitlement in such a confrontation. Taking this fact under consideration may lead to the strengthening or weakening of the original entitlement on the part of the deontic scorekeeper and become a mitigating factor for semantic foundationalism in legal interpretation by challenging the entitlement and extending justificatory requirements on the part of decision-makers. Finally, decision-makers can be in a relation of *incompatibility*, that is, when by virtue of being committed to some consequences they are not entitled to a given claim about *ratio legis*. Interestingly for eliciting *ratio legis*, the agent's practical commitment to legal action may prove the decision-makers' commitment to be right or wrong, and thus it may help to rectify the incompatibility relation and remedy instrumentalism.

Action *for* legal reasons takes place when the agent's acknowledgment of practical commitment is elicited by proper legal reasoning, and particular reasons function as causes for acting. Since the difference between acting for reasons and acting with reasons is a matter of degree to which the agent's practical reasoning is 'proper', or complete, the same relations between the results of a decision-maker's moves and practical deontic status, as characterised with regard to acting with reasons, would occur. The only difference might concern the applicability of the rule that grants doxastic commitments precedence before practical ones. A complete version of an agent's reasoning would also have to include, next to status-related reasons for action, a sufficient doxastic commitment, which may include the purpose of the rule that defines the legal status of an agent. This puts the agent on the same ground as the decision-makers or interpreters in the space of legal reasons, and the only difference between them is that of institutional position, which leaves the decision-makers with the final say. But the final say is not the same as the ultimate

Table 2 Impact of deontic status of an agent on deontic status of interpreters/decision-makers, considering the type of action

Deontic status of an interpreter/decision-maker (S)	Type of action	Deontic status of an agent (A)	Impact of deontic status of an agent on deontic status of interpreters/decision-makers
If S is committed to *p*, then S is committed to *q* (commitment-preserving relation)	Intentional legal action	A is committed to *q*	*None*
	Action with/for legal reasons	A is entitled to *q*	*None*
		A is not entitled to *q*	*None*
If S is entitled to *p*, then S is *prima facie* entitled to *q* (entitlement-preserving relation)	Intentional legal action	A is committed to *q*	*Entitlement-preserving relation strengthened*
	Action with/for legal reasons	A is entitled to *q*	*None*
		A is not entitled to *q*	*None or entitlement-preserving relation to be re-examined*
If S is committed to *p*, then S is not entitled to *q* (incompatibility relation)	Intentional legal action	A is committed to *q*	*Incompatibility relation weakened*
	Action with/for legal reasons	A is entitled to *q*	*Incompatibility relation weakened or to be re-examined*
		A is not entitled to *q*	*Incompatibility relation strengthened*

reason, and thus, by embracing the agent's complete practical reasoning, the decision-makers are offered an extended check on the conceptual content they commit themselves to in understanding the law, including the *ratio legis*. With Brandom's ideas applied, our theoretical approach can be broadened to embrace the rich network of normative relations in law and still not lose the objective dimension of these practices in law. This is summarily illustrated in Table 2.

Brandom's idea is that living in a human society is moving within a rich network of normative social relationships and enjoying many kinds of normative statuses, which reach into many dimensions. The tendency to integrate these dimensions in legal theory can be made successful by many different approaches, of which inferential pragmatism is just one. The present discussion of *ratio legis* illustrates that linguistic problems with which analytically oriented theory and philosophy is bound can indeed be tackled more effectively, thanks to the tools developed by inferential pragmatism. An approach that allows for the ability to keep track of our own and fellow speakers' and agents' statuses to find its way into our law-related practices is worth pursuing.

References

Anscombe GEM (1957) Intention. Basil Blackwell, Oxford

Audi R (2001) Doxastic voluntarism and the ethics of belief. In: Steup M (ed) Knowledge, truth, and duty. Oxford University Press, Oxford, pp 93–111

Bogucki O (2016) Model wykładni funkcjonalnej w derywacyjnej koncepcji wykładni prawa. Poligres Multimedia, Szczecin

Borowicz A (2009) Argumentacja oparta na odwołaniu się do racji normy prawnej. Państwo i Prawo 3:48–59

Brandom RB (1994) Making it explicit. Reasoning, representing and discursive commitment. Harvard University Press, Cambridge

Brandom RB (2000) Articulating reasons: an introduction to inferentialism. Harvard University Press, Cambridge

Brandom RB (2008) Between saying and doing. Towards an analytic pragmatism. Oxford University Press, Oxford

Brandom RB (2009) Reason in philosophy: animating ideas. Belknap Harvard University Press, Cambridge

Brandom RB (2014) A Hegelian model of legal concept determination: the normative fine structure of the judges' chain novel. In: Hubbs G, Lind D (eds) Pragmatism, law and language. Routledge, New York, pp 19–39

Bulygin E (2015) The objectivity of the law. In: Bernal C et al (eds) Essays in legal philosophy. Oxford University Press, Oxford, pp 302–310

Canale D, Tuzet G (2010) What is the reason for this rule? An inferential account of the Ratio Legis. Argumentation 24:197–210

Chomsky N (1965) Aspects of the theory of syntax. MIT Press, Cambridge

Chomsky N (1972) Studies on semantics in generative grammar. Mouton, The Hague

DeWitt RM (2000) Beyond equilibrium theory: theories of social action and social change applied to a study of power sharing in transition. University Press of America, Lanham

Dworkin R (1986) Law's empire. Harvard University Press, Cambridge

Field HH (1975) Conventionalism and instrumentalism in semantics. Noûs 9:375–405

Finnis J (1990) Natural law and legal reasoning. Cleveland State Law Rev 38:1–13

Finnis J (2002) Natural law: the classical tradition. In: Coleman J, Shapiro S (eds) The Oxford handbook of jurisprudence and philosophy of law. Oxford University Press, Oxford, pp 1–60

Finnis J (2011) Philosophy of law: collected essays, vol IV. Oxford University Press, Oxford

Gizbert-Studnicki T (1985) Wykładnia celowościowa. Studia Prawnicze 3–4:51–70

Greenawalt K (2002) Constitutional and statutory interpretation. In: Coleman J, Shapiro S (eds) The Oxford handbook of jurisprudence and philosophy of law. Oxford University Press, Oxford, pp 268–310

Jeshion R (2010) Singular thought: acquaintance, semantic instrumentalism, and cognitivism. In: Jeshion R (ed) New essays on singular thought. Oxford University Press, Oxford, pp 105–140

Katz JJ, Postal PM (1964) An integrated theory of linguistic descriptions. M.I.T. Press, Cambridge

Ladyman J (2002) Understanding philosophy of science. Routledge, London

Lang W (1986) Moral valuation and justification of law. In: Studies in the theory and philosophy of law, vol 1. Zakład Narodowy im. Ossolińskich, Wrocław

Lübbe-Wolff G (1981) Rechtsfolgen und Realfolgen. Welche Rolle können Folgenerwägungen in der juristischen Regel- und Begriffsbildung spielen? Freiburg

MacCormick N, Weinberger O (1986) An institutional theory of law: new approaches to legal positivism. Kluwer Academic Publishers, Dordrecht

Marmor A (2014) The language of law. Oxford University Press, Oxford

Mathis K (2011) Consequentialism in law. In: Mathis K (ed) Efficiency, sustainability, and justice to future generations. Springer, Berlin, pp 3–28

Moore MS (2016) Semantics, metaphysics, and objectivity in law. In: Keil G, Poscher R (eds) Blurred boundaries: vagueness and the law. Oxford University Press, Oxford

Morawski L (2002) Wykładnia w orzecznictwie sądów polskich. TNOiK Dom Organizatora, Toruń

Newmeyer F (1986) Linguistic theory in America, 2nd edn. Academic, San Diego

Nowak L (1973) Interpretacja prawnicza: studium z metodologii prawoznawstwa. Państwowe Wydawnictwo Naukowe, Warszawa

Peczenik A (1989) On law and reason. Springer, Dordrecht

Posner R (1995) Overcoming law. Harvard University Press, Cambridge
Raz J (2009) Between authority and interpretation: on the theory of law and practical reason. Oxford University Press, Oxford
Rhonheimer M (2008) The cognitive structure of the natural law and the truth of subjectivity. In: Murphy WF Jr (ed) The perspective of the acting person: essays in the renewal of Thomistic moral philosophy. The Catholic University of America Press, Washington, pp 158–194
Russell B (1956) Logic and knowledge: essays, 1901–1950. George Allen and Unwin, London
Savigny FC (1867) System of the modern roman law (trans: Holloway W), vol I. J. Higginbotham, Madras
Scalia A (1996) A matter of interpretation: federal courts and the law. An essay. Princeton University Press, Princeton
Sellars WS (1953) Inference and meaning. Mind 62:313–338
Sellars WS (1963) Science, perception, and reality. Routledge & Kegan Paul Ltd, London
Shah N (2002) Clearing space for doxastic voluntarism. The Monist 85(3):436–445
Smolak M (1998) Prawo, fakt, instytucja. Koncepcje teoretycznoprawne Prawniczego Pozytywizmu Instytucjonalnego. Poznań, Wydawnictwo Naukowe UAM
Smolak M (2010) Uzasadnienie decyzji interpretacyjnej jako praktyczne rozumowanie prawnicze. In: Choduń A, Czepita S (eds) W poszukiwaniu dobra wspólnego. Księga jubileuszowa Profesora Macieja Zielińskiego. Wydawnictwo Naukowe Uniwersytetu Szczecińskiego, Szczecin, pp 151–164
Smolak M (2012) Wykładnia celowościowa z perspektywy pragmatycznej. Wolters Kluwer, Warszawa
Soames S (2008) Interpreting legal texts: what is, and what is not, special about the law. In: Philosophical essays, vol 1: Natural language: what it means and how we use it. Princeton University Press, Princeton, pp 403–424
Solum L (2013) Communicative content and legal content. Notre Dame Law Rev 89:479–520
Tamanaha BZ (1996) Pragmatism in U.S. legal theory: its application to normative jurisprudence, sociolegal studies, and the fact-value distinction. Am J Jurisprudence 41:315–355
von Wright GH (1978) On so-called practical inference. In: Raz J (ed) Practical reasoning. Oxford University Press, Oxford, pp 46–62
Waldron J (2009) Dignity, rank and rights. In: The Tanner lectures on human values, University of California, Berkeley. Available at: https://tannerlectures.utah.edu/_documents/a-to-z/w/Waldron_09.pdf
Warner R (2005) Adjudication and legal reasoning. In: Golding MP, Edmundson WA (eds) The Blackwell guide to the philosophy of law and legal theory. Blackwell, Malden, pp 259–270
Wittgenstein L (2005) Philosophical investigations. The German text with a revised English translation (trans: Anscombe GEM), 7th edn. Blackwell, Oxford
Wróblewski J (1959) Zagadnienia teorii wykładni prawa ludowego. Wydawnictwo Prawnicze, Warszawa
Wróblewski J (1983) In: Aarnio A (ed) Meaning and truth in judicial decision. Juridica, Helsinki
Zieliński M (1972) Interpretacja jako proces dekodowania tekstu prawnego. Wydawnictwo Naukowe UAM, Poznań
Zieliński M (1998) Wyznaczniki reguł wykładni prawa. Ruch Prawniczy, Ekonomiczny i Socjologiczny 3–4:1–20
Zieliński M (2002) Wykładnia prawa. Zasady, reguły, wskazówki, 1st edn. Lexis Nexis, Warszawa
Ziembiński Z (1960) Przepis prawny a norma prawna. Ruch Prawniczy, Ekonomiczny i Socjologiczny 1:105–122
Ziembiński Z (1987) O pojmowaniu celu, zadania, roli i funkcji prawa. Państwo i Prawo 12:15–25

Maciej Dybowski is a lawyer and a philosopher, working as an assistant professor at the Department of Legal Theory and Philosophy, Faculty of Law and Administration, Adam Mickiewicz University in Poznań, Poland. His main fields of research include philosophy of law, neo-pragmatism, law and language, philosophy of human rights. The text is an extended version of a paper presented at the 2017 IVR World Congress in Lisbon during a special workshop organised by Maciej Dybowski and Verena Klappstein.

Legislative History, Ratio Legis, and the Concept of the Rational Legislator

Michał Krotoszyński

Abstract In Polish legal theory, the concept of the *rational legislator*—an ideal type of lawmaker that fulfills certain assumptions regarding its knowledge and values—plays a profound role in the process of legal interpretation. In this context, the concept of the rational lawmaker is best understood as a set of methodological directives that govern the process of legal analysis. These rules enable the translation of ambiguous and often inconsistent texts of legal statutes into a coherent system of unequivocal legal norms.

Yet if the concept of the rational legislator is accepted as the basis of legal interpretation, the *ratio legis* of a statute must be determined using sources that can be conventionally attributed to the rational lawmaker. These include the text of the statute in question, its preamble, and the values that can be decoded from other legal texts, primarily from the constitution.

Nevertheless, as an ontological gap exists between the rational lawmaker and actual legislators, the use of legislative history in the process of the analysis of *ratio legis* is somewhat questionable. Aside from providing methodological background for the concepts of *humanistic interpretation* and the *rational legislator*, this article explores the difficulties involved in applying legislative history to the abovementioned paradigm of legal interpretation and aims to assess how, if at all, this can be reconciled with the idea of the rational lawmaker.

1 Introductory Remarks

One of the outstanding dilemmas of legal interpretation is the issue of using legislative history in the process of legal analysis. Undoubtedly, the examination of legislative materials for documentation of a lawmaking procedure is relevant for the assessment of the validity of a certain statute or regulation or, in systems with an institutionalized

M. Krotoszyński (✉)
Adam Mickiewicz University, Faculty of Law and Administration, Poznań, Poland
e-mail: michal.krotoszynski@amu.edu.pl

V. Klappstein, M. Dybowski (eds.), *Ratio Legis*,
https://doi.org/10.1007/978-3-319-74271-7_4

constitutional review, the consistency of a specific act with the constitution (Tobor 2016, p. 173; for other uses of legislative record, see Whisner 2013).

Yet the question remains whether, how, and to what extent legislative history should be considered when interpreting the law. Those who support the use of such materials for legal reasoning most often see them as a source for understanding the *intent* of the lawgiver. Therefore, such scholars perceive legislative history as a prime tool for establishing *ratio legis*. Conversely, as will be shown, even if the belief that the interpretation should seek to establish the intent of the lawgiver is accepted, this does not necessarily mean that legislative materials should be acknowledged as documents expressing such intent.

In fact, as Raz (1996) points out, the acceptance of the premise that the interpretation of legislation stemming from deliberate lawmaking should reflect the intentions of its lawgiver, which Raz calls "The Authoritative Intention Thesis," does not presuppose any interpretative theory. The will to interpret law according to the intent of the lawgiver may be based only on the fact that the idea of the legislative authority must assume the power to introduce laws consistent with the lawmaker's will (pp. 256–260). The thesis stems from "the essential idea that legislators have control over the law" (p. 267) and solely serves a legitimizing purpose. What guides the understanding of law are the prevailing *conventions of interpretation* (p. 271). Raz makes it clear that the idea of intent should only apply to actual lawmakers, whether individual or institutionalized (p. 263). Yet this paper intends to demonstrate that the prevailing conventions of interpretation that Raz writes about can equip the lawmaker with idealizing features, therefore creating a nonexistent, ideal type of a legislator. In this case, the actual legislation is conventionally attributed to such an ideal lawmaker, and the wish to establish the intent of such a lawmaker is based not only on the nature of legislation itself but also on a much broader, theoretical, and ethical dimension (for a detailed explanation of the role of social conventions in establishing *ratio legis*, see Smolak 2012).

Before discussing these problems in more detail, some linguistic remarks are in order. Firstly, as is apparent, terms such as "legislator" and "lawgiver" can take on more than one meaning. The individuals who actually influence the shape and content of enacted provisions may be called *real* or *actual legislators*. The collective legislative bodies composed of actual legislators involved in processes, such as a parliamentary committee, may be referred to as *institutional legislators*. Those two terms should be distinguished from a *formal legislator* (a subject authorized by legal norms to enact provisions and to whom the law is conventionally attributed). Finally, *the rational legislator*, which will be described in detail later, can be defined as an ideal type *of lawgiver* that is assumed to meet certain criteria and is conventionally believed to enact law based on its knowledge and axiological system (Wronkowska 1987, pp. 148–150; Zieliński 2017, pp. 258–259).

It is also useful to distinguish *subjective theories* of legal interpretation, which aim to establish the intent of factual or institutional legislators from *objective theories* that construct the meaning of a legal text based on linguistic rules and social context. Whether subjective or objective, the *static* approach is a theory of interpretation claiming that the meaning of a legal provision is determined at the moment of enactment and cannot change over time. On the other hand, according to the *dynamic approach*, the proper understanding of law can alter together with the will of an actual lawmaker (subjective theories) or with changes in language or social context (objective theories). Even though any combination of these interpretative concepts is theoretically possible, the subjective theories usually involve a static approach, whereas objective theories tend to state that the meaning of a legal provision can evolve over time (Wróblewski 1959; Zieliński 2017, pp. 217–220).

This paper aims to present the dilemmas encountered when legislative history is considered as a source of knowledge of the intent of such an ideal lawmaker. To do so, a brief overview of the varying approaches for using legislative materials during legal analysis is presented below. Then the concept of the rational legislator, concentrating on its evolution and its meaning for legal interpretation, is described. Finally, the difficulties encountered in the application of legislative history in the abovementioned paradigm are discussed and assessed as to how, if at all, it can be reconciled with the idea of the rational lawmaker.

2 Legislative History and Legal Interpretation

2.1 The Definition of Legislative History

Legislative history can be defined as "any and all public documents relating to the law when it was still a bill in the legislature" (Davis et al. 2007, p. 586; see also Scott 2010, p. 378; Tobor 2016, p. 171). These may include, *inter alia*, (1) the official statement of purpose of the bill; (2) the note on the foreseen effects of the bill on the economy, employment, public safety, health care, or other core areas, including the predicted fiscal impact of the law; (3) legal opinions and other documents produced by experts in the legislative process; (4) the history of the amendments to the bill; (5) the recordings or the minutes of the meetings of the legislative body or its committees; (6) the majority and minority reports; and (7) the voting records (Davis et al. 2007, pp. 586 and 594–597; Tobor 2016, p. 171). Available legislative history varies from legal system to legal system. For example, in the United States, federal courts can rely on detailed legislative material, whereas in some states the availability of lawmaking records is scarce (Bielska-Brodziak 2012, p. 146).

2.2 Between Intentionalism and Textualism

The question of the use of legislative records for legal interpretation has gained much attention from legal scholars, especially in the United States. The two main theories on how the statutes should be interpreted are the *intentionalist approach* and *new textualism*.

In line with remarks made by Raz, *intentionalists* from the US and abroad see the discovery of a lawmaker's intent as the aim of statutory interpretation. The intentionalists generally believe that even if the lawmaker is a bicameral legislative body, it is still possible to attribute an intent to such an entity (Breyer 1992, pp. 864–866; Raz 1996, p. 263)—if not in psychological terms, then by the use of the concepts of collective intentionality or institutional facts (Borowicz 2009, pp. 17–20; Tobor 2013, pp. 63–65).

According to the intentionalists, *ratio legis* can be discovered using the legislative record. These materials can be consulted in at least six circumstances: (1) to avoid an absurd interpretative result, (2) to fix a legislative error, (3) to understand the meaning of a specialized term, (4) to find the purpose of a certain provision, (5) to choose between several possible interpretations of a statute (Breyer 1992, pp. 848–861), or (6) to confirm the literal meaning of the law. The use of legislative history cannot lead to the rejection of a clear meaning of statutory provisions (Scott 2010, p. 379), unless (1) or (2) of the above is true. It can be argued that to prevent any postenactment inclusions to legislative history (Starr 1987, p. 377), the courts should only take into account materials publicly available before the vote.

As noted, the search for the intent of actual or institutional lawgivers may be defended with the concept of *legislative authority* (Raz 1996). It can also be supported from a democratic perspective as in modern democracies, it is the lawmakers—in general, in contrast to the judiciary—who are freely elected. Therefore, neglect of the legislative intent may lead to violation of the separation of powers. The intentionalists also argue that grounding legal analysis in the concept of an intent prevents the courts from arbitrary reinterpretation of laws (Brzeziński 2006, pp. 24–28; Borowicz 2009, pp. 21–23; Tobor 2013, pp. 94–101). Overall, intentionalism seems to accept a static approach to legal interpretation, and its rejection of the concept of the ideal legislator as an unnecessary legal fiction (Raz 1996, p. 256; Tobor 2013, pp. 86–87) places it closer to the subjective theories, even if the notion of the legislative intent is also socially constructed.

Based on British interpretative legacy, *new textualism* either believes that "the objective indication of the words, rather than the intent of the legislature, is what constitutes the law" and therefore rejects "intent of the legislature as the proper criterion of the law" (Scalia 1998, pp. 29 and 31) or views statutes and regulations as the only source of legislative intent. After all, it is the bill and not the legislative record that is put to vote. This leads new textualism to "discard legislative history as an illegitimate source of authority" (Scott 2010, p. 348). The new textualists resort to other laws or dictionaries and reject manifestly absurd meanings but refuse to interpret the words of the legislator through the perspective of an equally ambiguous or arbitrary lawmaking record.

This approach stresses, *inter alia*, that (1) the majority of actual legislators are most often oblivious of the purpose of a bill and, therefore, *ratio legis* present in legislative history is in fact the intent of the bill's sponsors; (2) a lawmaking record can be misleading as the authors of a bill may choose not to disclose their true intent in order to maximize the chance of a bill's acceptance; (3) legislative history is often inconclusive, permitting judges to choose the meaning they prefer and, therefore, usurp the power of the legislature; (4) the need to interpret the lawmaking record takes much time and raises the costs of legal proceedings (Starr 1987; Brzeziński 2006, pp. 30–35; Costelloe 2015; for a rebuttal, see Breyer 1992, pp. 861–869; Tobor 2013, pp. 258–277; Bielska-Brodziak 2015). Therefore, the new textualism, as an objective theory of interpretation, prefers to see intent as a meaning that a rational person may reconstruct from a set of words used in legal provisions (Scalia 1998, p. 17).

Apart from these two paradigms, there are other theories concerning the methods of legal interpretation and the use of legislative history (Brzeziński 2006). For instance, the *pragmatic theory* views the process of decision making, such as legislation, as polycentric and, therefore, accepts varying materials as authoritative sources of legal analysis. This eclectic, "all hands on deck" position considers, *inter alia,* the wording of statutory provisions, basic legal and social values, legislative intent, and lawmaking history. The sources need to be juxtaposed upon one another and the interpreter should weigh all possible arguments to holistically arrive at the final conclusion (Scott 2010, pp. 348–349 and 406–408).

2.3 The Use of Legislative History in Different Legal Systems

The acceptance of lawmaking records as a tool of legal analysis varies around the globe. In the US, ten states have explicitly accepted in their codified cannons of interpretation the use of legislative history for legal interpretation, when the text of a statute is ambiguous, while Texas even permits such use whether the statutory provisions are clear or not. No state forbids the application of legislative record. Moreover, seven states accept only the materials that were available before the bill was enacted (Scott 2010, pp. 378–383 and 419–420). Both federal and state courts take legislative history into account, albeit with changing frequency (Breyer 1992, p. 846; Davis et al. 2007, pp. 587–588; Costelloe 2015, pp. 307–312).

In the United Kingdom, the common law rules of legal interpretation used to specifically bar judges from using legislative history, yet after the 1992 landmark case *Pepper v. Hart*, the courts were permitted to resort to lawmaking records when the provision is obscure or ambiguous or its literal meaning is manifestly absurd (Scott 2010, pp. 346–347; Costelloe 2015, pp. 312–324). In South Africa, article 39 (2) of the 1996 Constitution orders every court to promote the spirit, purport, and objects of the Bill of Rights during the interpretation of any legislation. As this approach includes the analysis of historical origins of the Bill of Rights or the statutory provisions stemming from it (*Minister of Land Affairs v. Slamdien*, paras. 13–14), the use of legislative record is accepted, at least regarding constitutional interpretation (de Ville 1999).

In France, courts may resort to lawmaking history if the text of the statute is unclear and the context fails to remove ambiguity. Finally, in Sweden, where the statutory provisions are abstract and concise, the use of legislative record is very common. The available material from the lawmaking process is officially published, and the statute is sometimes said to play the role of a heading for legislative history (Bielska-Brodziak 2012, pp. 147–149).

2.4 Legislative History as Viewed by the Polish Judiciary and Jurisprudence

The opinion of Polish courts on the use of legislative record in legal interpretation is far from coherent. In its notable ruling from January 2001, the Polish Supreme Court bluntly rejected the need to inquire into the intent of actual lawmakers. Instead, the court stated that even in cases where the intent of a lawgiver needs to be analyzed, "it is not [the intent of] a real, factual legislator, who cannot limit the granted interpretative freedom of the court, as the bond between such a lawgiver and the provision of law was shattered the moment the provision was enacted (. . .) – but [an intent of] the constructed, so called rational legislator. Thus, 'the will of a lawgiver' has to be deducted only from the text of the statute and should be rationalized and objectivized, e.g. by relating it to the aims (functions) of legal institutions established by the law" (III CZP 49/00; see also Borowicz 2009, p. 10).

This line of reasoning, which will be explored further, is not universally accepted by the Polish judiciary. Although the references to legislative history are not typical for verdicts of Polish courts, they are also far from being extraordinary. The judiciary may decide to establish the intent of the lawgiver by using statements of purpose (III UK 5/10, III SA/Kr 185/17), especially when few changes were made to a bill during the legislative process (III SPP 42/04). The history of the bill, including the rejected amendments, is also taken into account (P 7/08). The course of parliamentary discussion (I KZP 20/04, III CZP 89/09), the minutes from committee meetings (VI ACa 1057/14), and legal opinions on the draft law (III AUa 396/16) may also be examined. Sometimes the courts refuse to rely on the available material, for instance when "the statement of purpose does not match the content of the provision" (I KZP 18/09). General remarks on the application of legislative history are few, although the Polish Constitutional Court has accepted such use, provided it does not trump the plain meaning acquired by using linguistic and systemic interpretation (P 32/06).

The diversity of opinions among the judiciary leads to the question of whether the problem of the use of legislative history has been resolved by the Polish jurisprudence. From the legislative history perspective, at least three approaches to legal analysis should be acknowledged in Polish theory of law: (1) the clarification concept of legal interpretation, (2) the derivative concept, and (3) the intentionalist approach. The first two are the dominant theories of legal interpretation existing in Polish legal culture, whereas the third is directly connected with the intentionalist theory that was previously described.

According to the *clarification concept of legal interpretation*, which was developed in 1959 by Jerzy Wróblewski, the goal of legal analysis is to establish the meaning of a legal norm, understood here as a pattern of expected conduct. However, the interpreter, including the courts, need to clarify such a meaning only to the extent necessary to resolve a legal dispute or to decide a case. In fact, as many legal provisions are clear and therefore directly understandable, the interpretation is only necessary if the legal text is ambiguous (Lat.: *clara non sunt interpretanda*). Wróblewski notes that when legal interpretation aims to establish the will of a legislator from the time the law was enacted (static interpretation), the lawmaking record can provide the context in which such a will can be properly attributed. However, if the interpreter intends to establish the meaning of the provision based on the understanding of the text in current social and political circumstances (dynamic interpretation), the use of legislative material is unnecessary. The author of the clarification concept does not prescribe a specific approach, although he notes that with the passage of time and change of circumstances, the use of dynamic interpretation becomes more probable (Wróblewski 1959).

Maciej Zieliński's *derivative concept of legal interpretation* is based on a distinction between a *legal provision*, understood as a basic unit of a statute or other legal text, and a *legal norm*, which can be defined as a phrase with which the lawmaker either orders or forbids certain subjects in prescribed circumstances to act in a specific manner (Ziembiński 1960). As legal provisions are formulated in a standard language, they share the ambiguity of the vocabulary and grammar used to compose them. Legal norms, on the other hand, are unequivocal expressions that the lawgiver codes into the language of legal provisions. Therefore, legal interpretation consists of translation of ambiguous and often inconsistent texts of legal statutes into a coherent system of unequivocal legal norms. No legal provisions can be understood without a proper process of interpretation (Lat.: *omnia sunt interpretanda*). As described in more detail below, the normative principles that govern this process (*interpretative directives*) are based on certain assumptions regarding the language, knowledge, and axiology of this ideal type of lawgiver, the *rational legislator*. These directives can be divided into linguistic, systemic, and functional ones. The first group is related to the language of legal texts. Systemic directives are concerned with the relations between norms in a legal system. Finally, functional directives are employed to interpret legal provisions in such a way as to obtain legal norms that are best justified by the knowledge and axiology attributed to the rational legislator (Zieliński 1972, 2017; for an English introduction to the concept, see Zieliński 1987, Choduń 2015).

The derivative approach, as formulated by Maciej Zieliński, is skeptical toward the use of legislative history in legal interpretation. Zielinski warns that using such materials as a tool for establishing *ratio legis* in the course of functional interpretation is diminished by the fact that "it is highly debatable to what extent the specific assumptions (statements and values) [about the lawgiver] can be reconstructed based on the course of the discussion of a respective legislative committee, or the fact that such a committee accepted a particular linguistic form of a specific legal provision," as there is often little correlation between the overall tone of the debate and the result of the final vote (Zieliński 2017, p. 269).

Bogucki (2016, pp. 117–120 and 205–211), who further develops the use of functional directives, remains cautious when it comes to legislative history. He accepts the use of lawmaking record during functional interpretation only when the *ratio legis* of a certain provision cannot be established based solely on legal texts or by reference to the views of the judiciary or the legal doctrine. Bogucki also notes the difficulties with attributing the intent expressed in legislative history to the rational legislator.

In line with some of the intentionalist theories abroad, the *intentionalist approach*, developed in Poland by Tobor (2013), sees the establishment of legislative intent as the aim of legal interpretation. The intent should not be understood strictly psychologically but instead ought to be seen as a construct that is created by analysis of all materials that shed light on the goals of the lawgiver, perceived here as a certain public institution. Yet no idealizing conditions are to be applied to such a legislator. Following this approach, both legislative record and legal texts, including the history of their amendments, can be used to establish the will of the lawmaker. The large variety of available lawmaking material, including the votes and minutes from the meetings of parliamentary committees, which Tobor sees as the most reliable source of legislative intent, may be used to confirm the literal meaning of a legal provision, remove its ambiguity, or correct a legislative error.

In contrast to English and American works on legislative history, there are surprisingly few publications relating to this problem in Polish legal theory. Two dominant theories of legal interpretation, clarification and derivative, treat the question of lawmaking record marginally. Olgierd Bogucki's concept, however promising, is too new to be considered canonical, and the approach supported by Zygmunt Tobor is not widespread among Polish scholars. Even though the courts rely on legislative materials, there are no general rules concerning the scope of their use. In the next section of the article, I argue that at least when it comes to the derivative concept of legal interpretation—an approach to analysis of law I concur with—such a situation may be considered an understandable side effect of an adaptive nature of interpretation and the profound role that the concept of the rational legislator plays in legal analysis.

3 The Concept of Rational Legislator

3.1 Humanistic Interpretation

One of the main goals of humanistic studies, regardless of whether it is history, literature, or visual arts, is to explain the reasons that inspire various human activities. Even though such inquiries are often coined in psychological terms, in practice researchers do not engage in the psychological study of the motives of the concerned individuals. Instead, according to Kmita (1971, see also Kmita and Nowak 1968, 1970), scientists base their research, albeit often unconsciously, on the idea of a rational subject.

To put forth an example, to attempt to explain why Christopher Columbus decided to sail westward instead of following Vasco do Gama's route to India around Africa in 1492, researchers obviously would not occupy themselves with the impossible task of studying Columbus' state of mind at that time. Instead, they create the notion of a *rational subject* that, equipped with the knowledge and axiology that can be attributable to the Genoese sailor, would ultimately arrive at the same decision that Christopher Columbus made. This method of discerning why a specific action occurred is known as *humanistic interpretation.*

According to the *rationality assumption,* which serves as a base for humanistic interpretation, if, in a specific moment in time, "X has to undertake one of the actions $C_1, \ldots, C_n$, which according to his knowledge (...) exclude each other and add up (all) together, and unfailingly lead to the results $S_1, \ldots, S_m$ respectively (while $m \leq n$), and the said results $S_1, \ldots, S_m$ are ordered by the relation of preference characteristic for X," then X will undertake the action that leads to the result that has the highest preference, i.e., the result that X prefers the most (Kmita and Nowak 1970, p. 51). If the scientist also knows that a certain result S_k has the highest preference for X and that X knows that the action C_k unfailingly leads to the result S_k, then the scientist can finally explain why X decides to take the action C_k. To put it simply, a rational subject follows a course of action that leads to the result preferred by such a subject over other possible outcomes.

One should note that the rationality assumption is what one may call an *idealizational claim.* Not only does it counterfactually presume a definite link between an action and a result—in most cases, this relation is only probable—but it also equips the subject with properties that it may or may not realistically possess. The rationality assumption states, *inter alia,* that the rational subject has the best knowledge when it comes to possible actions and their results and that those outcomes form a system that is linearly ordered by the preferences of such a subject. The use of the idealizing conditions makes it obvious that humanistic interpretation is yet another instance of the procedures of idealization and concretization, typical for developed empirical sciences (Kmita 1971, a list of idealizing conditions available in Patryas 1979; for an English introduction to the idealizational concept of science, see Nowak 1992).

Humanistic interpretation can be divided into a historical and an adaptive one. *Historical interpretation* seeks to explain the activities of a certain individual or a group of individuals based on their knowledge and preferences. The reasons that led a subject to perform a specific action are verified with empirical data. This procedure is commonly used in historical analysis, including for the history of art and literature. On the other hand, *adaptive interpretation* does not seek to establish the intent of an action but instead rationalizes it to show its current cultural meaning. For instance, a literary critic may interpret a renaissance poem not to explore the author's actual intention but rather to show the meaning of the poem to a contemporary audience. In such a case, the knowledge and the preferences of the subject are not empirically tested (Kmita 1971, pp. 81–83; Nowak 1973, pp. 175–178).

3.2 The Concept of Rational Legislator

Even though lawyers speak of legislative intent, the examination of the character of legal sciences, or at least of Polish jurisprudence, leads to the conclusion that in law, as in other fields of humanities, researchers and interpreters do not engage in the practice of psychology but rather accept the theories of rational behavior. To be more precise, legal analysis is not concerned with the motives of real or institutional lawmakers but is entrenched in the concept of the rational legislator.

The rational legislator can be defined as an ideal type of lawgiver that acts in line with the rationality assumption, enacting the law that, according to its knowledge, leads to results that the rational lawmaker prefers the most (Nowak 1973, 1987). Even though the concept was developed as an explanatory tool allowing the discovery of a deep structure of legal reasoning (see also Borowicz 2009, pp. 11–14), it has become the base for at least two normative conceptions. The rational legislator may be looked upon as a model for actual lawmakers (Wronkowska 1987) or as a methodological foundation of the derivative concept of legal interpretation. Here, I concentrate on the latter.

The idealizing claims that construct the ideal type of rational legislator for the purpose of legal interpretation include (1) four rudimentary logical assumptions, (2) the intellectual premises, and (3) the axiological assertions. According to *basic logical claims*, the knowledge of the rational lawmaker forms a system and is not self-contradictory, whereas preferences are both asymmetrical and transitive (Nowak 1973, p. 39).

The *intellectual premises* are a group of various assertions regarding the linguistic, legal, and general knowledge of the rational legislator. The legislator is assumed to be *linguistically rational*, which means the lawgiver (1) treats legal provisions as an instrument of enacting unequivocal legal norms, (2) has the best knowledge regarding the features of legal texts, and (3) is aware of interpretative directives existing in the legal culture and expects the interpreters to follow them. The assertions concerning the *legal knowledge* of the rational legislator include the assumptions that the lawgiver (1) is aware of the rules of proper legislation and adheres to them, (2) has the best knowledge about the views of contemporary jurisprudence and the rulings of the judiciary and takes them into account while formulating the law, and (3) enacts legal norms consistent with the norms superior to them in the hierarchy of the legal system. The rational legislator is also attributed with contemporary *general knowledge*, as well as with expertise in the area under regulation. Finally, *axiological assertions* stipulate that the rational legislator creates the law in line with its hierarchical system of values. These values are mainly decoded from legal texts, primarily from the constitution (Zieliński 2017, pp. 259–270), although common social values should also be considered (Potrzeszcz 2016).

In principle, the rationality assumption "is not a falsifiable hypothesis but an irrefutable dogma" (Nowak 1987, p. 144). The lawyer simply "can never state that such and such juridical problem is unsolvable because the legislator is unreasonable" but instead must interpret the law as to equip it with the sense it may lack (Nowak 1987, p. 138). Yet the idealizing claims presented above do not have the same force. For instance, in the rare cases where the clear result of the linguistic interpretation fundamentally violates basic values attributed to the rational lawmaker, it is possible to trump the literal meaning as the assumption of the axiological rationality is stronger than that of the linguistic one (Zieliński 2017, pp. 267–268).

It is important to understand that when it comes to legal analysis, the concept of the rational legislator does not include any claims about actual lawmakers. Instead, the concept is best understood as a set of basic rules concerning the process of legal interpretation. As Ziembiński (1980, pp. 271–272) points out, the rational legislator "is a mental construct applied by lawyers as a fiction useful for the establishment of a legal system based on the accepted sources of law.... 'Rational legislator' as a work of legal thought will have such features as we attribute to it." Thus, to assume that the law is enacted by the rational legislator is the same as to declare that during legal analysis, one will follow certain methodological rules (Kmita 1990, p. 416). These rules structure the process of legal interpretation leading to the establishment of a coherent, effective, and axiologically legitimized system of legal norms (Ziembiński 1980, pp. 273–274). The concept may also set limits to the interpretative freedom of courts, grounding legal analysis in a set of fixed methodological assumptions. One may therefore say that the concept of rational legislator also has an ethical dimension.

3.3 Interpretation of Law as an Adaptive Interpretation

Despite lawyers often speaking of establishing a legislator's intent, in practice, the law is interpreted not to gain historical knowledge of the reasons for its enactment but to acquire a coherent system of unequivocal legal norms capable of guiding people's current conduct. Thus, the interpretation of law is yet another example of adaptive interpretation (Nowak 1973). This is especially visible in the derivative concept of legal analysis as it employs the notion of a rational legislator. This being the case, the interpretation of law by the derivative approach is both objective, as it neglects the historical intent of real lawgivers, as well as dynamic, as the meaning of legal provisions is established in relation to contemporary social context and can therefore change over time (Zieliński 2017, pp. 217–220).

Even though the derivative approach shares with new textualism a focus on the objective meaning of a legal text, one should note that the derivative concept also includes axiological deliberations that compare the literal meaning of the text with the values attributed to the rational lawmaker. These considerations may lead to the choice of one of varying possible outcomes of linguistic interpretation or even to the abandonment of a literal meaning inconsistent with the basic values of the rational legislator. The derivative approach may be therefore seen as more lenient than new textualism.

The genealogy of the concept of a rational lawmaker is a striking example of how an idea that began as being purely explanatory can develop into normative criteria. One of the reasons for its popularity may be its consistency with the domestic legal culture. What is more, even though Raz seems to be right, that the wish to establish the intent of the legislator does not presuppose any interpretative conventions, the history of the concept of the rational legislator shows that the prevailing conventions of interpretation can in fact influence the understanding of the lawmaker's intent.

4 Legislative History and the Concept of Rational Legislator

As mentioned, the derivative concept of legal interpretation is cautious when it comes to the use of legislative history as a tool of establishing *ratio legis*. Because an ontological gap between the rational lawmaker and actual legislators exists, the main dilemma is the interpretation of the intent of individuals or institutions active in the legislative process as the will of the rational legislator. The proponents of the derivative approach are highly aware of this fact. Speaking of the intent of the rational legislator, Ziembiński (1980, p. 271) notes that such an intent can only be judged based on legal texts, which are the sole materials that can be attributed to the lawmaker. Yet the interpretation of these texts "cannot be verified by comparing it to an honest statement of a historical lawgiver about his or her intentions"—it can only be contrasted against other, competing methods of legal analysis (Ziembiński 1980, p. 271; see also Potrzeszcz 2016, p. 70).

Incorporating legislative history into his model of derivative functional interpretation, Bogucki (2016, p. 119) notes the abovementioned difficulties. Nevertheless, he claims that "the acceptance of the construct of the rational legislator does not automatically deem the consideration of the aims and other values of an actual lawgiver unacceptable – one may answer this dilemma by attributing in certain circumstances the aims and other values of a real lawmaker to the rational legislator." I agree with Bogucki's assertion yet also believe that there is a need to assure that the concept of the rational lawmaker remains internally coherent. Therefore, my aim is to propose a general structure of reasoning that allows for such an attribution. Then I wish to stipulate some specific requirements for the use of legislative record for a particular case.

4.1 General Structure of the Attribution

First, one should note that according to one of the linguistic rationality assumptions, the rational legislator is aware of the interpretative directives existing in the legal culture and expects the interpreters to follow them (Zieliński 2017, p. 262; see also Smolak 2012, p. 204). I fully agree with this premise yet believe it is applicable when it comes not only to linguistic interpretation but also to the functional one, including the process of the establishment of *ratio legis*. After all, it is reasonable to claim that the rational legislator—that, according to another assumption, has the best knowledge of the views of the contemporary jurisprudence and the rulings of the judiciary and takes them into account while formulating the law—is also aware of the interpretative methods aimed at determining the intent of the rational legislator that are used by courts or are prescribed by the jurisprudence. This must, in turn, include adequate knowledge about the scope of the judicial use of legislative history and the contemporary theoretical debate on its role in legal analysis.

It may be argued that the rational legislator, who also has the best knowledge about the course of a legislative procedure, must be aware that if the legislative history is clear, the intent that is ascribed to the proposed provision in question or to the bill in its entirety may be attributed to the provision or provisions of the enacted law. If, nevertheless, the law is passed in the proposed form, it is reasonable to assume that the rational lawgiver at least accepts the fact that its provisions may be interpreted in line with its legislative history. One can argue that if the legislator was opposed to this result, the form of the law would be changed to clearly indicate such a fact. The act of voting may be therefore seen as constituting an assumption that the rational legislator accepts the possibility of the use of clear lawmaking record as a subsidiary source for the establishment of *ratio legis*.

I agree with Bogucki that the role of legislative material must remain subsidiary as the abovementioned argument is plausible only if there are no primary sources, such as the preamble or legal texts, that make it possible to determine the intent of the rational lawmaker. After all, the rational legislator may decide to enact a law in the form discussed during the legislative process, not because it can be interpreted in line with the intent present in the lawmaking material but because it is reasonable to believe that the proper use of other interpretative directives will lead to the establishment of a different intent. In such a case, the rational legislator may simply ignore legislative history, assuming there are other sources that clearly indicate *ratio legis*.

Therefore, the structure of the discussed argument can be formulated as follows:

/P1/ The rational legislator is aware of the interpretative conventions existing in the legal culture, including the possibility of the use of legislative history in legal interpretation.

/P2/ The rational legislator is not aware of any primary sources—including the preamble of the act or any legal texts—that would permit the establishment of the ratio legis in question contrary to the intent expressed in legislative history.

/P3/ The rational legislator is aware that, as the legislative history of a certain provision or the bill in its entirety is clear, it is possible that the enactment of the law in a form consistent with the one discussed during the legislative procedure may lead to the establishment of ratio legis in line with the clear intent available in legislative materials.

/P4/ The rational legislator decides to enact a provision or a bill in a form consistent with the one discussed during the legislative procedure.

/C/ The rational legislator accepts the fact that the ratio legis of the provision in question may be established in line with the clear intent available in legislative materials.

One might say that incorporating legislative history into the process of determining *ratio legis* is too much of a concession toward the internationalist approach. Yet it is important to note that the use of legislative history is subsidiary to other means of functional interpretation, including the analysis of the intent of the rational legislator expressed in legal texts. In case of inconsistency between the values present in legislative history and those available from legal texts, the latter must prevail as they can be attributed directly to the rational legislator (Bogucki 2016, p. 119). What is more, even in Maciej Zieliński's canonical version of the derivative concept of legal interpretation, the result of the analysis of legislative history can sometimes be used indirectly. As noted, when the legal text is ambiguous, the interpreter should assume the meaning unanimously accepted by the judiciary and the jurisprudence. Nevertheless, this uncontested opinion might have evolved with the use of legislative history, thus influencing current interpretative decisions.

4.2 *The Conditions of Use*

Finally, I would like to address some of the issues concerning the conditions of using legislative history for a specific case. Here, I will rely on the requirements articulated in legal literature, including those discussed by Bogucki (2016, pp. 205–211).

Firstly, if legislative history is to be used for legal interpretation, it must be publicly available. If the purpose of lawmaking material is to determine how the law should be interpreted, it must be accessible just as the law is. In minimum, it should be available for public inspection, with any relevant public institution having an openly accessible register of such material provided. To assure transparency and minimalize risk of postvote changes, full, preenactment Internet availability should be the ultimate goal. Secondly, it must also be proven that all legislative materials were accessible to the members of the legislative body before the vote. Without this, it is simply not possible to attribute the intent expressed in legislative history to the individuals voting for the law and, eventually, to the rational legislator.

Thirdly, if legislative history is to help translate ambiguous legal provisions into unequivocal legal norms, it must itself be straightforward enough. This means that the court must examine the whole of the legislative process to determine what values and aims can be attributed to the rational lawmaker. Only those values that are in line with the results of previous stages of legal interpretation and are consistent with the values that are expressed in the laws superior to the ones examined are to be taken in account. Finally, due consideration needs to be given to any amendments of a bill. If a bill was changed during the legislative process, it must be critically analyzed as to whether the intent expressed at the previous stages of the lawmaking procedure can still be attributed to the form of the final provision.

References

Bielska-Brodziak A (2012) Materiały legislacyjne w dyskursie interpretacyjnym z perspektywy brytyjskiej, amerykańskiej, francuskiej, szwedzkiej i polskiej [Legislative history in the interpretative discourse from British, American, French, Swedish and Polish perspective]. In: Nawrot O, Sykuna S, Zajadło J (eds) Konwergencja czy dywergencja kultur i systemów prawnych? [Convergence or divergence of cultures and legal systems?]. C.H. Beck, Warszawa, pp 144–154

Bielska-Brodziak A (2015) Argumenty interpretacyjne w kontekście wartości państwa prawa [Interpretative arguments in the context of the values of a state ruled by law]. In: Andruszkiewicz M, Breczko A, Oliwiniak S (eds) Filozoficzne i teoretyczne zagadnienia demokratycznego państwa prawa [Philosophical and theoretical questions of a democratic state ruled by law]. Temida 2, Białystok, pp 183–192

Bogucki O (2016) Model wykładni funkcjonalnej w derywacyjnej koncepcji wykładni prawa [Model of functional interpretation in derivative theory of legal interpretation]. Polgres Multimedia, Szczecin

Borowicz A (2009) Argument interpretacyjny odwołujący się do woli rzeczywistego prawodawcy [Interpretative argument based on the intentions of the lawgiver]. Studia Prawno-Ekonomiczne 79:9–28

Breyer S (1992) On the uses of legislative history in interpreting statutes. South Calif Law Rev 65:845–874

Brzeziński B (2006) Współczesne amerykańskie teorie wykładni prawa [Contemporary American theories of law interpretation]. Państwo i Prawo 7:22–39

Choduń A (2015) Maciej Zieliński's (derivative) concept of legal interpretation. Studia Prawa Publicznego 2(10):111–125

Davis B, Kelly K, Ford K (2007) Use of legislative history: willow witching for legislative intent. Idaho Law Rev 43:585–600

De Ville JR (1999) Legislative history and constitutional interpretation. J S Afr Law 2:211–223

Kmita J (1971) Z metodologicznych problemów interpretacji humanistycznej [On the methodological problems of humanistic interpretation]. Państwowe Wydawnictwo Naukowe, Warszawa

Kmita J (1990) Etyczny aspekt koncepcji racjonalnego prawodawcy [The ethical dimension of the concept of the rational legislator]. In: Wronkowska S, Zieliński M (eds) Szkice z teorii prawa i szczegółowych nauk prawnych [Sketches on legal theory and particular legal sciences]. Uniwersytet im. Adama Mickiewicza, Poznań, pp 413–429

Kmita J, Nowak L (1968) Studia nad teoretycznymi podstawami humanistyki [Studies on the theoretical foundations of the humanities]. Uniwersytet im. Adama Mickiewicza, Poznań

Kmita J, Nowak L (1970) The rationality assumption in human sciences. The Polish. Sociol Bull 1:43–68

Nowak L (1973) Interpretacja prawnicza. Studium z metodologii prawoznawstwa [Legal interpretation. A study in the methodology of jurisprudence]. Państwowe Wydawnictwo Naukowe, Warszawa

Nowak L (1987) A concept of rational legislator. In: Ziembiński Z (ed) Polish contributions to the theory and philosophy of law. Rodopi, Amsterdam, pp 137–145

Nowak L (1992) The idealizational approach to science: a survey. In: Brzeziński J, Nowak L (eds) Idealization III: approximation and truth. Rodopi, Amsterdam, pp 9–63

Patryas W (1979) Idealizacyjny charakter interpretacji humanistycznej [Idealizational character of humanistic interpretation]. Wydawnictwo Naukowe UAM, Poznań

Potrzeszcz J (2016) Racjonalność aksjologiczna prawodawcy jako założenie interpretacyjne [The axiological rationality of the lawmaker as an interpretative assumption]. In: Hermann M, Sykuna S (eds) Wykładnia prawa. Tradycja i perspektywy [Legal interpretation. Tradition and prospects]. C.H. Beck, Warszawa, pp 53–72

Raz J (1996) Intention in interpretation. In: George R (ed) The autonomy of law. Essays on legal positivism. Clarendon Press, Oxford, pp 249–286

Scalia A (1998) A matter of interpretation: federal courts and the law. Princeton University Press, Princeton

Scott J (2010) Codified canons and the common law of interpretation. Georgetown Law J 98:341–431

Smolak M (2012) Wykładnia celowościowa z perspektywy pragmatycznej [Purposive interpretation from pragmatic point of view]. Wolters Kluwer, Warszawa

Starr K (1987) Observations about the use of legislative history. Duke Law J:371–379

Tobor Z (2013) W poszukiwaniu intencji prawodawcy [The search for legislative intent]. Wolters Kluwer, Warszawa
Tobor Z (2016) Rola materiałów legislacyjnych w porządku prawnym [The role of legislative history in legal order]. Acta Universitatis Wratislaviensis, Przegląd Prawa i Administracji 104:171–181
Whisner M (2013) Other uses of legislative history. Law Libr J 105(2):243–254
Wróblewski J (1959) Zagadnienia teorii wykładni praw ludowego [Problems of the theory of interpretation of people's law]. Wydawnictwo Prawnicze, Warszawa
Wronkowska S (1987) The rational legislator as a model for the real lawmaker. In: Ziembiński Z (ed) Polish contributions to the theory and philosophy of law. Rodopi, Amsterdam, pp 147–163
Zieliński M (1972) Interpretacja jako proces dekodowania tekstu prawnego [Interpretation as a process of decoding of legal text]. Wydawnictwo Naukowe UAM, Poznań
Zieliński M (1987) Decoding legal text. In: Ziembiński Z (ed) Polish contributions to the theory and philosophy of law. Rodopi, Amsterdam, pp 165–177
Zieliński M (2017) Wykładnia prawa. Zasady, reguły, wskazówki [Legal interpretation. Principles, rules, hints], 7th edn. Wolters Kluwer, Warszawa
Ziembiński Z (1960) Przepis prawny a norma prawna [Legal provision and legal norm]. Ruch Prawniczy, Ekonomiczny i Socjologiczny 1:105–122
Ziembiński Z (1980) Problemy podstawowe prawoznawstwa [The basic problems of jurisprudence]. Państwowe Wydawnictwo Naukowe, Warszawa

Court Rulings

Poland

Supreme Court Resolution of 17 January 2001 (III CZP 49/00).
Supreme Court Resolution of 29 September 2004 (I KZP 20/04).
Supreme Court Resolution of 16 November 2004 (III SPP 42/04).
Constitutional Court Verdict of 15 October 2008 (P 32/06).
Constitutional Court Verdict of 7 April 2009 (P 7/08).
Supreme Court Decision of 23 September 2009 (I KZP 18/09).
Supreme Court Resolution of 17 November 2009 (III CZP 89/09).
Supreme Court Verdict of 10 November 2010 (III UK 5/10).
Warsaw Appellate Court Verdict of 16 June 2015 (VI ACa 1057/14).
Gdańsk Appellate Court Verdict of 6 July 2016 (III AUa 396/16).
Cracow District Administrative Court Verdict of 20 April 2017 (III SA/Kr 185/17).

South Africa

Minister of Land Affairs of the Republic of South Africa and Another v Slamdien and Others, South Africa Land Claims Court Verdict of 10 February 1999 (LCC107/98)

United Kingdom

Pepper v. Hart, House of Lords Decision of 26 November 1992 (UKHL 3)
Costelloe S (2015) The need for conditions limiting the use of legislative history in statutory interpretation: lessons from the British courts. Notre Dame J Law Ethics & Pub Pol'y 29:299–327

Michał Krotoszyński is an assistant professor at the Chair of Theory and Philosophy of Law, Faculty of Law and Administration, Adam Mickiewicz University in Poznań, Poland. His main fields of research include transitional justice, legal theory, and health care law. The above text was presented at the 2017 IVR World Congress in Lisbon during a special workshop organized by Maciej Dybowski and Verena Klappstein.

Part II
What Can *Ratio Legis* Be?

The Concept of Purpose in *Kant's* Metaphysical Elements of Justice

Verena Klappstein

Abstract *Kantian* philosophy of law impressed today's modern European legal systems. In *his* Metaphysical Elements of Justice (Doctrine of Right or Science of Right), *Kant* develops a legal system to ensure individual rights based upon different aspects of purpose. However, one cannot understand the concept of purpose as set out in the "Metaphysical Elements of Justice" as part of "The Metaphysics of Morals" without *Kant's* Doctrine of Virtue. Both are evolved in the "The Groundwork of the Metaphysics of Morals" in an intertwined way. In the latter, *he* not only stresses in the second and fourth formulations of the categorical imperative (the Formula of Humanity and the Kingdom of Ends Formulation) to treat humanity as an end in itself but also enables the deduction of duties. As *Kantian* philosophy impressed modern European legal systems, the question arises whether *his* concept of purpose could have any impact on the modern discourse of *ratio legis*—in the widest sense understood, as well as the legal consequence and purpose of a legal rule. Can *Kantian* philosophy hint at certain aspects of *ratio legis*, understood in the widest sense as legal consequence, underlying values, and purposes of rules of law, and thus shed light on the modern discussion of it?

To answer this question, the different kinds of purposes as set out with respect to hypothetical, categorical and legal categorical imperatives will be defined and explained with regard to their different functions and a set of four different purposes (Sect. 1). Further, both *Kant's* Doctrine of Right and Doctrine of Virtue—and their intertwined interconnection—will be briefly addressed to fully understand both their functions and to systemize four classes of duties (Sect. 2). From this basis, the question of how different kinds of purposes as found in *Kant's* Doctrine of Right and Doctrine of Virtue might matter in modern jurisprudence can be answered (Sect. 3).

V. Klappstein (✉)
Faculty of Law, Department for German and European Private Law, Civil Procedural Law, and Legal Theory of Prof. Dr. Thomas Riehm, University of Passau, Passau, Germany
e-mail: Verena.Klappstein@uni-passau.de

V. Klappstein, M. Dybowski (eds.), *Ratio Legis*,
https://doi.org/10.1007/978-3-319-74271-7_5

1 Endless Purposes as Aimed for with Hypothetical, Categorical, and Legal Categorical Imperatives

"The Metaphysics of Morals" of 1797 by *Kant* has two major topics, the Doctrine of Right[1] (*Rechtslehre*) and the Doctrine of Virtue[2] (*Tugendlehre*). In the former, *Kant* explains with which natural rights people are born and develops the legal categorical imperative as an instrument to show which rights they might acquire. In the latter, *Kant* sets out to show which purposes people ought to attain.

In *his* work, three kinds of imperatives are to be distinguished: hypothetical and categorical imperatives[3] and legal categorical imperatives. An imperative is any conclusion that predicates an omission or act to be necessary.[4]

Kant classified in *his* moral and legal philosophy several categories for purposes. They regard, firstly, the *effect* and *aim* they can have; secondly, their *necessity*; thirdly, their *achievability*; and, fourthly, their *directness*. Of course, this choice of purposes is nonexclusive, but each has their basis in *Kant's* work.

With regard to their *effect* and *aim*, *Kant* classifies three kinds of ends or purposes of which one is negative and two are positive. The first positive purpose ($purpose^{p1}$) is an end that can bring about a "product" in the widest sense in the world, e.g. reducing hunger, writing an article. The second positive purpose ($purpose^{p2}$) is an aim, which can be only furthered, constituted, cultivated, or even realized by actions, e.g. becoming a legal scholar. The third sense of purpose is a negative one ($purpose^{n}$). $Purposes^{n}$ limit the pursuit of other $purposes^{p\&p1\&n}$, e.g. self-preservation, which limits how to aim for other purposes.

The second differentiation regards the *necessity* of purposes and therewith subjective and objective purposes ($purpose^{s}$ and $purpose^{o}$): $purposes^{o}$, any rational

---

[1]Gregor (1996), p. 37; other translations of the term *Rechtslehre* are: Science of Right (Hastie 1887) or Metaphysical Elements of Justice (Ladd 1999).

[2]Gregor (1996), p. 139.

[3]"*Alle Imperativen nun gebieten entweder hypothetisch, oder kategorisch. Jene stellen die praktische Nothwendigkeit einer möglichen Handlung als Mittel zu etwas anderem, was man will (oder doch möglich ist, daß man es wolle), zu gelangen vor. Der kategorische Imperativ würde der sein, welcher eine Handlung als für sich selbst, ohne Beziehung auf einen andern Zweck, als objectiv=nothwendig vorstellte.*" Kant AA IV 414, available at: https://korpora.zim.uni-duisburg-essen.de/kant/aa04/414.html—"Now, all imperatives command either hypothetically or categorically. The former represent the practical necessity of a possible action as a means to attain something else that one wills (or yet is possible that one wills it). The categorical imperative would be one which represented an action as for itself, without reference to another end, as objectively necessary."—translation by Orr (2015), p. 39, available at: http://groundlaying.appspot.com/pdf/gms1786v_kant-scholar.pdf.

[4]"*Die Vorstellung eines objectiven Princips, sofern es für einen Willen nöthigend ist, heißt ein Gebot (der Vernunft) und die Formel des Gebots heißt Imperativ.*" Kant AA IV 413—"The representation of an objective principle, insofar as it is necessitating for a will, is called a command (of reason), and the formula of the command is called imperative."—translation by Orr (2015), p. 37.

agent must have, e.g. self-preservation, and *purposes*^{s}, not every rational agent must have, e.g. always run to get to a place.[5]

As third differentiation, *Kant* offers the *achievability* of the purpose as an underlying principle. Either it is a problematically practical principle if only a merely possible purpose (*purpose*^{p}) can be achieved, or it is an assertorically practical principle if an actual purpose (*purpose*^{a}) can be attained.[6]

To make all of the different kinds of purposes more manageable, I will add as fourth distinction their *directness*. Direct purposes are those purposes that the agent directly aims for and wants to attain (*purpose*^{d}), e.g. play the piano. They will sometimes need subordinate/interim or indirect purposes as intermediate steps to achieve them (*purposes*^{i}), e.g. look for methods to learn, acquire these methods, and set them into action. Any indirect *purpose*^{i} can easily be turned into a direct one if the agent directly aims for it. Thus, the classification is relative and flexible. Yet adding such a differentiation is not at all *unKantian* because in *his* works, *Kant* looked for an ultimate purpose (*purpose*^{u}) as well, thus offering a way that the directness of the purposes might be relevant as well.

Each of the three different imperatives *Kant* assigned a function to, which must have a bearing on the different purposes as well. Hence, they will be equally assessed.

1.1 Two Kinds of Hypothetical Imperatives: Endless Purposes

Hypothetical imperatives "represent the practical necessity of a possible action as a means to attain something else that one wills (or yet is possible that one wills it)."[7] As rules, they combine any of the agent's ends/purposes based on their desires or inclinations with the conditions/requirements that need to be fulfilled to achieve these particular ends.[8] Hence, specific hypothetical imperatives can only be applied by those agents that already have decided on specific purposes. If they have not done so, they cannot apply them.[9]

Hypothetical imperatives may only be decided and acted according to the agent's efforts and the purposes as decided by him, which are thus *purposes*^{s}. There cannot be an obligation to act according to any hypothetical imperative unless the agent thinks the purposes to be advantageous. This is why they can only order the agent to

[5]Instead of all see: Johnson and Cureton (2017); Koorsgard (2000), pp. 17 et seq.

[6]"*Der hypothetische Imperativ sagt also nur, daß die Handlung zu irgend einer möglichen oder wirklichen Absicht gut sei. Im erstern Falle ist er ein problematisch=, im zweiten ein assertorisch=praktisches Princip*" Kant AA IV 414 et seq.—"The hypothetical imperative thus says only that the action is good for some possible or actual purpose. In the first case, it is a problematic, in the second assertoric-practical principle"—translation by Orr (2015), p. 40.

[7]Translation by Orr (2015), p. 39.

[8]Kalscheuer (2014), pp. 11 et seq. and 14 et seq.; von der Pfordten (2009), p. 30.

[9]See Cholbi (2016), p. 14 et seq.

do something but not oblige him to do so. Furthermore, they are prone to be abused if the agents set tainted purposes, and they are potentially suggestive regarding their means as there are different ways to achieve these presumably tainted purposes. The agent does not even have to rationally choose one of the different means.[10] However, if the hypothetical imperative in itself *is* rational, it serves to achieve the purposes that the agent wanted in the first place.[11] Their function is to connect a purpose and action, commanding the agent to realize the possible acts to achieve certain purposes. Hypothetical imperatives have the form: "If you will purpose P, then act A (which is one possible means to P)." The purpose P then is the *purpose*^{d} as chosen by the agent. With regard to their effects and aims, they can be *purposes*$^{p\&p1\&n}$.

They can have both *purposes*^{p} or *purposes*^{a} as the agent can think of them as mere possibility or actuality.[12]

According to *Kant*, there are two different types of hypothetical imperatives. Thus, *he* differentiates between Rules of Skills (*Imperativ der Geschicklichkeit*) and Counsels of Prudence (*Rathschläge der Klugheit*).[13] The former consist of the specific purposes as individually set by the agents, hence *purposes*^{s}. It is their function to specify the purposes according to each agent's personal wishes/desires/ inclinations. As rules, they contain the requirements that need to be fulfilled to realize this individually set purpose. They are acquired by experience: if the agent's goal is to allay his or her hunger, he/she knows *a posteriori* that the requirements and conditions for this purpose are to eat bread. There can be a chain of hypothetical imperatives, if the actions are broken down into the tiniest steps, such as shopping, bringing it home, storing, taking a knife and a cutting board out, slicing, taking a plate, taking the slice in the hand, biting, chewing, swallowing. With each action, the completion of the set *purpose*^{d} draws nearer, and further *interim purposes*^{i} to fulfill the *purpose*^{d} will be accomplished as well. Hence, each of the *purposes*$^{d\&i}$ forms a relative system of directness. What is more, all these purposes need not only be individually set, but also there are diverse methods to achieve them due to the different perspectives and experiences each individual has. Yet there is one rational end and *purpose*^{u} that each and every agent looks for at last: happiness.[14]

---

[10] Hruschka (2015), p. 172: "*Er kann seine Vernunft auch seinem Handeln dienstbar machen, nämlich die besten Wege zur Erreichung seiner Zwecke ermitteln. Aber er ist durch und durch Tier von den anderen Tieren, die ebenfalls Intelligenzleistungen erbringen, nur graduell unterschieden. Vor allem die Zwecke, die er sich setzt, sind ihm von seiner tierischen Natur vorgegeben. Infolgedessen ist er dabei durch seine sinnlichen Antriebe und Neigungen bestimmt*" and Hruschka (2015), p. 173: "*Als geistiges [...] Wesen hat der Mensch die Fähigkeit, »nach Prinzipien zu handeln«, [...] und demgemäß die Fähigkeit, sich von seiner tierischen Natur unabhängige Zwecke zu setzen*", citing Kant AA VI 420, available at: https://korpora.zim.uni-duisburg-essen.de/kant/aa06/411.html.

[11] Cholbi (2016), p. 17.

[12] See above n. 6.

[13] "*Regeln der Geschicklichkeit, oder Rathschläge der Klugheit*" Kant AA IV 416—"they were either *rules* of skill, or *counsels* of prudence"—translation by Orr (2015), p. 43.

[14] "*Also ist der Imperativ, der sich auf die Wahl der Mittel zur eigenen Glückseligkeit bezieht, d. i., die Vorschrift der Klugheit, noch immer hypothetisch; die Handlung wird nicht schlechthin, sondern nur als Mittel zu einer andern Absicht geboten.*" Kant AA IV 415—"Therefore, the

The latter, Counsels of Prudence, are goals universally sought after. Nevertheless, each agent must *individually* identify them; hence, they can only be *purposes*^{s} as well. Their function is to identify *purposes*^{s} or goals for the overall sake of the agent's goodwill. In the vein of this function, possible goals or purposes can be to be good, happy, or abide by religious rules. Other than Rules of Skills, Counsels of Prudence are deduced *a priori*, by pure reason. Here again, happiness is a universal goal, rational end or *purpose*^{u} to be achieved at last. Table 1 gives an overview of the 11 different parameters for hypothetical imperatives (decision, obligation, abuse, function, form (with *purpose*^{d}), acquirement, purposes regarding effect and aim, purposes regarding necessity, purposes regarding achievability, purposes regarding directness, and the rational end (*purpose*^{u}), as discussed in the main text.

Table 1 Hypothetical imperatives

	Hypothetical imperatives	
Decision	Made according to the agent's desires and benefits sought after, possibly *a posteriori* or *a priori*	
Obligation	no obligation to follow, link as an "ought" of goal and conditions	
Abuse	possibility to set tainted goals and diverse means to achieve any goal	
Function	connection of purpose and action	
Form (with *purpose*^{d})	If you will purpose P, then act A (which is one possible means to P).	
	Rules of skills	**Counsels of prudence**
Acquirement	*A posteriori* (derived from experience)	*A priori* (deduction from pure reason)
Purposes regarding effect and aim	*Purposes*$^{p1\&p2\&n}$	
Purposes regarding necessity	Specific to each agent's personal wishes/desires/inclinations (*purpose*^{s})	Universal goals for overall sake of the agent's goodwill (be good, be happy, please God) yet as individually identified (*purpose*^{s})
Purposes regarding achievability	Leading each to *purposes*^{p} (problematically practical principle) or *purposes*^{a} (assertorically practical principle)	
Purposes regarding directness	Leading each to *purposes*$^{d\&i}$ in a relative system	
Rational end (*purpose*^{u}): happiness	Commonly yet individually sought after	Universal goal yet as individually identified

imperative which refers to the choice of means to one's own happiness, i.e. the prescription of prudence, is still always *hypothetical*; the action is commanded not absolutely, but only as a means to another purpose"—translation by Orr (2015), p. 43; Hruschka (2015), p. 183.

1.2 Four Forms of Categorical Imperatives: Purposes for the Internal Legislation

While hypothetical imperatives connect purposes and means, they are unserviceable to distinguish *which* purpose the agent should select as they hold only *purposes*^{s}, without distinguishing *purposes*^{o}. This function—to identify the necessary personal ethics and purposes—is assigned to the categorical imperative[15]; hence, the outcome of the scrutiny must be *purposes*^{o}. Unlike hypothetical imperatives, categorical imperatives oblige agents to act upon them disregarding their personal desires and advantages because they motivate by a sense of duty.[16] This is why any agent has to respond to them no matter what he wants. To determine and develop a categorical imperative, the agents use pure practical reason *a priori*. As the agent's wishes and desires are irrelevant, the thus identified categorical imperatives are universally valid. They are to be applied for the "inner legislation" as a test for morally valid maxims to act in a rational manner.[17] The testing of the maxims according to the categorical imperative has the following form, identifying the *purpose*^{d}: firstly, formulate a maxim that perpetuates your reason for acting A to achieve purpose P. Secondly, think of this maxim as a universal law that governs all rational agents so that all act like A in the same way to achieve P. Thirdly, reflect whether your maxim is imaginable in a world in which everyone acts A. Fourthly, if affirmed, the question needs to be answered, whether an agent can rationally will to act A on such a maxim in such a world. Fifthly, if affirmed as well, the action upon such a maxim is morally permissible.[18] Of course, that *purpose*^{d} might have yet again actually interim *purposes*^{i} to be achieved as well, forming a system of relative purposes.

The thus identified *purposes*^{o} can hold both the positive and negative attributes (*purposes*$^{p1\&p2\&n}$), be they not only possible but actual as well (*purpose*$^{p\&a}$).

According to many of *Kant's* texts, the core of morality is a systematization of reason to achieve a prevalent goal, as the first *purpose*^{u}, for any human being: happiness.[19] For this overall rational end, the agents' inclinations need to be regulated in a manner that they can and do "live on shared, transparent terms – terms that enable them to act rationally, both individually and collaboratively, in the

[15] Hruschka (2015), pp. 175 et seq.; with different interpretations as to the scope of this function: Williams (1968), pp. 36 et seq.

[16] Herman (1981), p. 363.

[17] Brinkmann (2003), p. 12; Cholbi (2016), p. 201; Geismann (2006), pp. 25 et seq.; Kalscheuer (2014), pp. 107 et seq.; Stratton-Lake (2008), pp. 101 et seq.

[18] Instead of all: Brinkmann (2003), pp. 140 et seq.; Horn et al. (2007), p. 231; Johnson and Cureton (2017).

[19] Guyer (2000), p. 100.

pursuit of diverse ways of life"[20] and happiness.[21] *Kant's* intended function of the categorical imperative was to develop a serviceable method to achieve happiness; it is based on the presumption that "morality is grounded on the idea of universal happiness from free conduct."[22] Thus, the categorical imperative sets aside the contradiction residing in the conflicting happiness of one agent or all agents with the overall end to maximize the happiness of both the individual agent and the others as well.[23] The rational ends—or *purpose*[u]—that all agents must have are thus not their own[24] but the happiness of others in their free conduct, as well as self-perfection.[25]

---

[20]Cholbi (2016), p. 229; similarly: Guyer (2000), p. 100: "fit an inter- and intrapersonal system of happiness."

[21]"*Da nun die Sittlichkeit sich auf die idee der allgemeinen Glükseeligkeit aus freyem Verhalten Gründet, so werden wir genothigt, selbst die Ursache und Regirung der Welt nach einer idee, nemlich demjenigen, was alles Einstimig macht oder durch einstimige Bestrebung zur Glükseeligkeit auch diese selbst besorgt, zu gedenken; denn sonst hätte die moralische idee keine realität in der Erwartung und wäre ein blos vernünftelnder Begrif.*" Kant N. 6958, AA XIX 214, available at: https://korpora.zim.uni-duisburg-essen.de/kant/agb-initia/index.html—"Now since morality is grounded on the idea of universal happiness from free conduct, we are necessitated to conceive of even the cause and government of the world in accordance with an idea, namely that which makes everything harmonious or is concerned with happiness itself through harmonious efforts; for otherwise the moral idea would have no reality in expectation and would be a merely sophistical concept." – translation as cited by Guyer (2000), p. 101.

[22]Guyer (2000), p. 101.

[23]Guyer (2000), p. 102.

[24]"*Wenn es also auf Glückseligkeit ankommt, worauf als meinen Zweck hinzuwirken es Pflicht sein soll, so muß es die Glückseligkeit anderer Menschen sein, deren (erlaubten) Zweck ich hiemit auch zu dem meinigen mache. [...] Widerwärtigkeiten, Schmerz und Mangel sind große Versuchungen zu Übertretung seiner Pflicht. Wohlhabenheit, Stärke, Gesundheit und Wohlfahrt überhaupt, die jenem Einflusse entgegen stehen, können also auch, wie es scheint, als Zwecke angesehen werden, die zugleich Pflicht sind; nämlich seine eigene Glückseligkeit zu befördern und sie nicht blos auf Fremde zu richten.*" Kant AA VI 388 – Only the "happiness is merely a means for removing obstacles to his morality [...] Adversity, pain, and want are great temptations to violate one's duty. It might therefore seem that prosperity, strength, health, and well-being in general, which check the influence of these, could also be considered ends that are duties, so that one has a duty to promote one's own happiness and not just the happiness of others"– translation as cited by Cholbi (2016), p. 216.

[25]Kant AA VI 419 et seq.; "*Es ist keine bestimmte Regel der Zweke als die allgemeingültigkeit der Zweke der Natur und der Zweke der Menschen. d. i. aus dem Ganzen der Natur und der Zweke der Menschen. Auch wird dadurch auch die Beziehung auf Glükseeligkeit aus den eignen Handlungen der Menschen so wohl in Ansehung der Natur als in Ansehung einander auf bestimte Grundsätze gebracht. Der ist würdig der Glükseeligkeit, dessen freye Handlungen auf die Einstimung mit dem allgemeinen Grunde derselben darin sie allein gerichtet sind, der also derselben aus seiner eignen Handlung fähig ist. Aus der idee des Ganzen wird hier die glükseligkeit jedes theiles bestimt.*" Kant N. 7058, AA XIX 237—"There is no determinate rule of ends except the universal validity of the ends of nature and the ends of human beings, i.e., from the whole of nature and the ends of human beings. Thereby the relations to happiness in the individual actions of humans are brought under determinate principles with regard to nature as well as with regard to each other. He is worthy of happiness whose free actions are directed to harmony with the universal grounds of that, who is therefore capable of that from his own action. From the idea of the whole the happiness of each part

In this vein, categorical imperatives of any form can either lead to perfect duties, which are duties not to act in certain ways (prohibitions), or imperfect duties, which are duties to act in certain ways (commandments).[26] As perfect duties, they require to perform particular acts, can easily compel, and furthermore do never allow for any exception due to a mere inclination.[27] Imperfect duties, e.g. duty of beneficence or to promote the morally permissible ends of others), do *not* compel, require only adopting general ends while providing a multitude of possible how-tos,[28] and can only be followed voluntarily.[29] Furthermore, they need to be balanced with other maxims, which is why one cannot easily subsume or apply them,[30] but a special decisive competence, reason, and practice are necessary.[31] With regard to purposes, *Kant* made the following distinction: *purpose*^{p2} lead to imperfect duties, whereas *purposes*^{n} lead to perfect duties.[32]

Kant phrased different versions of the categorical imperative, each zooming in on different aspects, clarifying another function.[33] As Formula of Universality and the Law of Nature (categorical imperative^{1}) translates literally, "act only according to that maxim, through which you at the same time can will, that it becomes a universal law" and "act in this way, as if the maxim of your action were to become through your will a universal law of nature."[34] Here the agent has to treat his or her own

---

is here determined."—translation as cited by Guyer (2000), pp. 99 et seq.; Beck (2008), pp. 200 et seq.; Guyer (2000), p. 100: "Many texts demonstrate Kant's recognition that the essence of morality is nothing other than the use of reason to systematize happiness, that is, to regulate our attempts to satisfy our inclinations so that we satisfy only those which fit into an intra- and interpersonal system of happiness. We might take as a motto for all of Kant's remarks along these lines this sentence: "*The conformity of an action with a necessary and universal rule of satisfaction* [Wohlgefallens] *is morality*" (R 6805, 19;167; 1773-175)"; Koorsgard (2000), pp. 56 et seq. and 127 et seq.

[26]"*Nun wollen wir einige Pflichten herzählen, nach der gewöhnlichen Eintheilung derselben, in Pflichten gegen uns selbst und gegen andere Menschen, in vollkommene und unvollkommene Pflichten *).*" Kant AA IV 421—"Now we want to enumerate some duties according to the usual division of them into duties to ourselves and to other human beings, into perfect and imperfect duties.*)"—translation by Orr (2015), p. 53 et seq.

[27]"*Uebrigens verstehe ich hier unter einer vollkommenen Pflicht diejenige, die keine Ausnahme zum Vortheil der Neigung verstattet*" Kant AA IV 421 n—"Moreover, I understand here under a perfect duty that one which permits no exception to the advantage of inclination"—translation by Orr (2015), p. 53 note.

[28]Cholbi (2016), p. 211.

[29]Horn et al. (2007), pp. 239 and 241.

[30]Kalscheuer (2014), p. 47.

[31]Kant AA VI 411.

[32]See Johnson and Cureton (2017).

[33]It is contested whether or not and if affirmed which of the different Categorical Imperatives form *genera* or *species*: Csingár (2013), pp. 99 et seq.; Geismann (2002), pp. 375 et seq.; Oberer (1997), p. 164; Paton (1962), pp. 152 et seq.; Schmucker (1997), pp. 120 et seq.; Schönecker and Wood (2007), pp. 126 et seq. and 163 et seq.; Williams (1968), pp. 22 et seq. and 36.

[34]"*handle nur nach derjenigen Maxime, durch die du zugleich wollen kannst, daß sie ein allgemeines Gesetz werde [...] handle so, als ob die Maxime deiner Handlung durch deinen*

maxim as if it was objective law, universalizing it. Its assigned function is the universalization of a possible maxim. In this manner, the problematic subjectivity of purposes is reduced as far as possible, to gain "objective" purposes and maxims.[35]

According to the end-in-itself formula or the Formula of Humanity (categorical imperative^2), humans and humanity need to be "used" as their very own end and not means:

> If, then, there is thus to be a highest practical principle and in view of the human will a categorical imperative, then it must be one such that, from the representation of that which necessarily for everyone is an end because it is an *end in itself*, constitutes an *objective* principle of the will, therefore can serve as the universal practical law. The ground of this principle is: *rational nature exists as an end in itself.* In this way the human being necessarily conceives its own existence; so far is it thus a *subjective* principle of human actions.[36]

In the form of a categorical imperative, that means "Act in this way, that you use humanity in your own person, as well as in the person of every other, always at the same time as an end, never merely as a means."[37] Thus, the overall purpose—or end in itself—is not only any human being or humanity but even any rational being that might act on the categorical imperative. If an agent treats another person as means to his or her discretionary end, the perfect duty, e.g. a prohibition, of the categorical imperative^2 is violated. With the categorical imperative^2 as well, an imperfect duty may be deduced. This is the commandment to treat humans, humanity, or any rational being as an end in itself. If this is not accomplished while acting on behalf of the commandment, it can be violated as well. In this manner, categorical imperative^2 focuses on how other people are treated while the agent interacts with them. Its function is to include *Kant's* special concept of dignity[38] in the process of ethics.

The Formula of Autonomy (categorical imperative^3) combines the Formula for the Universal Law of Nature and the Formula of Humanity with regard to their objectivity (universalization test) and subjectivity. It is based on the "principle of each human will, as a will giving universal law through all its maxims."[39] By this

---

Willen zum allgemeinen Naturgesetze werden sollte" Kant AA IV 421—translation by Orr (2015), p. 52.

[35]See the critical assessment of: Williams (1968), p. 125.

[36]"*Wenn es denn also ein oberstes practisches Princip, und, in Ansehung des menschlichen Willens, einen categorischen Imperativ geben soll, so muß es ein solches seyn, das aus der Vorstellung dessen, was nothwendig für jedermann Zweck ist, weil es Zweck an sich selbst ist, ein objectives Princip des Willens ausmacht, mit hin zum allgemeinen practischen Gesetz dienen kann. Der Grund dieses Princips ist: die vernünftige Natur existirt als Zweck an sich selbst.*" Kant AA IV 428—translation by Orr (2015), p. 66.

[37]"*Handle so, daß du die Menschheit, sowol in deiner Person, als in der Person eines jeden andern, jederzeit zugleich als Zweck, niemals bloß als Mittel brauchest.*" Kant AA IV 429—translation by Orr (2015), pp. 67 et seq.

[38]See Cholbi (2016), pp. 107 et seq. with further references; Hruschka (2015), pp. 188 et seq.

[39]"*das Princip eines jeden menschlichen Willens, als eines durch alle seine Maximen allgemein gesetzgebenden Willens*" Kant AA IV 432—translation by Orr (2015), p. 72.

means, it veers towards a kind of golden rule of the categorical imperative, proposing that any person might ask what renders to be an *acceptable universal* law und thus testing the moral law he had just developed. The function here is to have the concept of dignity universalized.

The Kingdom of Ends Formulation (categorical imperative[4]) is a *Kantian* thought experiment. In such a kingdom, only rational beings exist that each act according to the categorical imperative. Hence, they treat all human beings as purposes and not as means to their own purposes and are thus systematically unified.[40] Its function is to make the Kingdom of Ends possible. While in the Kingdom of Ends, they themselves are as agents a sovereign and subject to the laws when they abide them. In so doing, it is formulated:

> Accordingly, any rational being must in this way act, as if it were through its maxims always a lawgiving member in the universal empire of ends. The formal principle of these maxims is: act in this way, as if your maxim at the same time were to serve as the universal law (of all rational beings).[41]

In this manner, there is a perfect duty not to act upon maxims that might not create such a Kingdom of Ends if universalized. And there is an imperfect duty to act upon maxims that further the stability of the Kingdom of Ends. Happiness as *purpose*^{u} or rational end forms a *purpose*^{a}, hence is achievable, while acting—rationally deduced—virtuously in the Kingdom of Ends.[42] That said, it means that happiness as the rational end is otherwise a mere *purpose*^{p}. It is a systematic unification of the first three imperatives, leading to politically mature agents in the visionary Kingdom of Ends. Table 2 gives an overview of the 12 different parameters for categorical imperatives (decision, obligation, abuse, function, form (with *purpose*^{d}), acquirement, aspects of function, purposes regarding effect and aim, purposes regarding necessity, purposes regarding achievability, purposes regarding directness, and the rational end (*purpose*^{u})), as discussed in the main text.

---

[40]"*Ich verstehe aber unter einem Reiche die systematische Verbindung verschiedener vernünftiger Wesen durch gemeinschaftliche Gesetze.*" Kant AA IV 433—"I understand, however, under an empire the systematic union of different rational beings through common laws"—translation by Orr (2015), p. 74.

[41]"*Demnach muß ein jedes vernünftiges Wesen so handeln, als ob es durch seine Maximen jederzeit ein gesetzgebendes Glied im allgemeinen Reiche der Zwecke wäre.*" Kant AA IV 438—translation by Orr (2015), pp. 83 et seq.

[42]Cholbi (2016), pp. 119 and 218 et seq.

Table 2 Categorical imperative

	Categorical imperative			
Decision	Made with the application of pure practical reason *a priori*, independent of any agent			
Obligation	obligation to follow under any circumstances—universal validity			
Abuse	impossible			
Function	developing which purpose should be chosen			
Form (with *purpose*^{d})	1. Formulate a maxim that perpetuates your reason for acting A to achieve purpose P. 2. Think of this maxim as a universal law that governs all rational agents so that all act in the same way. 3. Reflect whether your maxim is imaginable in a world in which everyone acts on it. 4. If affirmed, can an agent rationally will to act on such a maxim in such a world. 5. If affirmed as well, the action upon such a maxim is morally permissible.			
	CI^{1}	**CI^{2}**	**CI^{3}**	**CI^{4}**
Acquirement	Pure practical reason *a priori*			
Aspects of function	Universalization	Human/ rational being/ humanity	Universalized human will	Make the Kingdom of Ends possible
Purposes regarding effect and aim	*Purposes*$^{p1\&p2\&n}$ *Purposes*^{n} leading each to *perfect* and *purposes*^{p2} to *imperfect* duties			
Purposes regarding the necessity	*Purpose*^{o}			
Purposes regarding achievability	Leading each to *purposes*^{p} (problematically practical principle) or *purposes*^{a} (assertorically practical principle)			
Purposes regarding directness	Leading each to *purposes*$^{d\&i}$ in a relative system			
Rational end (*purpose*^{u}): happiness	Maximization of self-perfection and everyone's happiness in their free conduct as *purpose*^{p}			Achievable happiness while acting virtuously in the Kingdom of Ends as *purpose*^{a}

1.3 Legal Categorical Imperative: Purposes for the External Legislation

Whereas hypothetical imperatives connect possible purposes with possible actions, categorical imperatives test the moral permissibility of individual maxims as "inner legislation." The legislation and test of outward-bound actions[43] are governed by the legal categorical imperative.[44] It is a system *a priori*[45] analytically developed within the concept of the outer freedom[46] or civil rights of the agents.[47] As a categorical imperative, it cannot be abused.[48] Its form and function are to identify the conditions under which the conflicting actions of persons can be harmonized:

> Right, therefore, comprehends the whole of the conditions under which the voluntary actions of any one Person can be harmonized in reality with the voluntary actions of every other Person, according to a universal Law of Freedom.[49]

Hence, freedom can only be expanded and limited in a way that is admissible to the freedom of another person to not be unlawful. In other words, everything is permitted that is not forbidden.[50] Nevertheless, the function of the legal categorical imperative is not only the facilitation as an action but also prevention: the agents are prevented from compelling others to perform actions that are not a means to their own ends.

According to *Kant*, right needs three applicational requirements. The first one is the most rudimental one: right can only be in charge if there are at least two

---

[43]Geismann (2006), pp. 32 et seq.

[44]It is contested that *his* Law of Right is an Imperative as well see: Csingár (2013), pp. 48 et seq.; negation of an Imperative: Kersting (2007), p. 85: "*Das Rechtsgesetz ist also kein Imperativ*"—The Law of Right is no Imperative; Scholz (1972), p. 45: "*Das Rechtsgesetz ist weder ein hypotheticher noch ein kategorischer, also überhaupt kein Imperativ*"—The Law of Right is neither a Hypothetical nor a Categorical, hence not at all an Imperative; affirmation of an Imperative: Geismann (2010), p. 94; Ludwig (2005), p. 94: "*Das Rechtsgesetz* ist *ein Imperativ, und zwar ein kategorischer*"—The Law of Right is an Imperative, namely a Categorical.

[45]"*nämlich das Recht, was zum* a priori *entworfenen System gehört*" Kant AA VI 205—"the Principles of Right, which belong to the rational system"—translation by Hastie (1887), p. 4.

[46]Guyer (2000), p. 96, citing *Moral Mrongovius*, Kant's Lectures on Ethics, translated by Louis Infield, London 1930, AA 27:1482: "Freedom is a part of the capacity which gives all others their infinite usefulness, it is the highest degree of life, it is the property that is a necessary condition at the basis of all perfections. [. . .] if all creatures had a faculty of choice bound to sensuous drives, the world would have no value; the inner value of the world, the *summum bonum*, is the freedom to act in accordance with a faculty of choice that is not necessitated. Freedom is therefore the inner value of the world."

[47]Kant AA VI 396; Kant AA VII 270; Kant AA VIII 289 et seq.

[48]See above: Sect. 1.2., p. 82 et seq.

[49]"*Das Recht ist also der Inbegriff der Bedingungen, unter denen die Willkür des einen mit der Willkür des anderen nach einem allgemeinen Gesetze der Freiheit zusammen vereinigt werden kann.*" Kant AA VI 230—translation by Hastie (1887), p. 45.

[50]Kalscheuer (2014), p. 93; of different opinion: Brandt (1995), p. 78; Flikschuh (2004), p. 316; Kersting (2007), pp. 194 et seq.: permissible laws of *Kant's* Philosophy of Law are exceptional laws of a principly forbidden prohibition.

intentionally acting and responsive agents in a limited outside world.[51] Only in the outside world can a conflict of interest occur. It is the function of the legal categorical imperative to solve these conflicts[52] and develop outer freedom/civil rights. The practical pure reason can imagine exterior free agents, who live in a local and temporal combined community; only in this vein that they alternately restrict each other's freedom.[53] This is why the exterior freedom of every agent is only possible as being *per se* restricted by general laws.[54] Thus, the practical freedom of all agents is the *ratio essendi* and *ratio cognoscendi* of the law.[55]

The second requirement can be found in the relation of the act of will (*Willkür*)[56] of the other agent.[57] *Kant* means with the act of will the freedom to act, which must be related to the outside world. Differentiating between the act of will and needs, only those needs that require actions in the outside world are relevant for the law.[58] Neither a special beneficence nor a particular flintiness is an attribute of law; in other words, the needs of other agents do not have to be legally considered; they are not a public task.[59] A welfare state can thus only be created to secure the interior and exterior security of the legal state. The latter can as well be achieved by legislating in a way to facilitate the happiness—as need requiring action in the outside world—[60]

[51]"*Der Begriff des Rechts, sofern er sich auf eine ihm correspondirende Verbindlichkeit bezieht, (d. i. der moralische Begriff desselben) betrifft erstlich nur das äußere und zwar praktische Verhältnis einer Person gegen eine andere, sofern ihre Handlungen als Facta aufeinander (unmittelbar oder mittelbar) Einfluß haben können.*" Kant AA VI 223 & 230—"The conception of RIGHT, – as referring to a corresponding Obligation which is the moral aspect of it, – in the first place, has regard only to the external and practical relation of one Person to another, in so far as they can have influence upon each other, immediately or mediately, by their Actions as facts"—translation by Hastie (1887), pp. 45 et seq.; Brinkmann (2003), pp. 127 et seq.; Höffe (1999), pp. 50 et seq. and 59 et seq.; Schmitz (2004), p. 318.

[52]Brinkmann (2003), p. 130; Höffe (1999), p. 50.

[53]Sänger (1982), pp. 178 et seq.; Geismann (2006), p. 32.

[54]Kant AA VI 396.

[55]Kant AA V 4 & n. *, available at: https://korpora.zim.uni-duisburg-essen.de/kant/aa05/004.html.

[56]Kant AA VI 399; Hruschka (2015), p. 182: There are four steps from the act of will to an action (1. the idea of an possible action, 2. the emotion of (dis)inclination for the action or their consequences, 3. thus the act of will takes in interest in the action and leads 4. either to act or not to act).

[57]"*Aber zweitens bedeutet er nicht das Verhältniß der Willkür auf den Wunsch (folglich auch auf das bloße Bedürfniß) des Anderen, wie etwa in den Handlungen der Wohlthätigkeit oder Hartherzigkeit, sondern lediglich auf die Willkür des Anderen.*" *Kant, Immanuel,* Die Metaphysik der Sitten, AA VI 230—"In the second place, the conception of Right does not indicate the relation of the action of an individual to the wish or the mere desire of another, as in acts of benevolence or of unkindness, but only the relation of his free action to the freedom of action of the other"—translation by Hastie (1887), p. 45; Kalscheuer (2014), pp. 73 et seq.

[58]Brinkmann (2003), p. 133.

[59]Brinkmann (2003), pp. 132 et seq.

[60]See above text at and reference in fn. 58.

of the people,[61] which would then form a *purpose*$^{p2\&p}$. Though it is claimed neither in the "The Groundwork of the Metaphysics of Morals" nor in "The Metaphysics of Morals," that very idea can be found in several other *Kantian* texts. It is the function of the legal categorical imperative not only to facilitate happiness but also to create an internal and external perfect constitution, which is the only situation, in which mankind can materialize all of its beneficial assets.[62] Yet it is not the internal morality of the people that leads to a "good" constitution, but "the good moral condition of a nation is to be looked for, as one of the first fruits of such a constitution."[63]

The third requirement for the law is the relationship of the *form* the act of will takes—and not its *matter*.[64] The act of will's *matter* is the agent's intention. Those

[61]"*Wenn die oberste Macht Gesetze giebt, die zunächst auf die Glückseligkeit (die Wohlhabenheit der Bürger, die Bevölkerung u. dergl.) gerichtet sind: so geschieht dieses nicht als Zweck der Errichtung einer bürgerlichen Verfassung, sondern bloß als Mittel, den rechtlichen Zustand vornehmlich gegen äußere Feinde des Volks zu sichern. Hierüber muß das Staatsoberhaupt befugt sein selbst und allein zu urtheilen, ob dergleichen zum Flor des gemeinen Wesens gehöre, welcher erforderlich ist, um seine Stärke und Festigkeit sowohl innerlich, als wider äußere Feinde zu sichern.*" Kant AA VIII 298, available at: https://korpora.zim.uni-duisburg-essen.de/kant/aa08/298.html—If the supreme power gives laws which are directed at first to happiness (the prosperity of the citizens, the population, etc.), this does not serve the purpose of the establishment of a civic constitution, but merely as a means to the legal state primarily against external enemies of the people. On this point, the head of the state must be competent to judge for himself whether it belongs to the commonwealth, which is necessary in order to secure its strength and stability both internally and externally.

[62]"*Man kann die Geschichte der Menschengattung im Großen als die Vollziehung eines verborgenen Plans der Natur ansehen, um eine innerlich= und zu diesem Zwecke auch äußerlich vollkommene Staatsverfassung zu Stande zu bringen, als den einzigen Zustand, in welchem sie alle ihre Anlagen in der Menschheit völlig entwickeln kann*" Kant AA VIII 27, available at: https://korpora.zim.uni-duisburg-essen.de/kant/aa08/027.html—"The history of mankind can be seen, in the large, as the realization of Nature's secret plan to bring forth a perfectly constituted state as the only condition in which the capacities of mankind can be fully developed, and also bring forth that external relation among states which is perfectly adequate to this end"—translation by Beck (1963), available at https://www.marxists.org/reference/subject/ethics/kant/universal-history.htm.

[63]"*das Innere der Moralität davon sicherlich nicht die Ursache ist (wie denn auch nicht von dieser die gute Staatsverfassung), sondern vielmehr umgekehrt von der letzteren allererst die gute moralische Bildung eines Volks zu erwarten ist*" Kant AA VIII 366, available at: https://korpora.zim.uni-duisburg-essen.de/kant/aa08/366.html—"A good political constitution, however, is not to be expected as a result of progress in morality; but rather, conversely, the good moral condition of a nation is to be looked for, as one of the first fruits of such a constitution"—translation by Campbell Smith (1917), pp. 154 et seq.

[64]"*Drittens, in diesem wechselseitigen Verhältniß der Willkür kommt auch gar nicht die Materie der Willkür, d. i. der Zweck, den ein jeder mit dem Object, was er will, zur Absicht hat, in Betrachtung [...] sondern nur [...die...] Form im Verhältniß der beiderseitigen Willkür, sofern sie bloß als frei betrachtet wird, und ob durch die Handlung eines von beiden sich mit der Freiheit des andern nach einem allgemeinen Gesetze zusammen vereinigen lasse.*" Kant AA VI 230—"And, in the third place, in this reciprocal relation of voluntary actions, the conception of Right does not take into consideration the matter of the act of Will [. . .] but only the form of the transaction is taken into account, in considering the relation of the mutual acts of Will. Acts of Will or voluntary Choice are thus regarded only in so far as they are free, and as to whether the action of one can harmonize with the Freedom of another, according to a universal Law"—translation by Hastie (1887), p. 45.

intentions are irrelevant for the right as they cannot influence the actions.[65] But the form of the act of will—its being free—is what *Kant* supposes to be the relevant third requirement. And the thus act of free will of one agent needs to harmonize with the act of free will of other agents: hence, the freedom of the both of them must harmonize. In this manner, "Every Action is right which in itself, or in the maxim on which it proceeds, is such that it can co-exist along with the Freedom of the Will of each and all in action, according to a Universal Law."[66] The frame of reference is in this vein a universal law one can think of.

According to the legal categorical imperative, right must have yet another attribute: it must hold an obligation to compel (title or authority to compel).[67] Only if it holds an obligation to compel in the outside world can it be externally legislated. *Kant* identifies three possible duties of right or juridical duties (*Rechtspflichten*). Juridical duties can be externally legislated, which duties of virtue (*Tugendpflichten*) cannot because the latter have an end in itself and can only compel the agents from inside. No external legislation, may it be as powerful and compelling as possible, can cause such a purpose and change of intention; it can only set the mental conditions to apply the categorical imperative without having these as a special purpose.[68] The three positive duties of right are *Honeste vive* ("Do not make

[65]Brinkmann (2003), p. 134.

[66]"*Eine jede Handlung ist Recht, die oder nach deren Maxime die Freiheit der Willkür eines jeden mit jedermanns Freiheit nach einem allgemeinen Gesetze zusammen bestehen kann.*" Kant AA VI 230—translation by Hastie (1887), p. 45.

[67]"*Der Widerstand, der dem Hindernisse einer Wirkung entgegengesetzt wird, ist eine Beförderung dieser Wirkung und stimmt mit ihr zusammen. Nun ist alles, was unrecht ist, ein Hinderniß der Freiheit nach allgemeinen Gesetzen: der Zwang aber ist ein Hinderniß oder Widerstand, der der Freiheit geschieht. Folglich: wenn ein gewisser Gebrauch der Freiheit selbst ein Hinderniß der Freiheit nach allgemeinen Gesetzen (d. i. unrecht) ist, so ist der Zwang, der diesem entgegengesetzt wird, als Verhinderung eines Hindernisses der Freiheit mit der Freiheit nach allgemeinen Gesetzen zusammen stimmend, d. i. recht: mithin ist mit dem Rechte zugleich eine Befugniß, den, der ihm Abbruch thut, zu zwingen, nach dem Satze des Widerspruchs verknüpft.*" Kant AA VI 231—"The resistance which is opposed to any hindrance of an effect, is in reality a furtherance of this effect, and is in accordance with its accomplishment. Now, everything that is wrong is a hindrance of freedom, according to universal Laws; and Compulsion or Constraint of any kind is a hindrance or resistance made to Freedom. Consequently, if a certain exercise of Freedom is itself a hindrance of the Freedom that is according to universal Laws, it is wrong; and the compulsion or constraint which is opposed to it is right, as being a hindering of a hindrance of Freedom, and as being in accord with the Freedom which exists in accordance with universal Laws. Hence, according to the logical principle of Contradiction, all Right is accompanied with an implied Title or warrant to bring compulsion to bear on any one who may violate it in fact"—translation by Hastie (1887), p. 47.

[68]"*Alle Pflichten sind entweder Rechtspflichten (officia iuris), d. i. solche, für welche eine äußere Gesetzgebung möglich ist, oder Tugendpflichten (officia virtutis s. ethica), für welche eine solche nicht möglich ist; - die letztern können aber darum nur keiner äußeren Gesetzgebung unterworfen werden, weil sie auf einen Zweck gehen, der (oder welchen haben) zugleich Pflicht ist; sich aber einen Zweck vorzusetzen, das kann durch keine äußerliche Gesetzgebung bewirkt werden (weil es ein innerer Act des Gemüths ist); obgleich äußere Handlungen geboten werden mögen, die dahin führen, ohne doch daß das Subject sie sich zum Zweck macht.*" Kant AA VI 239—"All Duties are either Duties of Right, that is, JURIDICAL DUTIES (officia iuris), or Duties of Virtue, that is,

thyself a mere Means for the use of others, but be to them like wise an End"), *neminem laede* ("Do no Wrong to any one, even if thou shouldst be under the necessity, in observing this Duty, to cease from all connection with others and to avoid all Society"), and *suum cuique tribue* ("Enter into a state in which every one can have what is his own secured against the action of every other").[69]

Kant understands these three as *pars pro toto* of a system of juridical duties.[70] The first ones are "internal duties," according to which every agent needs to stand one's ground as a juridical person; the second ones are "external duties," according to which every agent has to respect the internal and external private law of every other person; the third ones are "connecting duties," according to which every agent must enable a public legal situation that can ensure internal and external duties likewise.[71]

The legal categorical imperative does *not* have happiness as an own rational end, but its *purpose*[u] is to facilitate the happiness of the people through laws, as a duty to others, and preserve outer freedom.[72] In this vein, empirical autonomy is fostered. Table 3 gives an overview of the 12 different parameters for legal categorical imperative (decision, obligation, abuse, function, form (with *purpose*[d]), acquirement, aspects of function, purposes regarding effect and aim, purposes regarding

---

ETHICAL DUTIES (officia virtutis s. ethica). Juridical Duties are such as may be promulgate by external Legislation; Ethical Duties are those for which such legislation is not possible. The reason why the latter cannot be properly made the subject of external Legislation is because they relate to an End or final purpose, which is itself, at the same time, embraced in these Duties, and which it is a Duty for the individual to have as such. But no external Legislation can cause any one to adopt a particular intention, or to propose to himself a certain purpose; for this depends upon an internal condition or act of the mind itself. However, external actions conducive to such a mental condition may be commanded, without its being implied, that the individual will of necessity make them an End to himself"—translation by Hastie (1887), pp. 24 et seq.

[69]"*honeste vive* [...] "*Lasse dich von anderen nicht zum Mittel machen, sondern sei für sie zugleich Zweck*", *neminem laede* [...] "*Verletze nicht das Recht anderer*", *suum cuique tribue* [...] "*Tritt in einen Zustand, in dem das Recht aller Individuen gesichert sein kann*"" Kant AA VI 236 et seq.—translation by Hastie (1887), pp. 54 et seq.

[70]"*Also sind obstehende drei classische Formeln zugleich Eintheilungsprincipien des Systems der Rechtspflichten in innere, äußere und in diejenigen, welche die Ableitung der letzteren vom Princip der ersteren durch Subsumtion enthalten.*" Kant AA VI 236—"These three classical Formula, at the same time, represent principles which suggest a Division of the System of Juridical Duties into Internal Duties, External Duties, and those Connecting Duties which contain the latter as deduced from the Principle of the former by subsumption"—translation by Hastie (1887), p. 55; see e.g. Kersting (2007), pp. 167 et seq.

[71]Geismann (2012a, b), p. 15.

[72]Guyer (2000), p. 98: "The value of freedom is not unconnected to happiness; rather, while happiness is the natural end of human beings, the *systematic distribution* of happiness, both in one's own life as a whole and in the whole community of human beings, thus the maximization of happiness, can be expected only if human actions are conducted in accordance with an ideal of reason that is a product of human freedom rather than a mere law of nature; moral law thus requires an *a priori* concept of the universality of happiness and can never be grounded merely on empirically given ends, but it does not require a disregard of the goal of happiness altogether and, indeed, makes no sense without reference to happiness".

Table 3 Legal categorical imperative

	Legal categorical imperative
Decision	Made with the application of pure practical reason *a priori*, independent of any agent
Obligation	Title or authority to compel
Abuse	Impossible
Function	Solving the conflict of (at least) two agents in the outside world—outer freedom and civil rights
Form (with *purpose*^{d})	Identify the whole of the conditions under which the voluntary actions of any agent can be harmonized in reality with the voluntary actions of every other agent, according to a universal law of freedom
Acquirement	Made with the application of pure practical reason *a priori*, independent of any agent
Aspects of function	1. internal and external perfect constitution, which is the only situation, in which mankind and every agent can materialize all of its beneficial assets 2. therewith good moral education of the people 3. external legislation of juridical duties, not moral duties
Purposes regarding effect and aim	*Purposes*$^{p1\&p2\&n}$ *Purposes*^{n} leading each to *perfect* and *purposes*^{p2} to *imperfect* duties As duties of right (juridical duties): internal duty (e.g. *honeste vive*), external duty (e.g. *neminem laede*), and connecting duty (e.g., *suum cuique tribue*)
Purposes regarding necessity	*Purpose*^{o}
Purposes regarding achievability	Leading each to *purposes*^{p} (problematically practical principle) or *purposes*^{a} (assertorically practical principle) but only for needs that require actions in the outside world
Purposes regarding directness	Leading each to *purposes*$^{d\&i}$ in a relative system
Rational end (*purpose*^{u}): happiness	Facilitation of the happiness of the people through laws but not as an own rational end; duty to others and outer freedom, and empirical autonomy

necessity, purposes regarding achievability, purposes regarding directness, and the rational end (*purpose*^{u})), as discussed in the main text.

2 Assessing the Interconnections of Both Doctrines and the Classification of Duties of Right and Duties of Virtue

To fully understand how happiness could be a rational end and which functions the different imperatives have, their relations and dependencies and thus those of the duties of virtue and right need to be assessed. Human beings function in the outward-bound world with hypothetical imperatives. The connection of purpose and action allows agents to act in a way to achieve their individually set goals. However, willing these purposes is—according to *Kant*—decided upon with the categorical imperative and putting them into action in the outward-bound world with the legal categorical imperative.

There are different contexts that both the latter can have: the context of effectiveness (*Wirksamkeitszusammenhang*) and the context of their foundations (*Begründungszusammenhang*). The former answers the question whether law needs for its validity to be abided from duty (*aus Pflicht*)—hence ethical reasons—or not; the latter answers the question of the reason for the legal categorical imperative.[73]

2.1 Two Different Contexts of Effectiveness (Legal Categorical Imperative ↛ Categorical Imperative; Categorical Imperative → Legal Categorical Imperative)

The duty of virtue and juridical duty, as set out by the (legal) categorical imperatives, can be classified. As both the latter are intertwined, their independences need to be illuminated to further understand the context and function that the different kinds of purposes might have. The context of effectiveness addresses two questions. On the one hand, the legal categorical imperative is neither an adequate nor a necessary condition for the categorical imperative but a *mere condition of development* and *of facilitation* for it (legal categorical imperative as developing and facilitating condition for the categorical imperative, legal categorical imperative ↛ categorical imperative). Why is that? It is because in the outward world, only an external freedom is necessary. Hence, it is impossible to say whether an agent acting in accordance with a legal categorical imperative does so only dutifully (*pflichtgemäß*) or from duty.[74] Due to this impossibility, the legal categorical imperative cannot be an *adequate* condition for the validity of the categorical imperative. What is more, an action from duty is even contingent if no action at all is feasible since the inexistence of external freedom does not lead to an inexistent internal freedom. That is why the validity of the legal categorical imperative cannot even be a *necessary* condition for the validity of the categorical imperative.[75]

But what does it mean to say that the legal categorical imperatives are/set the conditions of development for all of the categorical imperatives? The legal categorical imperative fosters and facilitates the application of the categorical imperative, creating an environment in which agents are able to fully develop all of their dispositions, including their moral ones (*purposes^o*).[76] Hence, a "working and

[73]See: Kalscheuer (2014), p. 145 et seq. & 185 et seq.

[74]Cholbi (2016), p. 202; Csingár (2013), p. 42 et seq.

[75]Kalscheuer (2014), p. et seq.

[76]Kant AA VIII 27, see note 62; Kalscheuer (2014), p. 166 et seq.

good" constitution cannot be developed because an internal morality of each and every agent exists. On the contrary, because of a good constitution, a sound moral education of the people is to be expected.[77] With the legal categorical imperative, agents can be compelled to act obligatorily; thus, agents are exonerated as they do not have to morally decide and apply all the time the categorical imperatives.[78] Nevertheless, this mere exoneration does not provide sufficient context for a connection of effectiveness because if an agent is compelled to act dutifully, he or she does not have to understand and act upon the categorical imperative, but his/her inclination is rather different: the reformation of his/her disposition (*Reform der Sinnesart*) will only take place if his/her morals and his/her heart are transformed as well.[79] However, even an only compelled dutiful act does not only exonerate the agents but has positive effects for the agent and anyone observing the agent. The observer cannot decide whether or not the compelled agent acts dutifully or from duty because his maxim is unobservable.[80] Thus, the compelled agent aspires to be a role model even against his or her will.[81]

On the other hand, the *effectiveness* of the legal categorical imperative depends on the categorical imperative in a limited way, creating an *interdependency* (*Wechselwirkung*, categorical imperative as a limited condition for the legal categorical imperative, categorical imperative → legal categorical imperative). Whether or not the legal categorical imperative is *fully independent* of the categorical

[77] Kant AA VIII 366 see n. 63.

[78] Kalscheuer (2014), p. 170; Kersting (2007), p. 87 n. 19.

[79] Kant AA VI 47, available at: https://korpora.zim.uni-duisburg-essen.de/kant/aa06/047.html; Kalscheuer (2014), p. 170.

[80] Kant AA VI 20: "*die Maximen kann man nicht beobachten*"—one cannot observe maxims; Kant AA III 489, available at: https://korpora.zim.uni-duisburg-essen.de/kant/aa03/489.html: "*keiner durch die Schminke der Anständigkeit, Ehrbarkeit und Sittsamkeit durchdringen konnte* [...] *an vermeintlich ächten Beispielen des Guten, die er um sich sah, eine Schule der Besserung für sich selbst*"—no one could penetrate the make-up of decency, honesty, and modesty [...] in supposedly genuine examples of the good which one saw around him, a school of improvement for himself; Kant AA IV 407: "*In der That ist es schlechterdings unmöglich, durch Erfahrung einen einzigen Fall mit völliger Gewißheit auszumachen, da die Maxime einer sonst pflichtmäßigen Handlung lediglich auf moralischen Gründen und auf der Vorstellung seiner Pflicht beruht habe.*"—"In fact it is absolutely impossible to make out through experience with complete certainty a single case in which the maxim of an action otherwise in accordance with duty has rested solely on moral grounds and on the representation of one's duty."—translation by Orr (2015), p. 26; O'Neill (2014), p. 15; Kalscheuer (2014), p. 170.

[81] Kant AA VIII 22: "*in welcher Freiheit unter äußeren Gesetzen im größtmöglichen Grade mit unwiderstehlicher Gewalt verbunden angetroffen wird, d. i. eine vollkommen gerechte bürgerliche Verfassung*"—"in which freedom under external laws is associated in the highest degree with irresistible power, i.e., a perfectly just civic constitution" translation by Beck (1963); Kant AA VI 48: "*von guten Menschen (was die Gesetzmäßigkeit derselben betrifft)*"—Of good people (as far as its legality is concerned); Kalscheuer (2014), p. 170.

imperative,[82] *fully dependent,*[83] or only *dependent in a limited way*[84] is highly contested. An argument supporting the limited dependence can be derived from *Kant's* passage of devils in *his* "Perpetual Peace" (*Zum ewigen Frieden*).[85] According to *Kant*, devils own an intellect (*Verstand*), have the evil as an *impetus* for their maxims, and reverse each and every moral command without any

[82]Csingár (2013), pp. 106 et seq. and 128; Ebbinghaus (1988), p. 297 et seq.: "*Ob aber dieses Gesetz der ‚sittlichen Autonomie' eine Idee von möglicher Realität für den Menschen oder eine bloße ‚hochfliegende Phantasterei' ist, ist eine Frage, von deren Bejahung oder Verneinung die Gültigkeit jenes der Erfahrung entnommenen negativen Begriffes von praktischer Freiheit, den Kant seiner Rechtslehre zu Grunde gelegt hat, in keiner Weise berührt wird. [...] Was aber die ‚sittliche Freiheit' anlangt, deren Gesetz das der Selbstgesetzgebung der reinen praktischen Vernunft sein müßte, so ist deren Möglichkeit in keiner Weise die Voraussetzung für die Gültigkeit des von Kants Rechtslehre vorausgesetzten negativen Freiheitsbegriffs.*"; Ebbinghaus (1968), p. 114: "*Ich verzichte hier auf den Nachweis, daß eine Norm, die ein Gesetz für alle möglichen Grundsätze des Willens sein soll, notwendig die allgemein bekannte Form des kategorischen Imperativs haben muß. Es geht aber auch aus der Forderung hervor, daß ein solches Gesetz notwendig das Gesetz einer Gesetzgebung des Willens durch sich selbst oder ein Gesetz der Autonomie des Willens in der allerwörtlichsten Bedeutung des Wortes ist. Folglich kann es keine Realität innerhalb der Grenzen der Natur haben. Denn die Kausalität einer Ursache unter Naturbedingungen – und auch der Wille ist eine Ursache – kann nicht durch diese Ursache selbst bestimmt werden, sondern bedarf zu dieser Bestimmung einer zeitlich vorhergehenden Ursache Also ist das Gesetz der Autonomie ein Gesetz der Freiheit in positivem Verstande, das nur in bezug auf eine mögliche intelligible Welt Realität haben kann*"; Ebbinghaus (1986), p. 357: "*[...] die reine Vernunftidee der Menschheit und ihres Rechts kann auch für denjenigen ein Gegenstand seiner Zwecksetzung sein, der von einer Motivierbarkeit des Menschen durch reine Vernunftideen nichts weiß oder nichts wissen will.*"; Geismann (1974), p. 56: "*Jeder hat das subjektive Recht, die Willkür jedes anderen in der angegebenen Weise einzuschränken, auf Grund des objektiven Rechts der alle gemeinsamen praktischen Vernunft, nach dem schon jedermann selber zu einer solchen Einschränkung verbunden ist. Der zureichende Grund für die Befugnis zu dieser Einschränkung liegt darin, daß die Bedingungen, auf welche die Freiheit der Willkür eingeschränkt wird, die einzigen sind, unter denen sie notwendig möglich ist. Umgekehrt würde ein Recht, sich einer solchen Einschränkung zu widersetzen, jede gesetzliche und also rechtliche Sicherung der Freiheit unmöglich machen und somit sich selbst widersprechen.*"; Geismann (2006), p. 111; Kersting (2004a), p. 284: "*Sittlichkeit ist weder Entstehungsvoraussetzung noch Erhaltungsbedingung eines rechtlichen Zustandes. Die Möglichkeit einer dem rechtlichen Vernunftentwurf entsprechenden äußeren Koexistenzordnung bedarf nicht einmal der Denkbarkeit der transzendentalen Freiheit.*"; Kersting (2004a), p. 31 et seq.: "*Sittlichkeit ist weder Entstehungsvoraussetzung noch Erhaltungsbedingung eines rechtlichen Zustandes. [...] Weil es keiner moralischen Gesinnung, keines engelhaften Charakters bedarf, um das Recht zu verwirklichen [...]*" & p. 35: "*Reine Moral und reines Recht sind für Kant verbindlichkeitstheoretische Schicksalsgenossen.*" & p. 36: "*Beide [Recht und Moral] entstammen demselben Ursprung, der reinen praktischen gesetzgebenden Vernunft.*"; Müller (1996), pp. 103 et seq.; Reich (2001), p. 157: "*die rein rationale Rechtslehre [...] führt gewiß nicht auf das Prinzip der Autonomie des Willens*".

[83]Brandt (1997), p. 235; Pawlik (2006), p. 283; Vosgerau (1999), p. 244; Willascheck (2009), p. 57.

[84]Ludwig (1997), p. 226 n. 17; Niesen (2001), p. 588: "*Das Problem der republikanischen Staatserrichtung lautet [. . .], der Ausübung politischer Autonomie einen Rahmen vorzugeben, innerhalb dessen strategische Aktivitäten der Bürger sich so rational auswirken können, ‚als ob sie keine solche böse Gesinnungen hätten*'".

[85]Kant AA VIII 366.

consideration for their own interests.[86] In such a setup, devils need to think and operate according to moral categories:

> The problem of the *formation of the state*, hard as it may sound, is not insoluble, even *for* a race of devils, granted that they have intelligence. It may be put thus: – "Given a multitude of rational beings who, in a body, require general laws for their own preservation, but each of whom, as an individual, is secretly inclined to exempt himself from this restraint: how are we to order their affairs and how establish for them a constitution such that, although their private dispositions may be really antagonistic, they may yet so act as a check upon one another, that, in their public relations, the effect is the same as if they had no such evil sentiments."[87]

Thus, to form a state is only possible "*for* a race of devils" not *by* them,[88] which means that a state can only be formed by moral entities. Nevertheless, even devils are able to learn morality to sustain such a state.[89] Hence, on the one hand, the forms of a state for the race of devils need to connect the general rule of law (*allgemeines Rechtsgesetz*) as the natural contract, the principles of a republic, and the categorical imperative; on the other hand, the devils must be able to learn morality to sustain such a republican state.[90] Finally, any sustainability of the state has three moral aspects[91]: first, there must be the correct terms of the nature of the possible constitution; thus, the nature of the constitution itself helps to sustain it with a kind of moral substitution (*moralische Substitution*); second, the organization of the state must be of a kind that any human being, even if not morally good, can be compelled

[86]Kant AA VIII 366; see as well: Kalscheuer (2014), p. 179; Niesen (2001), p. 585; Pawlik (2006), p. 270; Römpp (1991), p. 305, n. 13.

[87]"*Das Problem der* ***Staatserrichtung*** *ist, so hart wie es auch klingt, selbst* ***für*** *ein Volk von Teufeln (wenn sie nur Verstand haben) auflösbar und lautet so: "Eine Menge von vernünftigen Wesen, die insgesammt allgemeine Gesetze für ihre Erhaltung verlangen, deren jedes aber insgeheim sich davon auszunehmen geneigt ist, so zu ordnen und ihre Verfassung einzurichten, daß, obgleich sie in ihren Privatgesinnungen einander entgegen streben, diese einander doch so aufhalten, daß in ihrem öffentlichen Verhalten der Erfolg eben derselbe ist, als ob sie keine solche böse Gesinnungen hätten.*"" Kant AA VIII 366, citations omitted – translation by Campbell Smith (1917), pp. 153 et seq., available at: http://www.gutenberg.org/files/50922/50922-h/50922-h.htm.

[88]Ludwig (1997), p. 226 n. 17.

[89]Kant AA VIII 366.

[90]Kalscheuer (2014), p. 181; Niesen (2001), p. 589.

[91]1. "*richtige Begriffe von der Natur einer möglichen Verfassung*" 2. "*große durch viele Weltläufe geübte Erfahrenheit*" und 3. "*über das alles, ein zur Annehmung derselben vorbereiteter guter Wille*" Kant AA VIII 23 – 1. correct concepts of the nature of a possible constitution. 2. great experience practiced by many courses of the world 3. above all, a goodwill prepared for the acceptance of them.

to be a good citizen.[92] The scale to measure whether citizens are good citizens is their success regarding their actions; "although their private dispositions may be really antagonistic, they may yet so act as a check upon one another, that, in their public relations, the effect is the same as if they had no such evil sentiments."[93] This second necessary moral aspect can be called moral simulation (*moralische Simulation*). The third moral aspect is the moral effect of such a setup (*moralische Wirkung*)[94]: a good moral "condition" or—better phrased—education of the people is to be expected.[95] Even to just sustain such a constitutional state, some kind of moral acceptance is necessary.[96] This conclusion sounds like a *petitio principii* as morality is not only the effect but also the condition of a just political regime.[97] However, such a *petitio principii* can be solved with an existing interdependence of morality and just political order. In this manner, the legal categorical imperative is a mere developing and facilitating condition for the categorical imperative. Like the legal categorical imperative—or the legal order—develops and facilitates the categorical imperative—or the morality of the people—so does the categorical imperative—or the morality of the people—develop and facilitate the legal categorical imperative—or the political order.[98]

2.2 *The Context of Their Foundation*

The context of each of the foundations of legal and categorical imperatives asks for their inferability. Can the legal categorical imperative be derived from the categorical imperative? Again, the answer to this question is contested: some argue for a *full*

---

[92]"*wenn gleich nicht ein moralisch=guter Mensch, dennoch ein guter Bürger zu sein gezwungen wird*" Kant, AA VIII 366—"But now nature comes to the aid of the universal, reason-derived will which, much as we honour it, is in practice powerless. And this she does, by means of these very self-seeking propensities, so that it only depends—and so much lies within the power of man—on a good organisation of the state for their forces to be so pitted against one another, that the one may check the destructive activity of the other or neutralise its effect. And hence, from the standpoint of reason, the result will be the same as if both forces did not exist, and each individual is compelled to be, if not a morally good man, yet at least a good citizen"—translation by Campbell Smith (1917), p. 153.

[93]"*in ihrem öffentlichen Verhalten der Erfolg eben derselbe ist, als ob sie keine [...] bösen Gesinnungen hätten*" Kant AA VIII 366—translation by Campbell Smith (1917), p. 154.

[94]See: Kalscheuer (2014), pp. 181 et seq.

[95]*Kant, Immanuel*, Zum ewigen Frieden, AA VIII 366.

[96]Guyer (2009), p. 131; Kalscheuer (2014), p. 183.

[97]Kalscheuer (2014), p. 184; Kleingeld (1995), p. 26; van der Linden (1988), pp. 108 et seq.

[98]Kalscheuer (2014), p. 185.

independence[99] of the legal categorical imperative, some for a *full dependence.*[100] Looking at the structure of *Kant's* Metaphysics, the Doctrine of Right is a part of the Doctrine of Virtue. The latter cannot only be found in *his* "Metaphysics of Morals" but is also based on *his* earlier work dating back to 1785, "The Groundwork of the Metaphysic of Moral." What is more, the categorical imperative is the supreme principle of the Doctrine of Virtue.[101] Already this composition hints at the possibility that *Kant* intended the legal categorical imperative to be derived from the categorical imperative. However, this inferability can be found with regard to the content as well in the following passage:

> The universal Law of Right may then be expressed, thus: "Act externally in such a manner that the free exercise of thy Will may be able to co-exist with the Freedom of all others, according to a universal Law." This is undoubtedly a Law which imposes obligation upon me; but it does not at all imply and still less command that I *ought,* merely on account of this obligation, to limit my freedom to these very conditions. Reason in this connection says only that it *is* restricted thus far by its Idea, and may be likewise thus limited in fact by others; and it lays this down as a Postulate which is not capable of further proof.[102]

---

[99]Total independence but negation of a necessary condition: Guyer (2002), p. 26: "Thus the universal principle of right my not be derived from the Categorical Imperative, but it certainly is derived from the conception of freedom and its value that is the fundamental principle of Kantian morality." & as well n. 7; Höffe (1995), pp. 79 et seq.; Pogge (2002), p. 151: "Kant establishes merely a one-sided dependence of M on R; he establishes that R's failure would entail the failure of M, that M cannot stand without R. And this does not imply, of course, that R is dependent upon (cannot stand without) M."; Willascheck (1997), p. 223; Willascheck (2009), p. 67; Wood (2002), p. 9: "Kant's theory of right falls under or can be derived from the principle of morality. That is, this may be said in so far as juridical duties are regarded not merely as juridical but also as ethical duties. Considered simply as juridical duties, however, they belong to a branch of the metaphysics of morals that is entirely independent of ethics and also of its supreme principle."; Wood (2005), pp. 171 et seq.

Total independence but negation of an adequate condition: Alexy (2005), p. 102 n. 37; Höffe (2001), pp. 117 et seq.; Kersting (2004a, b), p. 41: "*Der kategorische Imperativ ist als Prinzip des moralisch Notwendigen wie des moralisch Möglichen zugleich auch das Prinzip moralisch möglicher Zwangshandlungen wie legitim erzwingbarer moralisch notwendiger Handlungen. Das allgemeine Rechtsgesetz ist folglich eine Version des kategorischen Imperativs, die auf die Begründung von Pflichten, denen Zwangsbefugnisse korrespondieren, spezialisiert ist.*"; Kersting (2007), pp. 126 et seq.; Ripstein (2009), p. 358.

[100]Kalscheuer (2014), p. 201; Rosen 1993, pp. 12 et seq. and 50–55; similarly: Bielefeldt (2001), pp. 107 et seq.; Flikschuh (2004), pp. 318–324; Kaulbach 1970, p. 50: "*Die positive Rechtsgesetzgebung eignet aber nur dann "Autorität", wenn sie von einer Rechtsidee durchdrungen ist, die zuletzt ihre Wurzel im Moralgesetz hat.*"; Luf (2008), pp. 140 et seq.

[101]Kant AA VI 226: "*oberste Grundsatz der Sittenlehre*"—"SUPREME PRINCIPL of the Science of Morals"—translation by Hastie (1887), p. 35.

[102]"*Also ist das allgemeine Rechtsgesetz: handle äußerlich so, daß der freie Gebrauch deiner Willkür mit der Freiheit von jedermann nach einem allgemeinen Gesetze zusammen bestehen könne, zwar ein Gesetz, welches mir eine Verbindlichkeit auferlegt, aber ganz und gar nicht erwartet, noch weniger fordert, daß ich ganz um dieser Verbindlichkeit willen meine Freiheit auf jene Bedingungen selbst einschränken solle, sondern die Vernunft sagt nur, daß sie in ihrer Idee darauf eingeschränkt sei und von andern auch thätlich eingeschränkt werden dürfe; und dieses sagt sie als ein Postulat, welches gar keines Beweises weiter fähig ist.*" Kant AA VI 231—translation by Hastie (1887), p. 46; Willascheck (1997), p. 223; Willascheck (2009), p. 67.

Hence, the categorical imperative for the inner decision must be *extended* to the outward world—which is the function of the legal categorical imperative.

This relation is contested—again with regard to an otherwise existing inconsistency with the devil's passage: according to that interpretation, the citizens' self-interest legitimates any legal system, may it be one of public law, one of private law, or even anterior to any state.[103] This is why there should be no dependence but an *in*dependence of both. Even if this interpretation might hint at such a relation, the incoherence does not occur, if one looks at the devil's passage as being relevant only for the context of effectiveness but not for the context of the foundation, as the arguments drawn are those of effects and consequences.[104]

It is impossible to directly apply the categorical imperative in the outward world, which is why the legal categorical imperative is necessary: it converts the ethical duty of the categorical imperative into a legal competence to demand duty (*rechtliche Pflichteinforderungsbefugnis*).[105] The categorical imperative compels only the agent himself in the inward world, whereas the legal categorical imperative compels solely the outward directed compliance to act dutifully—and not from duty, which could anyways not be controlled.[106]

Hence, the legal categorical imperative serves to realize the actions in accordance with the categorical imperative in the outward world because the *rational* agents need to interact with each other. In this manner, the legal categorical imperative guarantees a legal range of protection,[107] enabling the agents to realize their moral duties in the way they developed them according to the categorical imperative (the thesis of realization—*Realisierungsthese*).[108]

---

[103]Csingár (2013), pp. 150 et seq.; Höffe (1995), pp. 79 et seq.; Müller (1996), pp. 182 et seq.

[104]Kalscheuer (2014), p. 188; Kersting (2004a, b), p. 32 n. 8: *Höffes Interpretation sei "mehr als eine marginale Fehlinterpretation"*—the interpretation by *Höffe* is more than a marginal misinterpretation; Geismann (2006), p. 111.

[105]Kalscheuer (2014), p. 213.

[106]Kant AA VI 20; Kalscheuer (2014), pp. 213 et seq.; Schadow (2013), p. 103.

[107]Kant AA VIII 22.

[108]Bauch (1968), pp. 218 et seq.: "*Als "Befugnis zu zwingen" hat das Recht also gerade die Freiheit zu unserer Bestimmung zu sichern, und diese rechtliche Regelung des staatlichen Lebens gibt dem Staate selber die hohe geistige Bestimmung, daß sich in ihm unsere Bestimmung darstelle und entfalte* [. . .] *Denn wenn wir sagen, die Macht verhalte sich zum Rechte, wie sich dieses verhalte zur Pflicht, so bedeutet das zugleich, daß die Macht ein Mittel zum Zwecke des Rechtes, als Macht, das Recht durchzusetzen, ist, wie das Recht ein Mittel zum Zwecke der Pflicht als Recht auf Pflichterfüllung ist.*"; Dulckeit (1932), pp. 4 et seq.: "*Demgemäß soll also beim Recht die empirische Willkür des einen eingeschränkt werden, damit die erscheinungsmäßigen Wirkungen der transzendentalen Freiheit des anderen* [...] *neben jener (im Einklang mit dem allgemeinen Freiheitsgesetze eingeschränkten) Willkür bestehen können.*"; Greco (2009), p. 37: "*obwohl Recht und Moral getrennt werden, bleibt es Zweck des Rechts, die Moral zu ermöglichen*"; Haensel (1926), p. 9: "*Recht als Recht auf Pflichterfüllung*" & Haensel (1926), pp. 11 et seq.: "*so liegt die in der Rechtsdefinition jener einzuschränkenden Freiheit des einen als schutzbedürftig gegenübergestellte Freiheit (Freiheit als Willkür) des anderen*"; Kalscheuer (2014), pp. 206 et seq.; Larenz (1943), p. 282: "*Das Recht schränkt die Willkür ein um der (transzendentalen) Freiheit willen. Kants "allgemeines Rechtsgesetz"* [...] *verlangt von jedem,*

2.3 *The Classification of Duties of Right and Duties of Virtue*

Bearing in mind the two different contexts of effectiveness (legal categorical imperative as developing and facilitating condition for the categorical imperative, legal categorical imperative $\nrightarrow$ categorical imperative, and dependence of the legal categorical imperative's *effectiveness* on the categorical imperative in a limited way creating an *interdependency*, categorical imperative as a limited condition for the legal categorical imperative, categorical imperative $\rightarrow$ legal categorical imperative) and the context of the foundation (thesis of realization), the duties of right and of virtue can be classified with regard to seven relevant yet nonconclusive parameters: the governing imperative, setting certain purposes as goals, objects, competence to compel third parties, accuracy of the necessary requirements, bindingness, and classification of obligation, thus leading to four classes of duty.

The first class is formed by the duties of right, which are governed by the legal categorical imperative. They hold the competence to compel even third parties. The objects they govern are external actions. Yet they can*not set* certain purposes as possible goals because the competence to compel for external actions cannot relate to goals.[109] The accuracy of the necessary requirements must be fitted and very precise to achieve an external subsumability. They bind perfectly and narrowly, leading to a legal obligation as first class of duty.[110]

The last three classes of duty are duties of virtue. They are oriented to purposes as all the three let the agents decide which purposes need to be aimed for. As all the three are governed by the categorical imperative, they can only imperfectly bind.[111] The second class of duty has the following further five parameters: their objects are

seine Willkür einzuschränken, nicht, wie am oft angenommen hat, damit die Willkür aller anderen in möglichst großem Umfange bestehen könne, sondern damit die transzendentale Freiheit eines jeden, genauer: ihre Auswirkung durch Handlungen in der Sinnenwelt, nicht behindert werde [...]. *Eingeschränkt wird nicht die (transzendentale) Freiheit, um deren willen das Rechtsgesetz besteht, sondern nur die (empirische) Freiheit der Willkür, an die es sich wendet, und zwar wird die Freiheit der Willkür insofern eingeschränkt, als sie dazu führen könnte, pflichtmäßige und daher echte freie Handlungen anderer zu hindern oder zu stören*"; Larenz (1933), pp. 100 et seq.; Marcic (1971), p. 306: "*Was das Recht als Zwangsgebot schützt, ist eben nicht die Willkür, sondern die Freiheit im Sinne des Sittengesetzes, die Selbstbestimmung nach dem Maße der Subjektivität. Das Recht ist der Dienstbote der Ethik.*"; Schreiber (1966), pp. 42 et seq.; similarly: Kersting (2004a, b), p. 53: "*Das Menschheitsrecht ist immer auch zugleich ein Recht auf Institutionalisierung der Bedingungen, die seine sichere Wahrnehmung garantieren. Diese Institutionalisierung bietet der Staat. Das ist aus vernunftrechtlicher Perspektive seine Definition, das ist seine Aufgabe: Der Staat ist die Wirklichkeits- und Wirksamkeitsbedingung des Vernunftrechts.*" and Kersting (2004a, b), p. 57: "*Wenn wir den Grundsatz der inhaltlichen Komplementarität von Recht und Pflicht zugrundelegen, muß sich diese erweiterte, die institutionellen Bedingungen seiner Realisierung einbeziehende Verständnis des Menschheitsrechts in der ihm zugeordneten inneren Rechtspflicht spiegeln*".

[109]Kant AA VI 239—translation by Hastie (1887), pp. 24 et seq. (passages cited above in n. 68); see as well: Csingár (2013), pp. 109 et seq.

[110]Kant AA IV 390; Geismann (2010), pp. 37 et seq.; O'Neill (2014), pp. 113 et seq.

[111]Kant AA IV 390.

Duties	Duties of virtue			Duties of right
Governing imperative	Categorical imperative			Legal categorical imperative
Setting certain purposes as goals	Yes			No
Object	Appetitive faculty	Internal inclinations	External actions	
Competence to compel third parties	No		Yes	
Accuracy of the necessary requirements	wide	Fitted and precise to be internally subsumable	Fitted and precise to be externally subsumable	Fitted and very precise to be subsumable
Bindingness	Imperfect (very wide)	Imperfect (wide)		Perfect (narrow)
Classification of obligation	Ethical obligation	Ethicalobligation to perform/ethical obligation to desist		Legal obligation
Classes of duties	IV	III	II	I

Fig. 1 Classification of duties of right and duties of virtue. Another chart with less attributes is structured by and depicted at O'Neill (2014), p. 135

external actions, and they must lead to a competence to compel third parties. They must be fitted and precise as their accuracy of the necessary requirements must be accomplished to be externally subsumable. These duties can only hold an imperfect and wide bindingness. The obligation they have can be classified as an ethical obligation to perform or desist.[112]

The third and fourth classes of duty have internal processes as objects and cannot possess the competence to compel third parties. Whereas the third class of duty regards internal inclinations, the accuracy of the necessary requirements yet again needs to be rather fitted and precise to achieve an internal subsumability, producing an imperfect and wide bindingness. Their obligation is to be classified as an ethical obligation to perform or desist.[113]

The fourth class of duty looks at the appetitive faculty (*Begehrungsvermögen*), only has a very wide accuracy of necessary requirements, binds only imperfectly and in a wide way, thus leading to an ethical obligation.[114]

Figure 1 gives an overview of the four classes of duties of right and virtue.

Whereas only the first and second classes of duties can command the (external) action, the third and fourth classes of duties command the (internal) maxims giving an instrument, which action the agent should take.[115] In this vein, the *Kantian*

[112]O'Neill (2014), pp. 113 et seq.

[113]O'Neill (2014), pp. 113 et seq.

[114]See as well: O'Neill (2014), pp. 113 et seq.

[115]Kant AA IV 390.

system of imperatives gains accuracy and concreteness following classes IV<I in the same way they hold the competence to compel third parties.[116]

3 How Do the Different Kinds of Purposes as Found in *Kant's* Doctrine of Right and Virtue Matter in Modern Jurisprudence, Especially with Regard to Understanding *Ratio Legis*?

Kant's three kinds of imperatives serve all different functions and lead to different kinds of purposes. If these interconnections, relations, and classifications are transferred and adapted to modern jurisprudence and legal systems, as *his* moral philosophy impressed on modern European jurisprudence,[117] what could that mean for purposes and *ratio legis*?

3.1 Hypothetical Imperatives and Ratio Legis

Starting out with the hypothetical imperatives, their function is to connect purpose and action. First of all, as agents, we constantly apply hypothetical imperatives. They are those we set for ourselves to achieve our own and self-referential ***purposes***$^{p1\&p2\&n/s/a/d}$, which can even be tainted. However, any goal that needs legal validity or legal compellation will have to be achieved according to the law. For example, if the agent wants to eat but is neither a farmer nor possesses the skill to forage, he or she needs to provide himself/herself with food. For this purpose, he or she can decide with the categorical imperative which way to choose: legal or illegal ones. In other words, he or she can enter into any contract or take/keep food without permission. For the former, he or she will have yet again to act according to simple sections of law in the form of hypothetical imperatives: submit a quote, receive an acceptance, thus form a contract and exchange the goods accordingly. It is their function to set legal requirements and legal consequences, connecting therewith a goal/purpose and necessary action. The chosen *purposes*$^{p1\&p2\&n/s/a/d}$ are specific to each agent's personal wishes/desires/inclinations. Thus, the legal purposes—exchange of the goods and the change of ownership—must turn into the *interim* ***purposes***^{i} that the agent needs to achieve so that the ***purposes***^{d}, e.g. to eat, can be accomplished.

The *purposes*^{d} are to be chosen by the agents according to their wishes, desires, or inclinations. Thus, there is an endless amount of possible *purposes*$^{s/d\&i}$. Yet there

[116] Geismann (2009), pp. 215 et seq. and 225 et seq.; Geismann (2010), pp. 36 et seq.

[117] For instance regarding Art. 1 of the German Constitution and dignity: Hruschka (2002), pp. 463 et seq.; Hruschka (2015), p. 169; Kalscheuer (2015), p. 9; see as well: Schmitz (2004), pp. 306 et seq.; Weber-Fas (1999), pp. 461 et seq. Critically though, e.g.: Prauss (2008), pp. 61 et seq. & for an action based critique Prauss (2008), pp. 100 et seq.

exists only one ***purpose***^{u}—or rational end—that is commonly yet individually sought after as an individual goal that can be identified by each agent individually: happiness.

With regard to modern jurisprudence, the *purposes*$^{p1\&p2\&n/s/a/d\&i}$ as individualized by every agent might form, if the law is needed to attain these purposes, the legal consequences as concretized. *Purposes*^{i} can be some further requirements as set by the law. Thus, hypothetical imperatives can be found in legal theory. If *ratio legis* is understood as the concrete legal consequence for each case, the purposes as classified for the *Kantian* moral and legal philosophy can be relevant. Nevertheless, they can be of value for legal theory.

3.2 The Categorical Imperative and Ratio Legis

The categorical imperative's function is to develop with rational tools which purpose should be chosen. Those purposes can be endless. In line with the four forms of the categorical imperative, there are four more concrete functions: (1) a universalization as a test, (2) to become a human/rational being and therewith making humanity possible, (3) to achieve a universalized human will, and (4) to make the Kingdom of Ends possible. Here again, an endless number of possible purposes can be found, with the five steps *Kant* proposed to identify morally valid ***purposes***$^{p1\&p2\&n/o/a/d\&i}$.[118] The overall ***purpose***$^{u/p}$ is the maximization of the agents' self-perfection and everyone's happiness, and with the fourth form of the categorical imperative, the ***purpose***$^{u/a}$ is an achievable happiness while acting virtuously in the Kingdom of Ends.

The categorical imperatives develop internally, which purpose or end should be chosen, e.g. to act legally or illegally (steal or contract), to eat quantitatively or qualitatively either healthy or unhealthy. Thus, it is a decisive instrument for the *moral inner decision*, what to want as purpose with universal validity. And this decision is made according to the people's referential ***purposes***^{o} and not only the single agent's ones (***purposes***^{s}).

Only the second class of duties derived from categorical imperatives can command external actions. In contrast, the third and fourth classes of duties command internal maxims. All three can *merely* lead to ethical obligations (to perform or desist). As ethical obligations, they can be a tool to analyze *ratio legis* in conceptions that do not separate but see at least some kind of relation of law and morality. In this vein, the classification as proposed here could be of interest for a positive law that has a connection to morality, such as rules regarding the violation of *bonos mores*, good faith, *bona fide*, etc.

[118] See above: Sect. 1.2., p. 82 et seq.

3.3 The Legal Categorical Imperative and Ratio Legis

The function assigned to the legal categorical imperative is to solve the conflict of (at least) two agents in the outside world. It is its function to identify the whole of the conditions under which the voluntary actions of any agent can be harmonized in reality with the voluntary actions of every other agent, according to a universal law of freedom. Hence, any ***purposes***$^{p1\&p2\&n/o/a/d\&i}$ identified has to serve a need that requires an action in the outside world, to be relevant for the law. This as well can be said for *ratio legis* so that the endless purposes, which could be identified with hypothetical and categorical imperatives, are thus reduced.

As the legal categorical imperative does not only facilitate but prevents actions as well—compelling others to perform actions, which are not a means to their own ends—***purposes***^{n} limit ***purposes***$^{p1\&p2}$ for other agents. This is an aspect that one can as well see in modern jurisprudence: negative freedoms have the ability to limit positive freedoms. In this vein, *rationes legis*, which fulfill negative or positive purposes, will be assessed by lawyers.

For the external world, ***purposes***^{n} lead to *perfect*, ***purposes***^{p2} to *imperfect* duties. Here again is a concept that is known in modern jurisprudence and *ratio legis* with regard to negative and positive aspects of general or special freedoms. Any negative aspect as *ratio legis*, e.g. sacredness of property, will lead to prohibitions—or in *Kantian* terms to perfect duties, e.g. prohibitions to act (such as assault and battery, theft, breach of contract). Positive aspects as *ratio legis*, e.g. positive aspects of property, to which the legal system aspires, will lead to commandments—or in *Kantian* terms imperfect duties, e.g. commandments to act (such as nonassistance of a person in danger, social-obligation norm concerning property).

The *Kantian* process to form any juridical duty was the following: the starting point is the rational social end, peace. From there special liberties or rights based on the universal freedom of all agents with a negative command can be rationally derived. Thus, first, private or natural rights can be established, and also public or civil rights, by positive laws, e.g. regarding property and freedom of contract. The three perfect duties of right[119] correlate with three further functions of the legal categorical imperative: firstly, to develop an internal and external perfect constitution, which is the only situation, in which mankind and every agent can materialize all of its beneficial assets; secondly, therewith, to guarantee good moral education of the people; and, thirdly, to accomplish the external legislation of juridical and *not* moral duties. Hence, here one can find only ***purposes***^{o}.

This third category of juridical duties has its own people referential purposes. And at least here, with positive laws, the commonly known *rationes legum* may be

[119]The three perfect Duties of Right are: (1) the internal and external perfect constitution, which is the only situation, in which mankind and every agent can materialize all of its beneficial assets (internal duty, e.g. *honeste vive*), (2) a good moral education of the people (external duty, e.g. *neminem laede*), and (3) an external legislation of juridical, not moral duties (connecting duty, e.g. *suum cuique tribue*). See above: Sect. 1.3., p. 87 et seq.

found, such as protection of minors/consumers or enabling the exchange of goods. Positive laws hold the abstract ***purposes***^{p} as initially assigned by the legislator and actualized in each decision by judges for the case to be the relevant ***purposes***^{a}. They might again abstractly be ***purposes***$^{d\&i}$; hence, some *rationes legum* not only are directly aimed for but also are aspects of another purpose, e.g. the prohibition and obligation to contract for the freedom of contract.

The overall ***purpose***^{u} or rational end is to facilitate the happiness of the people through laws and outer freedom, thus leading to empirical autonomy. The legal categorical imperative does *not* lead to happiness, though due to it happiness is facilitated. Their rational ends or *purpose*^{u} are to lead to social peace and empirical not the moral autonomy of the agents. In this vein, the function of the state or the determination of national objectives might be addressed.

Table 4 gives an overview by comparing the different parameters for hypothetical, categorical, and legal categorical imperatives with regard to the parameters: decision, obligation, abuse, function, form (with *purpose*^{d}), acquirement, purposes regarding effect and aim, purposes regarding necessity, purposes regarding achievability, purposes regarding directness, and the rational end (*purpose*^{u}).

3.4 A Possible Adaptation

Now if the classification of purposes is adapted for *ratio legis*, what does that mean? First of all, ***purpose***$^{p1\&p2\&n}$ can be found in modern legal theory as well. Whereas *purpose*^{p1} is a positive end that can be directly achieved in reality, e.g. a rule with legal requirements and consequences such as contracting, *purposes*^{p2} will be *rather*—behold but not only—found as indirect *purposes*^{i} within basic rights or principles,[120] which are the ends to be achieved by the means of material law, such as consumer protection or freedom of contract. It is here that a *ratio legis* as modernly understood might be found.[121] However, *purposes*^{n} can be found in any material law, e.g. criminal law, as well as in basic rights. It fits in this vein that *purposes*^{p2} will lead in the *Kantian* system to imperfect duties, which are a kind of commandments in modern jurisprudence. *Purposes*^{n} in the *Kantian* system lead to perfect duties, which fits, as they lead in modern jurisprudence to prohibitions, e.g. in criminal law.

With regard to ***purpose***$^{s\&o}$ (necessity of purposes), the contested question what kind of *ratio legis* could be found in legal interpretation might be addressed. Caution

[120]Alexy (1994), pp. 71 et seq.; Alexy (1995), pp. 222 et seq.; Dworkin (1977), pp. 40 et seq.; Esser (1990); similarly: Kalscheuer (2015), p. 18 with further references in n. 61.

[121]For the nowadays understanding of *ratio legis* see instead of all: Rüthers (2016), pp. 92 et seq. & 100 et seq. & 143 et seq. & 382 et seq. & 422 et seq. & 437 et seq.; see as well: Chirkowska-Smolak and Smolak (2018), pp. 137–157; Ciszewski (2018), pp. 119–136; Dybowski (2018), pp. 29–55; Dyrda (2018), pp. 3–17; Hermann (2018), pp. 187–205; Kordela (2018), pp. 19–28; Krotoszyński (2018), pp. 57–73; von Schütz (2018), pp. 161–186.

Table 4 Overview of the functions and purposes of hypothetical, categorical, and legal categorical imperatives

	Hypothetical[a] imperatives		Categorical[b] imperatives				Legal categorical[c] imperatives
Decision	Made according to the agent's desires and benefits sought after, possibly *a posteriori* or *a priori*		Made with the application of pure practical reason *a priori*, independent of any agent				Made with the application of pure practical reason *a priori*, independent of any agent
Obligation	No obligation to follow, link as an "ought" of goal and conditions		Obligation to follow under any circumstances—universal validity				Title or authority to compel
Abuse	Possibility to set tainted goals and diverse means to achieve any goal		Impossible				Impossible
Function	Connection of purpose and action		Developing which purpose should be chosen				Solving the conflict of (at least) two agents in the outside world—outer freedom and civil rights
Form (with *purpose*[d])	If you will purpose P, then act A (which is one possible means to P).		1. Formulate a maxim that perpetuates your reason for acting A to achieve purpose P. 2. Think of this maxim as a universal law that governs all rational agents so that all act in the same way. 3. Reflect whether your maxim is imaginable in a world in which everyone acts on it. 4. If affirmed, can an agent rationally will to act on such a maxim in such a world. 5. If affirmed as well, the action upon such a maxim is morally permissible.				Identify the whole of the conditions under which the voluntary actions of any agent can be harmonized in reality with the voluntary actions of every other agent, according to a universal law of freedom
	Rules of skills	**Counsels of prudence**	**CI^1**	**CI^2**	**CI^3**	**CI^4**	
Acquirement	*A posteriori* (derived from experience)	*A priori* (deduction from pure reason)	Pure practical reason *a priori*				Made with the application of pure practical reason *a priori*, independent of any agent

(continued)

Table 4 (continued)

	Hypothetical[a] imperatives		Categorical[b] imperatives				Legal categorical[c] imperatives
Goals/purposes (function)	Specific to each agent's personal wishes/desires/inclinations (*purpose*^{s})	universal goals for overall sake of the agent's goodwill (be good, be happy, please God) yet as individually identified (*purpose*^{s})	Universalization	Human/rational being/humanity	Universalized human will	Make the Kingdom of Ends possible	1. internal and external perfect constitution, which is the only situation, in which mankind and every agent can materialize all of its beneficial assets 2. therewith good moral education of the people 3. external legislation of juridical duties not moral duties
Purposes regarding effect and aim	*Purposes*$^{p1\&p2\&n}$						
	–		*Purposes*^{n} leading each to *perfect* and *purposes*^{p2} to *imperfect* duties				
			II. & III. & IV. classes of duty[d]				As duties of right (juridical duties) and I. class of duty[e]: internal duty (e.g., *honeste vive*), external duty (e.g., *neminem laede*), and connecting duty (e.g., *suum cuique tribue*)
Purposes regarding necessity	*Purposes*^{s}		*Purposes*^{o}				
Purposes regarding achievability	Leading each to *purposes*^{p} (problematically practical principle) or *purposes*^{a} (assertorically practical principle)						
							But only for needs that require actions in the outside world

Purposes regarding their directness	Leading each to *purposes*[d&i] in a relative system				
Rational end (*purpose*[u]): happiness	Commonly yet individually sought after	Universal goal yet as individually identified	Maximization of self-perfection and everyone's happiness in their free conduct as *purpose*[p]	Achievable happiness while acting virtuously in the Kingdom of Ends as *purpose*[a]	Facilitation of the happiness of the people through laws but not as an own rational end; duty to others and outer freedom, and empirical autonomy

[a]Specific to each agent's personal wishes/desires/inclinations with self-referential purposes
[b]Independent of each agent's personal wishes/desires/inclinations with self & people referential purposes as decisive instrument for moral inner decision what to want with universal validity
[c]Decisive instrument of what to do in the outward world with people referential purposes
[d]See Fig. 1, p. 102
[e]See Fig. 1, p. 102

is in need here as the German terms of the subjective and objective interpretations with regard to *ratio legis* are contraintuitive: subjective interpretation means in this context the purpose as set by the legislator and identified by the lawyer; objective interpretation means the purposes *only* as identified by the legal interpreter.[122] However, the same misunderstanding can easily follow from *Kant's* philosophy: as little as his *purposes*^{o} as identified with any of the categorical imperatives can be entirely objective, can the *rationes legum* as identified—no matter whether by the maker or interpreter of the law—be objective as *only* persons can identify?[123] Of course, one has to appreciate that both the methods chosen by *Kant*, as by modern jurisprudence, try to obliterate subjectivity via different means. However, hermeneutical research has shown that this is an impossible endeavor.

With regard to their achievability, one can again distinguish in modern jurisprudence between purposes that can and in the very instance are wanted to be attained, e.g. contracting, filing a lawsuit, and those that exist as a mere possibility, e.g. consumer protection. Whereas the former will be found rather in legal consequences, the latter is part of the discussion about *ratio legis*. Hence, *Kant's* differentiation between ***purposes***$^{\boldsymbol{a}}$ and ***purposes***$^{\boldsymbol{p}}$ could be adapted.

Let us look at the differentiation concerning the directness of purposes. Here, again, one can see how modern jurisprudence discusses ***purposes***$^{\boldsymbol{d\&i}}$, such as consumer protection as part of freedom of contract. This distinction opens a discussion of an internal system of *rationes legum* in respect of *genera* and *species* for certain purposes. Whereas *purposes*^{d} could be identified as a legal consequence for certain sections in the area of legal theory, connecting in *Kantian* terms with hypothetical imperatives action and purpose, *purposes*$^{d\&i}$ could be found in constitutional rights, as well as in *ratio legis* that need to be extracted in interpretational ways in substantive law.

What *Kant* identified as ***purposes***$^{\boldsymbol{u}}$, happiness, especially with regard to the legal categorical imperative and the facilitational aspect, could be as well of value for the discussion of *ratio legis* and the function of the legal system. In contrast, the general idea of *purpose*^{u} depends on the general premises set up within different jurisdictions and/or the underlying different legal philosophical concepts. Thus, one might find indicators of *Kant's* idea of happiness in the discussion of the determination of the national objectives. Nevertheless, for the legal categorical imperative, happiness is merely a *purpose*^{p2} as it should only be facilitated.

In a nutshell, the different concepts of purposes as categorized here within *Kant's* moral and legal philosophy are still addressed in modern jurisprudence, though not only in different terms but even in different branches of science, e.g. legal theory and legal philosophy.

---

[122] See e.g.: Rüthers (2016), pp. 437 et seq. with further references.

[123] See e.g.: Williams (1968), pp. 125 et seq. with further references.

4 Theses

1. *Kant's* hypothetical, categorical, and legal categorical imperatives can be systemized with regard to their *function* and *four different*—nonconclusive evolved from *his* work—*kinds of purposes*: the effect and aim (positive *purposes*$^{p1\&p2}$ and negative *purpose*^{n}), their necessity (subjective *purpose*^{s} and objective *purpose*^{o}), their achievability (possible *purpose*^{p} and actual *purpose*^{a}), and their directness (direct *purpose*^{d}, indirect *purpose*^{i}, and ultimate *purpose*^{u}).[124]
2. Hypothetical imperatives have the function to connect action and purpose, either derived *a posteriori* (Rules of Skills) or deduced *a priori* (Counsels of Prudence). These purposes can be *purposes*$^{p1\&p2\&n}$ as they are individually identified only as *purposes*^{s}, *purposes*$^{p\&a}$, as well as *purpose*$^{d\&I}$, forming a relative concept of purposes. The *purpose*^{u} is happiness.[125]
3. The categorical imperative is the developing instrument to decide which of the different purposes should be chosen by pure practical reason *a priori*. Each of the four assessed formulas of categorical imperatives illuminates one special aspect of this function. They can have *purposes*$^{p1\&p2\&n}$, where *purposes*^{n} lead to perfect duties, *purposes*^{p2} to imperfect duties. The thus identified purposes can only be *purposes*^{o} but classified as *purposes*$^{p\&a}$ and *purposes*$^{d\&i}$, forming a relative concept of purposes. Here, again, the *purposes*^{u} are the maximization of everyone's happiness, as well as the agent's self-perfection.[126]
4. The legal categorical imperative solves the conflict of at least two agents in the outside world leading to outer freedom and civil rights. It is gained by applying pure practical reason *a priori*. Like the categorical imperative, the legal categorical imperative can lead to *purposes*$^{p1\&p2\&n}$, where *purposes*^{n} lead to perfect duties, *purposes*^{p2} to imperfect duties. The thus identified purposes can only be *purposes*^{o} but also *purposes*$^{p\&a}$ and *purposes*$^{d\&i}$. As *purposes*^{u}, the facilitation of happiness of the people through laws, the duty to others and outer freedom, as well as empirical autonomy could be identified.[127]
5. The *purposes*^{u} of the legal categorical imperative already hint at the two different contexts (of effectiveness and of their foundation) that categorical imperative and legal categorical imperative must have.[128]
   The *context of effectiveness* has two sides: on the one hand, the legal categorical imperative is neither an adequate nor a necessary condition for the categorical imperative but a *mere condition of development* and *of facilitation* for it (legal categorical imperative as developing and facilitating condition for the categorical imperative, legal categorical imperative $\nrightarrow$ categorical imperative).[129]

---

[124]See above: Sect. 1, p. 78 et seq.

[125]See above: Sect. 1.1, p. 79 et seq.

[126]See above: Sect. 1.2, p. 82 et seq.

[127]See above: Sect. 1.3, p. 87 et seq.

[128]See above: Sect. 2, p. 93 et seq.

[129]See above: Sect. 2.1, p. 94.

On the other hand, the *effectiveness* of the legal categorical imperative depends on the categorical imperative in a limited way, creating an *interdependency* (categorical imperative as a limited condition for the legal categorical imperative, categorical imperative → legal categorical imperative).[130] Like the legal categorical imperative develops and facilitates the categorical imperative—or the morality of the people—the categorical imperative—or the morality of the people—develops and facilitates the legal categorical imperative, which could be derived from *Kant's* passage of devils in *his* "Perpetual Peace."[131]

The *context of each of foundation* of legal and categorical imperatives asks for their inferability. The legal categorical imperative serves to realize the actions in accordance with the categorical imperative in the outward world as rational agents need to interact with each other. It guarantees a legal range of protection, enabling the agents to realize their moral duties as developed with the categorical imperative (*thesis of realization*).[132]

6. Bearing in mind the former two different contexts, duties of right (first class of duty, governed by the legal categorical imperative) and of virtue (second to third classes of duty, governed by the categorical imperative) could be classified with regard to seven—nonconclusive—parameters: the governing imperative, setting certain purposes as goals, objects, competence to compel third parties, accuracy of the necessary requirements, bindingness, and classification of obligation, thus leading to four different classes of duties. The thus classified *Kantian* system of imperatives gains accuracy and concreteness following classes IV<I in the same way they hold the competence to compel third parties.[133]
7. Regarding the classification of—possibly endless but tainted—purposes for hypothetical imperatives (*purposes*$^{p1\&p2\&n/s/a/d}$), they are the concretized legal requirements and consequences as in day-to-day life as agents opt for them, insofar as hypothetical imperatives can be found in modern jurisprudence and legal theory. For a discussion of *ratio legis*, they can only be of value in this area.[134]

   Categorical imperatives serve—again, possibly endless but untainted—*purposes*$^{p1\&p2\&n/o/a/d\&i}$. As second to fourth classes of duties, they merely lead to ethical obligations. Thus, the classification of purposes as proposed here can only have an impact to analyze *ratio legis* in conceptions that do not separate law and morality or for rules that are implicit parts of morality, such as the violation of *bonos mores*, good faith, *bona fide*, etc.[135]

[130] See above: Sect. 2.1, p. 95 et seq.

[131] See above: Sect. 2.1, p. 96 et seq.

[132] See above: Sect. 2.2, p. 98 et seq.

[133] See above: Sect. 2.3, p. 101 et seq.

[134] See above: Sect. 3.1, p. 103 et seq.

[135] See above: Sect. 3.2, p. 104 et seq.

Legal categorical imperatives have—untainted—*purposes*$^{p1\&p2\&n/o/a/d\&i}$. A correlation can be seen for *ratio legis* in that its *purposes*^{n} generate perfect duties that are prohibitions to act, whereas *purposes*^{p2} educe imperfect duties that are commandments to act. With regard to *Kant's* identified juridical duty (external legislation of juridical duties as connecting duty, e.g. *suum cuique tribue*), the *ratio legis* as analyzed in modern jurisprudence can be discussed here. *Kant's* concept of the overall *purpose*^{u} or rational end bears resemblance to the function of the state or the determination of national objectives.[136]

8. The different concepts of purposes, as categorized here within *Kant's* moral and legal philosophy, are still addressed in modern jurisprudence, though not only in different terms but even in different branches of science, e.g. legal theory and legal philosophy. They can be of value for the discussion of *ratio legis*, as suggested here. But further and more detailed research is needed.[137]

References

Alexy R (1994) Theorie der Grundrechte, 2nd edn. Suhrkamp, Frankfurt/Main

Alexy R (1995) Rechtssystem und praktische Vernunft. In: Alexy R (ed) Recht, Vernunft, Diskurs. Suhrkamp, Frankfurt/Main, pp 213–231

Alexy R (2005) Ralf Dreiers Interpretation der Kantischen Rechtsdefinition. In: Alexy R (ed) Integratives Verstehen – Zur Rechtsphilosophie Ralf Dreiers. Mohr Siebeck, Tübingen, pp 95–110

Bauch B (1968) Grundzüge der Ethik, 35th edn. Wiss. Buchgesellschaft, Darmstadt

Beck LW (1963) White, idea for a universal history with a cosmopolitan purpose, from Immanuel Kant, "On History", Indianapolis. https://www.marxists.org/reference/subject/ethics/kant/universal-history.htm. Accessed 1 Aug 2017

Beck G (2008) Fichte and Kant on freedom, right, and law. Lexington Books, Lanham

Bielefeldt H (2001) Kants Symbolik – Ein Schlüssel zur kritischen Freiheitsphilosophie. Alber, Freiburg

Brandt R (1995) Das Problem der Erlaubnisgesetze im Spätwerk Kants. In: Höffe O (ed) Immanuel Kant, Zum ewigen Frieden. Akademie Verlag, Berlin, pp 69–86

Brandt R (1997) Antwort auf Bernd Ludwig: Will die Natur unwiderstehlich die Republik? Kant-Studien 88(1997):229–237

Brinkmann W (2003) Praktische Notwendigkeit: Eine Formalisierung von Kants Kategorischem Imperativ. Mentis, Münster

Campbell Smith M (1917) Perpetual peace. A philosophical essay by Immanuel Kant. The Macimillan Company, New York. http://www.gutenberg.org/files/50922/50922-h/50922-h.htm. Accessed 1 Aug 2017

Chirkowska-Smolak T, Smolak M (2018) Is there an imitative *Ratio Legis*, and if so, how many are there? Psychological perspective. In: Klappstein V, Dybowski M (eds) Ratio Legis: philosophical and theoretical perspectives. Springer, Heidelberg, pp 137–157

Cholbi M (2016) Kant's ethics. Routledge, New York

Ciszewski W (2018) Nonconsequential conception of neutrality. In: Klappstein V, Dybowski M (eds) Ratio Legis: philosophical and theoretical perspectives. Springer, Heidelberg, pp 119–136

[136]See above: Sect. 3.3, p. 105 et seq.

[137]See above: Sect. 3.4, p. 106 et seq.

Csingár P (2013) Auswirkungen der Erkenntnistheorie und Ethik Kants auf seine Rechtsphilosophie. LIT, Berlin
Dulckeit G (1932) Naturrecht und positives Recht bei Kant. Abhandlungen der rechts- und staatswisenschaftliche Fakultät der Universität Göttingen, Leipzig
Dworkin RM (1977) Taking rights seriously. Harvard University Press, Cambridge
Dybowski M (2018) Articulating *Ratio Legis* and practical reasoning. In: Klappstein V, Dybowski M (eds) Ratio Legis: philosophical and theoretical perspectives. Springer, Heidelberg, pp 29–55
Dyrda A (2018) The real *Ratio Legis* and where to find it. In: Klappstein V, Dybowski M (eds) Ratio Legis: philosophical and theoretical perspectives. Springer, Heidelberg, pp 3–17
Ebbinghaus J (1968) Kant und das 20. Jahrhundert. In: Herb K, Oberer H (eds) Gesammelte Aufsätze, Vorträge und Reden. Wiss. Buchgesellschaft, Darmstadt, pp 97–119
Ebbinghaus J (1986) Positivismus – Recht der Menschheit – Naturrecht – Staatsbürgerrecht. In: Herb K, Oberer H (eds) Gesammelte Schriften, 1, Sittlichkeit und Recht. Bouvier, Bonn, pp 349–366
Ebbinghaus J (1988) Die Strafen für Tötung eines Menschen nach Prinzipien einer Rechtsphilosophie der Freiheit. In: Herb K, Oberer H (eds) Gesammelte Schriften, 2, Philosophie der Freiheit. Bouvier, Bonn, pp 283–380
Esser J (1990) Grundsatz und Norm, 4th edn. Mohr Siebeck, Tübingen
Flikschuh K (2004) Ist das rechtliche Postulat ein Postulat der reinen praktischen Vernunft? Jahrbuch für Recht und Ethik 12(2004):299–330
Geismann G (1974) Ethik und Herrschaftsordnung: ein Beitrag zum Problem der Legitimation. J. C. B Mohr (Paul Siebeck), Tübingen
Geismann G (2002) Die Formeln des kategorischen Imperativs nach H. J. Paton, N.N. Klaus Reich und Julius Ebbinghaus. Kant-Studien 93(2002):374–384
Geismann G (2006) Recht und Moral in der Philosophie Kants. Jahrbuch für Recht und Ethik 14 (2006):3–124
Geismann G (2009) Studien zur Moral-, Religions- und Geschichtsphilosophie. Königshausen & Neumann, Würzburg
Geismann G (2010) Studien zur Rechtsphilosophie. Königshausen & Neumann, Würzburg
Geismann G (2012a) Pax Kantiana oder Der Rechtsweg zum Weltfrieden. Königshausen & Neumann, Würzburg
Geismann G (2012b) Recht und Moral. In: Geismann G (ed) Kant und kein Ende, vol. 2, Studien zur Rechtsphilosophie. Königshausen & Neumann, Würzburg, pp 11–146
Greco L (2009) Lebendigs und Totes in Feuerbachs Straftheorie. Ein Beitrag zur gegenwärtigen strafrechtlichen Grundlagendiskussion. Duncker & Humblot, Berlin
Gregor MJ (1996) Translation of the metaphysics of morals. In: The metaphysics of morals, Cambridge texts in the history of philosophy, 2nd edn. Cambridge University Press, New York
Guyer P (2000) Kant on freedom, law, and happiness. Cambridge University Press, New York
Guyer P (2002) Kant's deduction of the principles of right. In: Timmons M (ed) Kant's metaphysics of morals. New American Library, New York, pp 23–64
Guyer P (2009) The crooked timber of mankind. In: Rorty AO, Schmidt J (eds) Kant's Idea for a universal history with a cosmopolitan aim – a critical guide. Cambridge University Press, Cambridge, pp 129–149
Haensel W (1926) Kants Lehre vom Widerstandsrecht. Pan-Verlag, Berlin
Hastie W (1887) The philosophy of law. Clark, Edinburgh
Herman B (1981) On the value of acting from the motive of duty. Philos Rev 90(1981):359–382
Hermann M (2018) How can *Ratio Legis* help a lawyer to interpret a legal text? Employing the purpose of a regulation for legal interpretation. In: Klappstein V, Dybowski M (eds) Ratio Legis: philosophical and theoretical perspectives. Springer, Heidelberg, pp 187–205
Höffe O (1995) Kategorische Rechtsprinzipien. Suhrkamp, Frankfurt/Main

Höffe O (1999) Der kategorische Rechtsimperativ, "Einleitung in die Rechtslehre". In: Höffe O (ed) Immanuel Kant, Metaphysische Anfangsgründe der Rechtslehre. De Gruyter, Berlin, pp 41–62

Höffe O (2001) "Königliche Völker" – Zu Kants kosmopolitischer Rechts- und Friedenstheorie. Suhrkamp, Frankfurt/Main

Horn C, Mieth C, Scarano N (2007) Grundlegung zur Metaphysik der Sitten. Suhrkamp, Frankfurt/Main

Hruschka J (2002) Die Würde des Menschen bei Kant. ARSP 88(2002):463–480

Hruschka J (2015) Kant und der Rechtsstaat und andere Essays zu Kants Rechtslehre und Ethik. Alber, Freiburg

Johnson R, Cureton A (2017) Kant's moral philosophy. In: Zalta EN (ed) The Stanford encyclopedia of philosophy, Edition Spring 2017. https://plato.stanford.edu/archives/spr2017/entries/kant-moral/. Accessed on 1 Aug 2017

Kalscheuer F (2014) Autonomie als Grund und Grenze des Rechts. De Gruyter, Berlin

Kalscheuer F (2015) Human dignity as justice in the face of injustice: on Kant's supplementary function of human dignity in law. In: Merle J-C, Trivisonno ATG (eds) Kant's theory of law. Steiner-Verlag, Stuttgart, pp 9–19

Kant I. Die Grundlegung der Metaphysik der Sitten, AA IV. https://korpora.zim.uni-duisburg-essen.de/kant/aa04/. Accessed on 1 Aug 2017

Kant I. Die Metaphysik der Sitten, AA VI. https://korpora.zim.uni-duisburg-essen.de/kant/aa06/203.html. Accessed on 1 Aug 2017

Kant I. Die Religion innerhalb der Grenzen der bloßen Vernunft, AA VI. https://korpora.zim.uni-duisburg-essen.de/kant/aa06/001.html. Accessed on 1 Aug 2017

Kant I. Erläuterungen zu A. G. Baumgartens "Initia philosophiae practicae primae" (1760), AA XIX. https://korpora.zim.uni-duisburg-essen.de/kant/agb-initia/index.html. Accessed on 1 Aug 2017

Kant I. Idee zu einer allgemeinen Geschichte in weltbürgerlicher Absicht, AA VIII. https://korpora.zim.uni-duisburg-essen.de/kant/aa08/015.html. Accessed on 1 Aug 2017

Kant I. Kritik der Reinen Vernunft, AA III. https://korpora.zim.uni-duisburg-essen.de/kant/aa03/Inhalt3.html. Accessed on 1 Aug 2017

Kant I. Kritik der praktischen Vernunft, AA V. https://korpora.zim.uni-duisburg-essen.de/kant/aa05/. Accessed on 1 Aug 2017

Kant I. Über den Gemeinspruch: Das mag in der Theorie richtig sein, taugt aber nicht für die Praxis, AA VIII. https://korpora.zim.uni-duisburg-essen.de/kant/aa08/273.html. Accessed on 1 Aug 2017

Kant I. Zum ewigen Frieden, AA VIII. https://korpora.zim.uni-duisburg-essen.de/kant/aa08/341.html. Accessed on 1 Aug 2017

Kaulbach F (1970) Moral und Recht in der Philosophie. In: Blühdorn J, Ritter J (eds) Recht und Ethik. Klostermann, Frankfurt/Main, pp 43–58

Kersting W (2004a) Kant über Recht. Mentis, Paderborn

Kersting W (2004b) Vernunft, Verbindlichkeit und Recht bei Kant. In: Ameriks K, Sturma D et al (eds) Kants Ethik. Mentis, Paderborn, pp 269–290

Kersting W (2007) Wohlgeordnete Freiheit, 3rd edn. Mentis, Paderborn

Kleingeld P (1995) Fortschritt und Vernunft – Zur Geschichtsphilosophie Kants. Königshausen und Neumann, Würzburg

Koorsgard CM (2000) Creating the kingdom of ends. Cambridge University Press, Cambridge

Kordela M (2018) *Ratio Legis* as a binding legal value. In: Klappstein V, Dybowski M (eds) Ratio Legis: philosophical and theoretical perspectives. Springer, Heidelberg, pp 19–28

Krotoszyński M (2018) Legislative history, Ratio Legis, and the concept of the rational legislator. In: Klappstein V, Dybowski M (eds) Ratio Legis: philosophical and theoretical perspectives. Springer, Heidelberg, pp 57–73

Ladd J (1999) Immanuel Kant, metaphysical elements of justice, the complete text of the metaphysics of morals, Part I, 2nd edn. Hackett Publishing Company, Inc., Indianapolis

Larenz K (1933) Die Rechts- und Staatsphilosophie des deutschen Idealismus und ihre Gegenwartsbedeutung. In: Baeumler A, Schröter M (eds) Handbuch der Philosophie, Abteilung IV, Staat und Geschichte. Beitrag D. Oldenbourg, München, pp 89–188

Larenz K (1943) Sittlichkeit und Recht – Untersuchungen zur Geschichte des deutschen Rechtsdenkens und zur Sittenlehre. In: Larenz K (ed) Reich und Recht in der deutschen Philosophie, vol 1. Kohlhammer, Stuttgart, pp 169–412

Ludwig B (1997) Will die Natur unwiderstehlich die Republik? Einige Reflexionen anlässlich einer rätselhaften Textpassage in Kants Friedensschrift. Kant-Studien 88(1997):218–228

Ludwig B (2005) Kants Rechtslehre. Meiner, Hamburg

Luf G (2008) Die Typik der reinen praktischen Urteilskraft. In: Luf G, Holzleithner E, Somek A (eds) Freiheit als Rechtsprinzip. facultas.wuv, Wien, pp 133–150

Marcic R (1971) Geschichte der Rechtsphilosophie. Rombach, Freiburg

Müller A (1996) Das Verhältnis von rechtlicher Freiheit und sittlicher Autonomie in Kants "Metaphysik der Sitten". Peter Lang, Frankfurt/Main

Niesen P (2001) Volk-von-Teufeln-Republikanismus. In: Wingert L (ed) Die Öffentlichkeit der Vernunft und die Vernunft der Öffentlichkeit. Suhrkamp, Frankfurt/Main, pp 568–604

Oberer H (1997) Sittengesetz und Rechtsgesetz a priori. In: Oberer H (ed) Kant. Analysen – Probleme – Kritik, vol 3. Königshausen und Neumann, Würzburg, pp 157–200

O'Neill O (2014) Acting on principle, an essay on Kantian ethics, 2nd edn. Cambridge University Press, Cambridge

Orr S (2015) Translation of groundlaying toward the metaphysics of morals by Immanuel Kant, 2nd edn. Riga 1786. http://groundlaying.appspot.com/pdf/gms1786v_kant-scholar.pdf. Accessed 1 Aug 2017

Paton HJ (1962) Der kategorische Imperativ, Eine Untersuchung über Kants Moralphilosophie. De Gruyter, Berlin

Pawlik M (2006) Kants Volk von Teufeln und sein Staat. Jahrbuch für Recht und Ethik 14 (2006):269–294

Pogge TW (2002) Is Kant's Rechtslehre a 'Comprehensive Liberalism'? In: Timmons M (ed) Kant's metaphysics of morals – interpretative essays. Oxford University Press, New York, pp 133–158

Prauss G (2008) Moral und Recht im Staat nach Kant und Hegel. Alber, Freiburg

Reich K (2001) Kant und Rousseau. In: Baum M, Reich K (eds) Gesammelte Schriften. Meiner, Hamburg, pp 147–165

Ripstein A (2009) Force and freedom – Kant's legal and political philosophy. Harvard University Press, Cambridge

Römpp G (1991) Moralische und rechtliche Freiheit, Zum Status der Rechtslehre in Kants praktischer Philosophie. Rechtstheorie 22(1991):287–305

Rosen AD (1993) Kant's theory of justice. Cornell University Press, Ithaca

Rüthers B (2016) Rechtstheorie, 9th edn. C.H. Beck, München

Sänger M (1982) Die kategoriale Systematik in den "Metaphysischen Anfangsgründen der Rechtslehre". De Gruyter, Berlin

Schadow S (2013) Recht und Ethik in Kants Metaphysik der Sitten. In: Trampota A (ed) Kant's "Tugendlehre" – a comprehensive commentary. De Gruyter, Berlin, pp 85–111

Schmitz HG (2004) Kantisches Vernunftrecht und seine gegenwärtige rechtsphilosophische Reinterpretation. In: Heidemann DH, Engelhard K (eds) Warum Kant heute? De Gruyter, Berlin, pp 306–327

Schmucker J (1997) Der Formalismus und die materialen Zweckprinzipien in der Ethik Kants. In: Oberer H (ed) Kant. Analysen – Probleme – Kritik, vol 3. Königshausen und Neumann, Würzburg, pp 99–155

Scholz G (1972) Das Problem des Rechts in Kants Moralphilosophie. Philosophische Fakultät der Universität zu Köln, Köln

Schönecker D, Wood AW (2007) Kants "Grundlegung zur Metaphysik der Sitten", Ein einführender Kommentar. Schöningh, Paderborn

Schreiber HL (1966) Der Begriff der Rechtspflicht. De Gruyter, Berlin
Stratton-Lake P (2008) Being virtuous and the virtues: two aspects of Kant's doctrine of virtue. In: Betzler M (ed) Kant's virtue ethics. De Gruyter, Berlin, pp 101–122
van der Linden H (1988) Kantian ethics and socialism. Hackett Publishing Company, Inc., Indianapolis
von Schütz K (2018) Immanent *Ratio Legis*? Legal forms and statutory interpretation. In: Klappstein V, Dybowski M (eds) Ratio Legis: philosophical and theoretical perspectives. Springer, Heidelberg, pp 161–186
von der Pfordten D (2009) Kants Rechtsbegriff. In: von der Pfordten D (ed) Menschenwürde, Recht und Staat bei Kant. Mentis, Paderborn, pp 27–40
Vosgerau U (1999) Der Begriff des Rechts bei Kant. Rechtstheorie 30(1999):227–250
Weber-Fas J (1999) Geistiger Vater der Rechtsstaatlichkeit, Dem Andenken Immanuel Kants. ZRP 1999:461–464
Willascheck M (1997) Why the doctrine of right does not belong in the metaphysics of morals. Jahrbuch für Recht und Ethik 5(1997):205–228
Willascheck M (2009) Right and coercion: can Kant's conception of right be derived from his moral theory. Int J Philos Stud 17(2009):49–70
Williams TC (1968) The concept of the categorical imperative, a study of the place of the categorical imperative in Kant's ethical theory. Clarendon Press, Oxford
Wood AW (2002) The final form of Kant's practical philosophy. In: Timmons M (ed) Kant's metaphysics of morals. Princeton University Press, New York, pp 1–21
Wood AW (2005) Kant. Blackwell, Malden

Verena Klappstein is *Habilitandin* at the University of Passau (Faculty of Law, Professorship for German and European Private Law, Civil Procedural Law, and Legal Theory of *Prof. Dr. Thomas Riehm*). The working title of her *Habilitation* based on *Kantian* Moral Philosophy is *Vertragsfreiheit durch Kontrahierungszwang und -verbot* (Freedom of Contract via Obligation to and Prohibition to contract). Her main research areas are private, company, and business law; legal philosophy; and philosophy of science. The article is the extended version of a speech, "The Concept of Purpose in Kant's Metaphysical Elements of Justice," given during the XXVIII World Congress of IVR—Peace Based on Human Rights, 16–21 July 2017, University of Lisbon, Portugal, in the Special Workshop "Is There a *Ratio Legis* and if So, How Many Are There? – The Most Powerful Method of Legal Reasoning Uncovered".

Nonconsequential Conception of Neutrality

Wojciech Ciszewski

Abstract In the paper, I focus on the nonconsequential conception of state neutrality. I claim that we can distinguish three such conceptions: justificatory neutrality, intentional neutrality, and expressive neutrality. Each of them is based on a different understanding of the rationale of an action. The idea of justificatory neutrality provides a constraint on the types of reasons that may legitimately support political decisions. Intentional neutrality refers to considerations that move political decision makers. Expressive neutrality states that the most important aspect of a political action is an attitude that this action expresses. The aim of my research is twofold. I would like, first, to clarify the meaning and distinctiveness of each conception and, second, to propose the defensible variant of state neutrality principle drawing on this classification.

1 Introductory Remarks

The idea of state neutrality toward different conceptions of the good is certainly one of the leading topics in contemporary legal and political philosophy. Since the publication of *A Theory of Justice* by John Rawls in 1971, a lot of academic work has been devoted to establishing the justification of the principle, clarifying its specific content, and repelling numerous objections raised against the idea of state neutrality. One of the crucial issues addressed in this debate concerns the conception of state neutrality, particularly the answer to the question "what does it mean for a state to be neutral?" There are two ways of responding to this question, which may be called consequential and nonconsequential conceptions of state neutrality. According to the former approach, state neutrality requires that political actions

---

The paper was supported by the Polish Ministry of Science and Higher Education under the research grant no 0120/NPRH3/H21/82/2014, "The Neutrality Principle" (*Zasada neutralności światopoglądowej*).

W. Ciszewski (✉)
Jagiellonian University, Krakow, Poland

V. Klappstein, M. Dybowski (eds.), *Ratio Legis*,
https://doi.org/10.1007/978-3-319-74271-7_6

should equally influence different conception of the good held by citizens in a given society. The latter approach depends on some other aspect of a political action than effects that it causes. The supporters of nonconsequential conception commonly point to some understanding of the rationale (or *ratio legis* in legal terminology) of an action.

Surprisingly, after almost 50 years of debate, there are still many problems and ambiguities with the typology of conceptions of state neutrality. Among theorists, there is no agreement on the number or substance of specific conceptions. One might rather notice a big conceptual confusion regarding these issues. Some theorists have used different terms for the same ideas; others have put the same label on different conceptions. Some of the available typologies are not adequate because of their briefness or unfairness to the idea of neutrality. Still, the issue seems to be an important one—the clarification of different conceptions is a crucial step in formulating a defensible principle of state neutrality.

In this paper, I would like to focus on nonconsequential conception of neutrality, which is commonly regarded as more plausible than alternative conceptions. In my opinion, we can distinguish three conceptions that provide a minimally credible account of state neutrality. Each of them is based on a different understanding of the rationale of an action. The aim of my research is twofold. I would like, first, to clarify the meaning and distinctiveness of each conception and, second, to propose the defensible variant of state neutrality principle drawing on this classification.

In the first part of this paper, I will shed some light on the philosophical background of the discussion between different conceptions of neutrality by presenting the opposition between two philosophical approaches: political perfectionism and antiperfectionism. In the second part, I will introduce a typology of different conceptions of state neutrality. The main object of interest will be three nonconsequential conceptions. These are justificatory neutrality, intentional neutrality, and expressive neutrality. In the third part, I will question how a defensible principle of state neutrality can be formulated on the basis of previous considerations.

2 The Philosophical Background of the Discussion

The issue of state neutrality is at the heart of the controversy between adherents of two philosophical approaches, namely political perfectionists and antiperfectionists. According to Jeremy Waldron:

> Political perfectionism is simply the view that legislators and officials may consider what is good and valuable in life and what is ignoble and depraved when drafting the laws and setting the framework for social and personal relationships.[1]

[1]Waldron (1989), p. 1102.

It may be useful to emphasize three elements of Waldron's definition. First, the idea of political perfectionism applies to different types of political actions and decisions. By these terms, one should understand actions performed by political actors and addressed to the public. In his definition, Waldron mentions just two apparent examples of such activities (drafting laws and setting a framework of the social order), but the perfectionist principle also applies to others, such as governors pursuing state policies or courts issuing judgments.

Second, political perfectionism provides legitimacy for state officials to consider values and ideals that refer to the nonpolitical aspect of citizens' lives. According to this view, political actors may rightfully consider what is good or bad in human life; what conceptions of the good one should adopt; what activities, relationships, practices, goals, or commitments make people's living better; which ideal of human flourishing is true and worth of engagement; etc. Perfectionists commonly claim that some individual conceptions of the good are more valuable than others. This thesis is not very controversial; however, it is usually followed by a much more contentious assertion that those valuable individual visions of the good are important components of political morality.[2]

Third, political perfectionism assumes that state officials may perform political actions on the basis of their conclusions about the value of different conceptions of the good. Hence, the moral status of these conceptions may legitimately inform political decisions. In other words, political perfectionists claim that valuable conceptions of the good may be promoted (or disapproved) in legal regulations, policies, and court judgments. According to this approach, state officials are justified in protecting and promoting particular ideals of human flourishing even if the value of such ideals is a matter of reasonable disagreement within the society. The contested status of an ideal is not an obstacle for favoring this ideal by political means.

One should note that particular conceptions of political perfectionism may differ in a number of aspects. For example, some versions of political perfectionism treat promotion of conceptions of the good as state officials' obligation, whereas other versions assert that state officials are only justified in performing actions of this kind.[3] Besides, distinct variants of perfectionism may be focused on different conceptions of the good. Relying on this criterion, one may recognize religious perfectionism, liberal perfectionism, feminist perfectionism, communitarian perfectionism, environmentalist perfectionism, nationalist perfectionism, and so on.[4] Furthermore, within the perfectionist theory, there is also a debate regarding permissible means of promoting valuable ideals of the good. Some theorists suggest that perfectionist policies may be enforced by any means, including administrative fines and penalties. Others are more cautious here and say that valuable conceptions

[2]Wall (1998), p. 8.

[3]Couto (2014), pp. 98–100.

[4]Arneson (2000), p. 39.

of the good should be promoted, but only by noncoercive measures, such as advertising campaigns, subsidies, or tax incentives.[5]

Therefore, the gist of political perfectionism is the legitimacy of state officials to consider and promote individual conceptions of the good while performing political actions. In turn, political antiperfectionism denies such a possibility. Ronald Dworkin defines the main idea of this view as follows:

> [...] political decisions must be, so far as is possible, independent of any particular conception of the good life, or of what gives value to life. Since the citizens of a society differ in their conceptions, the government does not treat them as equals if it prefers one conception to another, either because the officials believe that one is intrinsically superior, or because one is held by the more numerous or more powerful group.[6]

According to antiperfectionists, political actions cannot be based on the assertions about of what is good and bad in human life. In the quotation above, Dworkin suggests one route of justifying such stance. In his view, it is a typical feature of democratic societies for people to deeply differ in the values they hold. It is normal that no individual conception of the good is commonly followed by all citizens. In each democratic society exists a variety of such conceptions, most of which are at least minimally reasonable. Because democratic citizens are free and equal in their moral status, they have the power to decide which conception of the good is appropriate for them. Citizens may legitimately demand respect for their choices and to be treated with equal concern by governors. When state officials promote one of contested conceptions of the good, they disrespect citizens who do not share this conception. As a result, citizens are not treated as equals.[7]

Summarizing so far, the key question for debate between perfectionists and antiperfectionists is whether a general standard that forbids state officials from recognizing and promoting certain conceptions of what is good and bad in human life should be enforced. Antiperfectionists argue for such a standard, and perfectionists are against it. This contentious standard is, of course, the state neutrality principle.

3 Conceptions of State Neutrality

Among political antiperfectionists, there is an agreement that state neutrality principle is justified and desirable. However, at the same time, there is much less agreement with respect to the preferred content of this principle, or as it is called in philosophical discussion, the proper conception of state neutrality.

---

[5]Chan (2000), pp. 14–15.

[6]Dworkin (1986), p. 191.

[7]It should be clear that this is only one route of argumentation for political anti-perfectionism. For other arguments in favor of state neutrality, see: Caney (1991), pp. 457–477; Quong (2011), pp. 73–107.

In literature, one may find various attempts to classify conceptions of state neutrality. In my opinion, the best way to frame this issue is to distinguish between consequential and nonconsequential conceptions. According to the former, state officials should not do anything that would have the effect of favoring a conception of good life over other such conceptions. Therefore, each political action should have an equal (and, in this sense, neutral) impact on different ideals of the good held by citizens. The latter approach treats the effects of political actions as irrelevant from the perspective of neutrality. On this account, state neutrality relates to some other aspect of an action performed by a state official.

Consequential conceptions of state neutrality do not constitute a homogeneous category. These conceptions differ in at least two important aspects. First, each consequential conception must clarify *the scope* of consequences that are relevant for state neutrality. Should we be focused on direct or maybe long-term effects of political actions? Should the inquiry be limited only to consequences that are foreseeable by state officials (hence "normal" effects of political action), or should there be no such limitation?

Second, there is a question of proper *criterion* for assessing relevant consequences. One available criterion is the "popularity" of a conception of the good (that is, the number of adherents of a given conception.[8] According to this approach, political actions should not make any conception of the good more (or less) popular in society. For example, introduction of religious training in schools ought to be regarded as a violation of the neutrality principle because it increases the popularity of religious conception. Another available consequential criterion is "realizability," which is understood as the level of difficulty with which a conception of the good is pursued.[9] On this account, actions of state officials should not impede (or facilitate) the fulfillment of any particular conception of the good to a greater degree than any other conception of this kind.[10] For example, by supporting practices distinctive for one ideal of good life (such as subsidizing religious organizations), state officials make it easier for adherents of this ideal to realize their moral goals. This situation is a clear violation of state neutrality, according to the "realizability" criterion. The third available interpretation is based on the idea of "equal satisfaction."[11] From this point of view, state neutrality requires equalization of the level of satisfaction among adherents of different conceptions of the good. State officials should assure that followers of each conception handle fairly well in society. If a political action entails more satisfaction among adherents of one ideal of the good than others, then this action should be regarded as contrary to the neutrality principle.

It is commonly held that all consequential approaches to state neutrality are vulnerable to serious objections. Critics argue that it is not possible to satisfy the demands of those conceptions in political practice. According to this criticism,

---

[8]Raz (1986), pp. 112–115; Patten (2014), pp. 113–114.

[9]Raz (1986), pp. 112–115; Patten (2014), pp. 113–114.

[10]Kramer (2017), p. 13.

[11]Arneson (1990), p. 217.

political actions inevitably influence popularity, "realizability," and the level of satisfaction of each conception of the good, and this impact is unavoidably unequal.[12] Other theorists claim that even if the state of equal influence was achievable, in many circumstances it would not be a desirable ideal. In political spheres, we are mainly interested in the realization of different political values, such as fairness, equality, or solidarity. The pursuit of equal consequences could undermine these valuable ends.[13]

Although there are political theorists who maintain that some version of consequential neutrality may constitute a defensible ideal, nonconsequential conceptions are generally regarded as more plausible. As was said above, these conceptions refer to some other aspect of political action than effects caused by this action. The question then is, what "other aspect" may determine the neutral character of an action? Different theorists answer this question by indicating aims, justifications, intentions, procedures, or principles; however, the boundaries between these concepts are very unclear. There is neither consensus on the number nor agreement on the meaning of particular instances of nonconsequential neutrality.

In my opinion, we should distinguish three different nonconsequential conceptions of state neutrality. These are justificatory neutrality, intentional neutrality, and expressive neutrality. All these conceptions indicate an action's rationale (or *ratio legis* in legal terminology) as the feature that grounds neutrality of an action. However, on each account, this rationale is differently understood. The justificatory neutrality points to the best available justification of an action, the intentional neutrality indicates the motive that moves a political agent, and the expressive neutrality is focused on the meaning of an action in the eyes of the observers. In the next section, I will discuss these conceptions in more detail.

3.1 Justificatory Neutrality

According to the justificatory neutrality, a political action is neutral when it is supported by a neutral reason (or a set of neutral reasons). It is important to note that, apart from being neutral, the relevant reason (or set of reasons) must be also sufficient and flawless in order to ground the action. Hence, the justificatory neutrality is violated not only when there are no neutral arguments for an action but also when one can indicate neutral arguments, but these arguments are either not sufficient or grounded in flawed premises.

A justificatory account of state neutrality assumes that there are at least two different sets of reasons available in the political sphere: neutral and nonneutral. The plausibility of the conception depends on drawing a distinction between these two sets. One can apply one of two strategies here. The first one—the accessibility

[12] Kramer (2017), pp. 13–14; Rawls (1993), p. 194.

[13] Wall (1998), pp. 35–36.

strategy—states that a reason may count as neutral if it has a proper epistemological status. Namely, a neutral reason has to be epistemologically accessible to all citizens. Different theorists propose more specific criteria to determine the accessible character of a reason—they indicate intelligibility, replicability, or testability as the relevant threshold in this context. All accessibility accounts recognize arguments derived from scientific knowledge as the paradigmatic example of a neutral justification. In turn, reasons that are based on personal emotions or derived from a revelation are commonly regarded as nonneutral.[14]

The alternative proposition is the acceptability strategy. This approach states that a reason may count as neutral if it could be accepted by an ideal democratic citizenry. Proponents of this strategy usually base their argumentation on a hypothetical construction of an ideal democratic citizen. The acceptance of a hypothetical ideal citizen functions as a test for the neutrality of reasons. According to the most influential account of democratic citizenship, citizens are characterized by two basic capacities. The first is rationality, which is an ability to "have, to revise, and rationally to pursue a conception of the good (...) which specifies a person's conception of what is of value in human life."[15] The second is reasonableness—"the capacity to understand, to apply, and to act from (and not merely in accordance with) the principles of political justice that specifies fair terms of social cooperation."[16] Advocates of the acceptability strategy claim that idealized citizens would not commonly approve arguments derived from religious or ethical doctrines because each citizen is rational and specifies his or her own vision "of what is of value in human life." One should not reasonably expect any agreement on such comprehensive reasons in democratic circumstances. On the other hand, no ideal democratic citizens would reject values of democratic justice, freedom, or equality. Reasons derived from these democratic values and principles are paradigmatic examples of neutral considerations.[17]

It may be helpful to illustrate how the idea of justificatory neutrality works in practice. I guess that the reasoning of the US Supreme Court in the case of *McGowan v. Maryland* provides us with a good example.[18] The issue in *McGowan* concerns the constitutional validity of Maryland criminal statutes commonly known as "Sunday Closing Laws." The statutes under review proscribed conducting various business activities on Sundays. The regulation was challenged in court by a group of employees from Anne Arundel County. According to the facts of the case, the plaintiffs were convicted and fined five dollars for selling prohibited goods on Sunday.

What makes this issue problematic is that Sunday Closing Laws have clearly religious origins. Sunday is a holy day for Christians. In *McGowan*, the Supreme

[14]Bird (1996), p. 71; Greenawalt (1995), pp. 46–49; Vallier (2011), p. 387.

[15]Rawls (2000), p. 19.

[16]Rawls (2000), pp. 18–19.

[17]Quong (2011), p. 261; Freeman (2007), pp. 289–290.

[18]McGowan v. Maryland, 366 U.S. 420 (1961).

Court acknowledged that, historically, such laws were intended to favor Christian people and promote a Christian vision of good life.[19] Even today, the fact that business activities are prohibited on Sundays may be easily interpreted as supporting Christian doctrine. All this evidence poses a challenge to the conformity of Sunday Closing Laws to the First Amendment of the US Constitution.

The Supreme Court's answer in *McGowan* was that Sunday Closing Laws do not violate the First Amendment (in particular, the establishment clause). The reason for this judgment is that one can give an appropriate, nonreligious argumentation for the maintenance of these laws. This argumentation consists of two elements. First, the Supreme Court stated that providing citizens with a uniform day of rest is a legitimate political aim. Reasons of health protection, safety factors, recreation needs, and general well-being speak in favor of enacting such regulation.[20] Second, the Supreme Court argued that it is reasonable and pragmatically justified to choose Sunday for a uniform day of rest. In the Court's opinion, Sunday is commonly perceived as a day for recreation by all citizens (both religious and nonreligious). As a consequence, this day offers more opportunities for relaxation than any other day of the week. Therefore, the Supreme Court claimed that "It would seem unrealistic for enforcement purposes and perhaps detrimental to the general welfare to require a State to choose a common day of rest other than that which most persons would select of their own accord."[21]

Although many theorists support the conception of justificatory neutrality, several objections can be raised against this idea. Principally, it is argued that justificatory neutrality is too permissive. By focusing solely on an action's justification, one may come to see even intuitively nonneutral actions as neutral. Alan Patten considers the example of an establishment of religion (or church) by governors, and in his opinion, even such clearly nonneutral reform may satisfy the requirements of justificatory neutrality.[22] This is because the establishment of a religion may be supported by perfectly neutral considerations, such as, Patten claims, the need to enhance a state's authority and legitimacy in the eyes of citizens. Nevertheless, in spite of the neutral justification, such policy would still be seen as "the paradigmatic example of a departure from neutrality."[23] This example shows that all that justificatory neutrality can do here is prevent performing nonneutral actions for nonneutral reasons; however, it cannot do the same when such actions are neutrally justified.

In my opinion, Patten's objection is important, but it does not undermine the conception of justificatory neutrality. First of all, we should remember that for an action to be neutral, it is important not only that there are neutral reasons in favor of this action but also that these reasons are sufficient and free from flawed premises. Therefore, in order for the objection to succeed, it has to be true that the

[19] McGowan, p. 447.

[20] McGowan, 444.

[21] McGowan, 452.

[22] Patten (2014), p. 113.

[23] Patten (2014), p. 113.

establishment of a religion (or church) would positively influence state's authority and legitimacy in the eyes of citizens. I doubt whether this reason may be regarded as plausible and sufficient in well-ordered democracies characterized by reasonable pluralism. It seems to me that such an action would rather undermine a state's authority and legitimacy and not enhance it. In my opinion, it is hard to find a neutral argumentation that would adequately support the decision to establish a religion.

Second, we should keep in mind that the state neutrality principle is only one of several principles that regulate state–religion relations (or, more broadly, relations between a state and different conceptions of the good). Together with other principles (for example, religious freedom, nondiscrimination, and separation of state and church), the neutrality principle constitutes the doctrine of the secular state.[24] The crucial thing is that each of these principles provides some constraints on political actions regarding religious issues. Therefore, in Patten's case, religious establishment may be forbidden not necessarily because of state neutrality but for violating some related principle (for example, the principle of separation between church and state).

The other objection to justificatory neutrality goes in the opposite direction. One may claim that the justificatory conception precludes some political actions that are not controversial among citizens.[25] Some of these actions may be even commonly viewed as legitimized and desirable. In this context, critics usually give examples of state support to arts and culture, protection of national heritage, and financing liberal arts education. The problem with these activities is that they are ordinarily defended by different kinds of nonneutral arguments, like invoking the intrinsic quality of arts or the value of classical knowledge for human flourishing. These kinds of arguments are excluded by the conception of justificatory neutrality. Therefore, one may say that if we restrict permissible justifications of political actions only to neutral reasons, some valuable activities will be precluded.

The above objection seems to be sound. It is a fact that the most popular arguments supporting mentioned activities are essentially nonneutral. However, it should be emphasized that the ban on nonneutral argumentation does not lead to preclusion of the activities in question. Many of those actions may be also justified in a neutral way—by arguments, which are derived from generally acceptable and accessible considerations, such as the idea of equality of opportunity, the idea of intergenerational justice, economic benefits, or the reduction of social inequalities. Of course, this is only a very general reply. To fully answer the above concern, each problematic activity (and arguments in its favor) should be considered case by case.

[24] Laegaard (2013), pp. 127–128.

[25] Brighouse (1995), pp. 62–63.

3.2 Intentional Neutrality

Another nonconsequential conception of state neutrality is intentional neutrality. According to this conception, neutrality should provide a constraint on state officials' intentions for actions. State officials should not be guided by improper—that is, nonneutral—considerations. By nonneutral considerations I mean especially the aim of promoting (or discouraging) any conception of the good or giving special assistance (or hindrance) to the adherents of a particular conception.

The important difference with justificatory neutrality is that in case of the intentional conception, we are focused on a belief that moves the agent to perform an action. Under scrutiny here is the real motivation that stands behind one's activity. It is not relevant whether the activity in question is rationally and neutrally justifiable. Therefore, a decision enacted with a nonneutral intention should be regarded as nonneutral, even if there is a good neutral reason for the decision (and even if such reason was offered for this decision).

Once again, we can invoke a US Supreme Court opinion in order to illustrate the specificity of a conception. Let us take a look at the case of *Lukumi Babalu Aye v. City of Hialeah*.[26] The case concerned a church, Lukumi Babalu, which practices the Santería religion. Santería developed in the Caribbean as a mixture of Roman Catholic doctrine and African religious rituals. The important thing about this religion is that it employs animal sacrifice as one of its principal forms of devotion. Animal killing accompanies all major Santerían rituals.

According to the facts of the case, the Lukumi Babalu Church planned to establish a house of worship in Hialeah, Florida. In response, the city council of Hialeah held a session and passed a number of ordinances that prohibited ritual slaughter in the city limits and, in fact, preclude practicing Santería. In response to this, the church filed a suit against the city, alleging violations of the First Amendment of the US Constitution. Two lower courts ruled for the city and upheld the ordinances in question. The courts declared that laws in the case were based on appropriate and sufficient considerations (primarily, reasons of public health and the prevention of cruelty to animals). The consequences of these ordinances on Santerían religious practices were only "incidental to [their] secular purpose and effect."[27] However, the Supreme Court reversed the previous decisions. The majority opinion stated that the real motives of councilmen in the case were hidden and nonneutral.

The legislative history revealed that, regardless of the official justification, the real intent of councilmen was to target and disadvantage the Santería religion. The majority opinion indicated several facts that support this judgment. First, according to the Supreme Court, the circumstances of passing the ordinances in question were extraordinary. Efforts of Santerίans to establish a house of worship apparently influenced the activity of the council. The City Council held a public session just

[26]Lukumi Babalu v. City of Hialeah, 508 U.S. 520 (1993).

[27]Lukumi Babalu, p. 529.

to pass these regulations.[28] Second, the Supreme Court pointed to the statements of the councilors, which revealed their private motivations. All of these statements were announced during the public session. For example, Councilman Andres Mejides observed that the Bible does not allow this particular type of animal sacrifice practiced by Santeríans, and the president of the council, Herman Echevarria, asked, "What can we do to prevent the Church from opening?"[29] Some of these statements were met with applause from the public. Third, the ordinances did not explicitly mention the word "religion"; however, they used words with clearly religious connotations (such as "sacrifice" or "ritual").[30] Finally, the Supreme Court indicated that burdening Santerían religious practices was the only effect of the ordinances in question. Although the regulation was aimed at protecting animals, many violent practices were exempted from it (for example, kosher slaughterhouses, regular slaughterhouses, hunting, fishing, euthanasia of stray animals, and feeding live rabbits to greyhounds).[31]

Although the conception of intentional neutrality is popular in judicial practice, it is vulnerable to weighty objections. Primarily, there is a well-known problem with the ascription of an intention (in the above sense) to a political agent. The idea of intention is easily applicable in cases of individual conduct; however; in the political sphere, we often need to assess actions of group agents, such as parliaments, councils, or committees.[32] If we understand an intention as a consideration that moves an agent to act in a given way, then it becomes a question of whether such a thing exists in cases of group agents. Different participants in the group are usually guided by various motives; some of them may be moved by moral reasons, others by prudence, emotions, or prejudice.

What is more, even if we hypothetically assume that common intentions exist, we have to admit that it is extremely difficult to capture their content. Intentions in the above sense, even in cases of individuals, are not accessible from the perspective of the external observer. We do not possess any test that reveals the real motive behind political actions. In the *Lukumi Babalu* case, the Supreme Court based its judgment on different facts from the legislative history; however, this approach seems to be problematic. One may find the choice of facts arbitrary and biased. One may question whether evidence indicated by the Court reflects the real intentions of political agents. Additionally, one may be worried that giving courts the power to identify real intention behind political actions may strengthen the judiciary and, consequently, breach the proper balance between different powers.

Finally, some theorists claim that there is also a more general problem with intention-based moralities. Thomson argues that the idea that intentions play a role

[28]Lukumi Babalu, p. 526.

[29]Lukumi Babalu, p. 541.

[30]Lukumi Babalu, p. 534.

[31]Lukumi Babalu v. City of Hialeah, pp. 543–544.

[32]Koppelman (2013), pp. 86–87.

in fixing what a person may do is "odd."[33] Intention-based principles, such as intentional neutrality, are not action guiding. It is because an agent does not know what intention he or she will have at the time of an action. In this sense, one cannot predict his or her future intentions and, therefore, cannot plan his/her moral conduct.

3.3 *Expressive Neutrality*

The third nonconsequential conception of state neutrality is expressive neutrality. Pursuant to this approach, neutrality requires state officials to act in ways that express neutral attitudes toward different conceptions of the good. Only an action that is perceived as neutral by its observers may be regarded as a neutral one. Hence, on this account, an action might be properly justified, and it might arise from pure intentions but still be disapproved because of expressing a nonneutral attitude.

According to supporters of expressive neutrality, it is a common phenomenon that what people do and what their behavior expresses are two different things. Expressivists claim that attitudes of state officials send messages to citizens and that the content of a message is in the eyes of the beholder.[34] Anderson and Pildes argue that the standard of adequate attitude "is not met simply by intending to express those attitudes"—this standard is rather "public, set by objective criteria for determining the meaning of actions."[35] Thus, people have only limited control over their attitudes and the messages that those attitudes send.

Anderson and Pildes give three examples showing how an agent's behavior may express improper attitude in spite of his or her motives:

> First, they [people] might act negligently or thoughtlessly, by failing to notice or take certain considerations as reasons for action. Teenagers blaring their car horn late at night might be consciously intending only to signal a friend to join them. But in failing to consider or to take the neighbors' interests in peace and quiet as a reason for action, their behavior expresses inconsiderateness toward their neighbors. Second, people may act in ignorance of social conventions or norms that set public standards for expressing certain attitudes. Thus, a person from a different culture might not know he is expressing disrespect for another by failing to shake his hand. Third, people may act on attitudes or assumptions of which they are unaware. In reviewing a novel, the reviewer might contemptuously interpret the text in ways that make the author look simpleminded. The reviewer might not be aware of her contempt for the author. She may just have difficulty imagining that he is capable of sophistication, and therefore interprets the author's words accordingly.[36]

---

[33]Thomson (1993), p. 293.

[34]Nussbaum (2008), pp. 225–227; Laborde (2013), pp. 83–85; Anderson and Pildes (2000), p. 1550.

[35]Anderson and Pildes (2000), p. 1512.

[36]Anderson and Pildes (2000), pp. 1512–1513.

The well-known example of the application of this conception in legal practice is the US Supreme Court's opinion in the case *Lynch v. Donnelly*.[37] The case concerns the constitutional legality of an annual Christmas display placed in the shopping district in the city of Pawtucket, Rhode Island. The display consisted of a nativity scene with infant Jesus, Mary, and Joseph surrounded by angels, animals, Christmas trees, Santa Claus, reindeer, and a banner with a sign reading "Season's Greetings." This exhibition was challenged in court for violating the First Amendment of the US Constitution. Two lower courts, the District Court and the Court of Appeals, ruled for the plaintiffs.

The Supreme Court reversed previous decisions and argued for the constitutional permissibility of the Christmas display in Pawtucket. The majority opinion stated that the display in question had a legitimate secular purpose. From our point of view, more interesting than the majority opinion is the concurring opinion written by Justice Sandra Day O'Connor. In the concurring opinion, O'Connor clarified the idea of expressive neutrality. According to her argumentation, state actions can fail the neutrality test by communicating certain ideas (either consciously or unconsciously). A *prima facie* noncontroversial action may signal that some citizens are not full members of the political community by virtue of the conception of the good that they hold.[38] In democratic states, actions that convey such messages are inadmissible because all citizens have equal political status—there can be no first- and second-class citizens.

In the case of Pawtucket's crèche, O'Connor concluded that the objective observer would not find the Christmas exhibition as privileging a particular religion.[39] The main argument for this conclusion was that the display in question consisted of both religious and secular symbols, such as Santa Claus, reindeer, and a "Season's Greetings" banner. In her opinion, O'Connor claimed that these secular elements change the meaning of the whole display. They convey a less spiritual and nondiscriminatory message. People who are not Christians should not find the display—and hence the attitude of Pawtucket's governors—as promoting certain religious beliefs.

Many theorists support the idea of expressive neutrality; however, the conception is vulnerable to some criticism. Probably the main problem concerns the identification of observer's perspective, which is key to the process of approving political actions. It seems that there can be two ways of identifying this perspective—empirical and constructivist. Unfortunately, both these approaches reveal substantial weaknesses.

The first, an empirical (or sociological) way of identifying observer's perspective, states that we should focus on the opinions of the real citizenry—that is, on the beliefs of people as they are. According to this approach, a political action is neutral if it is perceived as such by real citizens who are subject to it. Therefore, if citizens

[37]Lynch v. Donnelly, 465 U.S 668 (1984).

[38]Lynch, pp. 688 and 692.

[39]Lynch, p. 692.

find as a matter of fact the official's attitude behind an action to be discriminatory and undermining the value of self-respect, then this action should be regarded as nonneutral.

But the empirical approach to expressive neutrality is very problematic.[40] First, by rejecting any restriction on the observer's perspective, the conception becomes dependent upon beliefs that may be mistaken or immoral, as well as fragile sensibilities. It is not controversial that at least some real citizens hold mistaken or immoral views, nor that we do not want such views to influence the legitimacy of political decisions. However, with the empirical approach, we have no tools for differentiating between justified and unjustified critique of state actions. Another precarious issue with this approach is that in many situations, it is impossible to predict how a given action will be perceived by citizens. In fact, we can assess those actions only after they are performed. This is problematic as we commonly expect legal principles to guide actions at the time of their performance.

The second, constructivist, way of identifying an observer's perspective may provide some answers to doubts revealed by the empirical approach. In accordance with this view, the expressive meaning of political actions may be tested from the standpoint of an "objective observer"—a hypothetical person with average sensitivity and ideal moral motivation. Such a test provides an opportunity for recognition of actions as neutral or nonneutral before their performance.

However, even the constructivist approach is not free of criticism.[41] Critics argue that this version of expressive neutrality is incoherent. It is indicated that the main aim of the conception is to secure real persons' self-respect and status in society. However, in order to realize this aim, theorists postulate a hypothetical, ideal observer, which does not necessarily reflect real citizens' concerns. For this reason, it is questionable whether the constructivist approach could satisfy the aim of the conception and secure real citizens' standing. There is also a problem with the vagueness of the test of objective observer. Because there are no rigid criteria, the application of the test may provide totally different results in very similar situations. For example, among adherents of expressive neutrality, there is a disagreement whether the test, applied in the case *Lynch v. Donnelly*, provides a result in favor or against the constitutionality of the Christmas display. As was said above, O'Connor's conclusion was positive, but many theorists claim that she was wrong and that the outcome should have been reversed.[42]

[40]Laegaard (2017), pp. 122–123.

[41]Smith (2001), pp. 560–562; Laegaard (2017), pp. 125–127.

[42]Eisgruber and Sager (2007), p. 134.

4 Toward the Principle of State Neutrality

After introducing three nonconsequential conceptions of state neutrality, we can ask about the content of the state neutrality principle. The question for now is how our previous considerations may be useful in establishing a defensible principle of state neutrality.

In my opinion, we can expect that a defensible principle of state neutrality will satisfy three main desiderata. The principle should be functional (by this I mean easily applicable to particular cases), action guiding (it should provide action guidelines for the political agent), and intuitively plausible (it should cohere with our intuitions concerning state neutrality). Relying on the presented typology of nonconsequential conceptions of neutrality, we can distinguish three alternative strategies for establishing the principle.

The first strategy consists in *putting together* all three nonconsequential conceptions in one formula of state neutrality. It is important to note that the conceptions presented above are not mutually exclusive; thus, one may have a principle of state neutrality that encompasses all three of them. According to this approach, a neutral political action should satisfy all three conditions at the same time: be supported by a neutral reason, be motivated by a neutral intent, and express a neutral attitude. Every time we investigate the neutrality of an action, we must recognize all three dimensions of this action as appropriate. In case any of the requirements are not fulfilled, the action should be regarded as violating the principle.

Nevertheless, the strategy of *putting together* conceptions of neutrality should be rejected. There are serious problems with two requirements recommended by this approach. As was argued in the previous section, intentional neutrality is a highly questionable conception because it is not functional in practice, especially in legal contexts. The issue is that we do not have access to other persons' intentions. Besides, the conception of intentional neutrality does not provide action guidelines for political agents as one cannot plan what intention he or she will have at the time of performing an action. In addition, there are also doubts regarding the expressive neutrality. In a previous section, I claimed that the empirical version of this conception lacks an action-guiding characteristic, whereas the alternative, a constructivist approach, may be nonfunctional (at least in some cases, the application of the conception does not lead to clear results).

The second available strategy is *choosing the most plausible conception of state neutrality among the three presented and rejecting two alternative approaches*. Here, we assume that only one conception provides a reliable criterion for assessing the neutrality of political actions, whereas two other propositions do not. Hence, according to this view, the state neutrality principle should be concerned exclusively with reasons, intentions, or expressions. Taking previous considerations into account, it seems that the conception of justificatory neutrality is the best candidate for this role. This conception is a source of action guidelines (one should only perform actions that are neutrally justifiable), and it seems to be functional (applicable to particular cases).

The weakness of the second strategy is that it may contradict our common intuitions and expectations regarding the state neutrality principle. As was discussed above, the main objections against justificatory neutrality refer to its intuitive plausibility. The conception recognizes as neutral actions those that are commonly regarded as nonneutral. It also excludes some uncontroversial political settlements for contradicting the idea of neutrality. It may be argued that by rejecting intentional and expressive aspects of neutrality, the principle of neutrality becomes even less sound. This is because both rejected approaches are based on sound intuitions that state that aims held by a political agent and values that his or her action manifests are relevant from the point of view of state neutrality. Ignoring these intuitions would undermine the plausibility of the principle.

I claim that the answer to the problems of the second strategy is a slight modification. The third strategy consists in *choosing the most reliable conception of neutrality and accommodating the other two conceptions*. In my opinion, the content of the state neutrality principle should be based on the conception of justificatory neutrality; however, the principle should also accommodate—as far as possible—the reasonable intuitions underlying two alternative approaches.

How can justificatory-based neutrality principle be reconciled with these intuitions? In my opinion, the claims of intentional neutrality might be accommodated by the justificatory conception by focusing the latter on reasons offered by a state official who performs an action in question. On this account, the scrutiny of political decisions is concerned solely with the reasons formulated and given by an agent. One should ask not whether an action is generally justifiable in neutral terms but whether arguments offered officially by a political agent were appropriate. Hence, according to the modified principle, even if there are sufficient neutral reasons for a political action, the action should be regarded as nonneutral, assuming that these reasons were not included in the official justification given by a political agent.

Finally, the justificatory-based neutrality principle should also accommodate the reasonable intuitions underlying the conception of expressive neutrality. There is a need to supplement the initial principle in two ways. First, the care about expressive dimension of actions speaks in favor of transparency of a state action's justifications. Particularly, state officials' reasons for political actions should be available to the public. The knowledge of the action's rationale (or at least its availability) affects the way that this action is seen by the public. The transparency of political actions should be understood here as a requirement of the state neutrality principle. Therefore, the violation of the transparency requirement (in this regard) is equal to breaching the neutrality. Second, the claims of expressive neutrality should also be reconciled with the justificatory conception by including expressive considerations into the range of neutral arguments permissible in political and legal discourse. The fact that an action will be perceived as neutral (or nonneutral) should be taken into account by a political decision maker. In this sense, it may provide a reason for (or against) performing an action. However, it does not mean that in each case, the reception of an action should be treated as a decisive argument in neutrality inquiry (this is what the conception of expressive neutrality demands). My proposition is more modest. I argue that expressive considerations might be included in the process of weighing reasons—they should be recognized as appropriate arguments. However, it is possible that in a particular case other arguments will prevail over expressive ones.

5 Conclusion

In this paper, I distinguished three nonconsequential conceptions of state neutrality (justificatory neutrality, intentional neutrality, and expressive neutrality) and discussed the main objections raised against these conceptions. In my opinion, justificatory neutrality is the most defensible of those conceptions and may provide a basis for the principle of state neutrality. However, as I argued, the principle should be modified in order to accommodate plausible intuitions of two alternative conceptions of neutrality. According to the modified version of the justificatory-based principle, an action is neutral when it is supported by a neutral reason (or by a set of neutral reasons) offered by a political agent in a transparent justification of his or her action. Stated in this way, the principle describes the features of the rationale (or *ratio legis*) that should be scrutinized in evaluating the neutrality of political actions.

References

Anderson ES, Pildes R (2000) Expressive theories of law: a general restatement. Univ Pa Law Rev 148:1503–1575

Arneson RJ (1990) Neutrality and utility. Can J Philos 20:215–240

Arneson RJ (2000) Perfectionism and politics. Ethics 111(2000):37–63

Bird C (1996) Mutual respect and neutral justification. Ethics 107(1996):62–96

Brighouse H (1995) Neutrality, publicity, and state funding of the arts. Philos Public Aff 24:35–63

Caney S (1991) Consequentialist defences of state neutrality. Philos Q 165:457–477

Chan J (2000) Legitimacy, unanimity, and perfectionism. Philos Public Aff **29**:5–42

Couto A (2014) Liberal perfectionism. De Gruyter, Berlin

Dworkin R (1986) A matter of principle. Clarendon Press, Oxford

Eisgruber CL, Sager LG (2007) Religious freedom and the constitution. Harvard University Press, Cambridge

Freeman S (2007) Rawls. Routledge, New York

Greenawalt K (1995) Private consciences and public reasons. Oxford University Press, Oxford

Koppelman A (2013) Defending American religious neutrality. Harvard University Press, Cambridge

Kramer M (2017) Liberalism with excellence. Oxford University Press, Oxford

Laborde C (2013) Political liberalism and religion: on separation and establishment. J Polit Philos 21:67–86

Laegaard S (2013) Secular religious establishment. A framework for discussing the compatibility of institutional religious establishment with political secularism. Philos Public Issues 3:119–157

Laegaard S (2017) What's the problem with symbolic religious establishment. The alienation and symbolic equality accounts. In: Laborde C, Bardon A (eds) Religion in liberal political philosophy. Oxford University Press, Oxford

Nussbaum M (2008) Liberty of conscience: in Defense of America's tradition of religious equality. Basic Books, New York
Patten A (2014) Equal recognition. The moral foundation of minority rights. Princeton University Press, Princeton
Quong J (2011) Liberalism without perfection. Oxford University Press, Oxford
Rawls J (1993) Political liberalism. Columbia University Press, New York
Rawls J (2000) Justice as fairness: a restatement. Belknap Press of Harvard University Press, Cambridge
Raz J (1986) The morality of freedom. Oxford University Press, Oxford
Smith S (2001) Expressivist jurisprudence and the depletion of meaning. Md Law Rev 60
Thomson JJ (1993) Self-defense. Philos Public Aff 20:283–310
Vallier K (2011) Against public reason liberalism's accessibility requirement. J Moral Philos 8:366–389
Waldron J (1989) Autonomy and perfectionism in Raz' morality of freedom. South Calif Law Rev 62(1989):1097–1153
Wall S (1998) Liberalism, perfectionism and restraint. Cambridge University Press, Cambridge

Court Rulings

Lukumi Babalu v. City of Hialeah, 508 U.S. 520 (1993).
Lynch v. Donnelly, 465 U.S. 668 (1984).
McGowan v. Maryland, 366 U.S. 420 (1961).

Wojciech Ciszewski is assistant professor at the Jagiellonian University in Cracow (Faculty of Law and Administration, Department of Legal Theory). His research interests include political philosophy, legal philosophy, and contemporary ethics. The paper is the extended version of a speech titled "Nonconsequential Conceptions of State Neutrality" delivered during the XXVIII World Congress of IVR—"Peace Based on Human Rights," July 16–21, 2017, University of Lisbon, Portugal, in the Special Workshop "Is There a *Ratio Legis* and if So, How Many Are They?—The Most Powerful Method of Legal Reasoning Uncovered."

Is There an Imitative *Ratio Legis*, and if so, How Many Are There? Psychological Perspective

Teresa Chirkowska-Smolak and Marek Smolak

Abstract This paper seeks to demonstrate that certain *ratio legis* in democratic countries where the rule of law is well established is inadmissible in view of its imitative nature. Imitative *ratio legis* is the purpose of the legislator that aims at an ostensible solution of a social problem. Ostensibility means absence of will on the part of the legislator to have their activity produce effects. The only thing in evidence is an intention to engender a conviction among the addressees of the norms that such an effect does arise.

If we agree that ostensibility is inadmissible, then the question is in what way we can reject imitative *ratio legis*. We discuss three types of reasons in support of inadmissibility of imitative *ratio legis*. These are as follows: first, given non-compliance of legislation with the moral standards of the political community (Dworkin); second, in view of the imitative goal of the legislator or absence of a link between a prescribed/prohibited behaviour and the ostensible nature of the legislator's goal (Fuller); third, lack of conventional-moral relationship between the substance of a prescriptive provision and the goal of the legislator (MacCormick).

All of these types of reasons rely on three assumptions: moral community of judges exist; judges possess special moral competences in assessing which *ratio legis* is admissible and which is not; their moral reasoning can be characterised as rational. We argue that in the light of the achievements of contemporary moral psychology, above mentioned assumptions are at least doubtful. We are of the opinion that when

This paper was produced within the framework of a research funded by the National Science Centre (Narodowe Centrum Nauki) (OPUS 8 2014/15/B/HS5/00650). This paper is partly based on our ideas presented in Polish in the Polish Journal *Ruch Prawniczy, Ekonomiczny i Socjologiczny* (The Legal, Economic and Sociological Review) 2, 2017.

T. Chirkowska-Smolak (✉)
Adam Mickiewicz University, Faculty of Social Sciences, Poznań, Poland
e-mail: chirko@amu.edu.pl

M. Smolak
Adam Mickiewicz University, Faculty of Law and Administration, Poznań, Poland
e-mail: smolak@amu.edu.pl

V. Klappstein, M. Dybowski (eds.), *Ratio Legis*,
https://doi.org/10.1007/978-3-319-74271-7_7

formulating moral judgments, judges are not equipped with any special moral competence for settling moral dilemmas. We are of the view that since people are usually unaware of the factors affecting their moral judgment, we may assume that judges are similarly unaware of what drives their moral judgments about inadmissibility of *ratio legis*, and thus the assumption that their decisions are rational is mistaken. If we assume that contemporary findings of moral psychology as to the role of intuitions in the moral judgments are correct, one arrives at an obvious and 'classic' question about which manner of argumentation should be adopted in order to convince the doubtful. Some hope can be found in reasoning based on the idea of public reason.

1 Introduction

In the following article, we would like to achieve four goals: first, demonstrate that certain *ratio legis* in democratic countries where the rule of law is well established is nevertheless inadmissible in view of their imitative nature; second, demonstrate the moral reasons in support of rejecting of imitative *ratio legis*; third, show the role of moral fundaments in formulating moral judgments; fourth, explain why so often judges' moral reasoning cannot be characterised as rational.

We believe that the achievements of contemporary moral psychology help us to answer to these questions and show us that when judges make moral judgments, they also make many mistakes, especially when they base their judgments on intuitions.

Let us start with the definition of imitative *ratio legis*. Imitative *ratio legis* is the purpose of the legislator that aims at an ostensible solution of a social problem. It is a surrogate, a substitute of a law that would in actual fact rectify a social, political or economic problem as opposed to feigning it. Ostensibility means absence of will on the part of the legislator to have their activity produce effects. The only thing in evidence is an intention to engender a conviction among the addressees of the norms that such an effect does arise.

A good example of an imitative *ratio legis* may be found in the so-called remedial enactment of 22 December 2015, on the amendment of the Law of the Constitutional Tribunal (CT, Tribunal), whose Article 2 (3) stipulates as follows: 'The dates of hearings or hearings in camera during which petitions are examined, shall be appointed following the chronological order in which cases have been filed and received by the Tribunal'.[1]

If we agree that imitative *ratio legis* is socially and politically inadmissible, the question is: what are the reasons in support of rejecting imitative *ratio legis*? The answer may be demonstrated by means of three modes of argumentation, that is, argumentation suggested by Dworkin, argumentation formulated by Fuller and argumentation based on the conventional-institutional nature of the political community formulated by MacCormick.

---

[1]Journal of Laws of 2015, item 2217.

2 Three Modes of Argumentation in Support of Rejecting Imitative *Ratio Legis*

Characterisation of the argumentation suggested by Dworkin (1986) should begin with a description of the checkerboard statutes. In his *Law's Empire*, Dworkin poses the following questions:

> Do the people of North Dakota disagree whether justice requires compensation for product defects that manufacturers could not reasonably have prevented? Then why should their legislature not impose this 'strict' liability on manufacturers of automobiles but not on manufacturers of washing machines? Do the people of Alabama disagree about the morality of racial discrimination? Why should their legislature not forbid racial discrimination on buses but permit it in restaurants? Do the British divide on the morality of abortions? Why should Parliament not make abortions criminal for pregnant women who were born in even years but not for those born in odd ones?[2]

This latter question in particular conveys the essence of the so-called checkerboard statutes. A checkerboard statute sets out a criterion for differentiating between subjects in a manner modelled after the black-and-white arrangement of tiles on the board. Even more importantly, its provides for criteria such as even and odd years (black or white colour on the board, respectively), which as Dworkin argues are unacceptable from the moral standpoint. Dworkin noted that statutes of that kind are enacted when it is impossible to reconcile two moral orders where abortion is approved in one but not in the other. The adoption of the even/odd day of birth criterion, which statutes adopt as a basis for rendering a person criminally liable for the felony of abortion or for not deeming the act criminally liable, results from a legislative compromise that cannot be supported by any moral standards. In other words, the paradigm of even and odd numbers possesses no inherent reason that would justify such a solution. Naturally, checkerboard statutes are enacted very seldom, but it does not mean that such laws are not passed at all. In his article, Raban quotes the vivid example in Chinese legislation, which prescribes that nurses smile showing exactly eight teeth.[3]

The above example of checkerboard statutes warrants the conclusion that imitative *ratio legis*, just as checkerboard laws, cannot be underpinned by any moral standards due to their ostensible nature. If the above approach is assumed to be apt and correct, there arises the question why ostensibility cannot be reconciled with any moral standard and thus with the idea of the rule of law.

In order to answer the question, one may take advantage of Dworkin's requirement for an integral conformity of law with one 'scheme of justice' where that scheme refers to the entire legal system. When this integrity requirement is adopted, it must be presumed that all decisions of the legislator have to comply with the same scheme of justice. Imitative *ratio legis* should be rejected because they violate moral principles derived from that scheme of justice. In a situation where judges, in the first

---

[2]Dworkin (1986), p. 178.

[3]Raban (2015), p. 26.

place, note that statutes do not concur with the moral standards of the political community and, second, discern their imitative nature, they should find a coherent system of principles governing rights and obligations, as well as the best constructive interpretation of the political structure and legal doctrine of a given political community in order to reject such statutes.[4]

Imitative *ratio legis* may be distinguished from non-imitative ones on the basis of moral standards to which given political community subscribes. It is therefore possible to provide a moral rationale behind a norm that prescribes setting a hearing date while having regard for the systemic importance of cases. However, no moral rationale can be provided for a norm that imposes fixing dates for hearings depending on the even or odd number of the case file. Furthermore, a viable moral justification can be found for those *ratio legis* that genuinely aim to resolve social issues, but we are incapable of providing a moral argument for those *ratio legis* that only purport to solve the problem. Naturally, the moral reason in favour of non-imitative *ratio legis* is recognising that authenticity and honesty of legal solutions represent a moral good shared by the political community. And conversely, all ostensible legislative action, just as acts in the law consisting in absolute simulation, are immoral (absolutely invalid). This is due to the fact that ostensibility and simulation of resolving actual social, political or systemic issues do not entail a moral reason that one could identify. For instance, it is believed that the order of adjudicated cases depending on their importance is dictated by a moral reason shared by the political community. Obviously, a justification of that kind does not have to be accepted. However, it has to be acknowledged that a statute that stipulates an order of examined cases in view of their significance for the state system harbours a 'kernel of moral common sense'. In the statute that stipulates that the order of cases examined by the CT be decided by the date on which they are received, the 'kernel of moral common sense' is absent. In other words, imitative *ratio legis* is inadmissible as it offers no moral rationale for its enactment due to immoral content or its ostensible nature.

One could ask why authenticity of actions of the legislature is a moral good desirable in the public sphere and complies with the rule of law, whereas ostensibility of legislative actions is morally unacceptable, but given the tremendous number of pertinent publications (for instance, those concerned with the idea of social contractarianism), we feel excused from having to provide broader argumentation to that effect.

Since the above reservations can, to a certain extent, be recognised as valid, there is another argumentation to fall back upon, which circumvents the problems associated with adopting moral standards that a political community would have to share. What we have in mind is the value of the purpose of law advanced by Fuller. According to Fuller, drawing on the moral standard may be misleading because the crux of the matter lies in the inadmissibility of the goal of the legislator, as opposed to lack of moral dimension to the prescription itself. In other words, it is the appraisal of the goal of the legislator who designs to streamline the working of the Tribunal rather

[4]Dworkin (1986), p. 178.

than evaluation of the means in the form of prescription to hear cases as they are filed, which has a decisive significance in the assessment of whether the decision of the legislator is admissible or not.[5] In point of fact, an imitative *ratio legis* is inadmissible in view of the imitative goal of the legislator. In itself, the aim of rendering the work of the Tribunal more efficiently is acceptable, but the crucial element here is that the actual purpose of the legislator is unrelated to the prescribed behaviour. In the regulation that provides that 'dates of hearing shall be set while taking into consideration the date of their receipt', the legislator does not aim to recognise that the cases that were received at the most recent date are the most important, nor do they intend to assert that the most current cases have a novelty value. The goal is to reduce the efficiency of the Constitutional Tribunal. This is how we actually think about law: if laws lead towards accomplishing a goal, a goal that is inadmissible due to its ostensibility, it is unlikely that such statutes will be received with approval.

Incidentally, Fuller was of the opinion that formal requirements of law, such as public promulgation, sufficient generality and prospectiveness, to mention only a few, may substantially restrict the possibility of enacting imitative *ratio legis*. As we know, Fuller observed that under certain conditions, formal requirements of law inhibit taking legislative decisions that, apart from being irrational, do not conform to moral norms as well.[6]

The third mode of argumentation, which holds that certain *ratio legis* is permanently inadmissible due to its imitative nature, relies on the existence of a conventional-normative community based on the mutually shared conviction that a conventional-normative relationship occurs between the prescriptive provision and its goal.[7] Let us recall yet again the norm contained in the remedial enactment: 'The dates of hearings or hearings in camera during which petitions are examined, shall be set following the chronological order in which cases have been filed and received by the Tribunal.' Assuming that the aim of the rule is to render the judicial activities of the Tribunal more efficiently, the whole difficulty lies in determining the knowledge and the patterns of reasoning on the grounds of which it would be possible to justify the causal relationship between the above injunction and the aim asserted by the legislator. In order for a relationship to exist between a provision stipulating that 'the dates of hearings or hearings in camera during which petitions are examined, shall be set following the chronological order in which cases have been filed and received by the Tribunal' and the goal of the legislator—improvement/correction of the functioning of the Tribunal—a certain conventional-normative connection must occur. The connection derives from the fact that a relevant community respects specific conventional social practice, a practice founded on intentional, reciprocal expectations of the members of the community, anticipating certain and not other behaviours within the said community.

[5]Fuller (1964), pp. 46–88.

[6]Fuller (1964), pp. 77–78.

[7]MacCormick (2007), p. 18.

Let us illustrate the above conclusion using the following example. If a norm in force prescribes that 'dates of hearing or hearings in camera, during which petitions are examined, shall be set in regard to systemic importance of cases', then by virtue of collective intentionality we recognise that the legislator's aim behind the rule is to protect the systemic order of the state. The legislator knows that they will achieve that goal by enacting a rule formulated in that particular manner; both the interpreter and the legislator know of each other that they are aware of the particular aim of the rule, namely 'protection of the systemic order of state'. As may be seen, the above social practice is a kind of knowledge comprising information addressed to all members of the community: information on how one should proceed in particular situations so as to achieve particular results.

Consequently, implementation of the rule stating that 'the criterion of systemic importance shall be adopted as the criterion determining the order of cases to be heard by the CT' will necessarily depend on the potency of mutual social expectations that 'protection of the systemic order of state' counts as the goal of the regulation. Clearly, imitative *ratio legis* fails to meet that condition because mutual expectations of the members of a political community cannot effectively serve to demonstrate the conventional relationship between 'the dates of hearings or hearings in camera during which petitions are examined, shall be set following the chronological order in which cases have been filed and received by the Tribunal' and the aim of such provision: 'improvement of the functioning of the Tribunal'. Naturally, these expectations may vary from individual to individual. However, as a rule, a reference to mutual convictions, understood here as a reason for undertaking particular action, is made implicitly only when the interpreter belongs (which is usually the case) to the same community of social practice as the legislator. The specificity of that conventional-narrative community lies therein that effective achievement of the legislator's goals is necessarily contingent on respecting the community's reciprocal expectations as to the exact course of these actions. The aim can only be accomplished when other members of the conventional-normative community interpret those actions as serving to meet the objective of a given legal text while relying on appropriate mutual intentional convictions that they and the subject in question respect. This conventionalist approach is therefore founded on the notion that general conformity of human behaviours with a social rule is not only indispensable for the rule to exist, but it also determines the rule's capacity to create a reason for action, which it supplies to everyone whose behaviour is within the scope governed by the rule.[8]

To recapitulate the findings so far, the following has to be stated—imitative *ratio legis* is inadmissible in democratic countries where the rule of law is well established due to the inconsistency of *ratio legis* with moral standards of the political community (Dworkin); the imitative goal of the legislation or absence of a connection between the prescribed/prohibited behaviour and the goal of the legislator, which in fact constitutes an ostensible goal (Fuller); the absence of a conventional-normative link between the content of a prescriptive provision and its goal (MacCormick).

[8]Gizbert-Studnicki et al. (2016), pp. 343–344.

3 Formulating Moral Judgments by Judges. Psychological Perspective

These modes of argumentations, which hold that *ratio legis* is permanently inadmissible due to its imitative nature, rely on the existence of some kind of a conventional-normative community of judges based on the mutually shared moral judgments. But in the light of the above deliberations, one arrives at an obvious question: if judges are morally reasonable and community of judges respects specific conventional social practice, a practice founded on intentional, mutual moral judgments, why do they often have a different point of view about inadmissibility of *ratio legis*? An inquisitive reader may ask another question: on what grounds does one recognise that a given objective is inadmissible or cannot be admitted in the light of the concept of the rule of law? Why are efficiency and cohesion of the activities of judicial bodies an asset worthy of constitutional protection? Why do we recognise the efficiency and cohesion of the judicature as a desirable value that deserves constitutional safeguards?

As one could easily find, all of the above questions are essentially concerned with the moral fundaments upon which our moral judgments are validated. Since people are usually unaware of the factors affecting their moral judgment, we assume that judges are similarly unaware of the basis upon which our moral judgments are validated. They are unaware of what drives their moral judgments concerning inadmissibility of *ratio legis* as it offers no moral rationale for its enactment due to immoral content or its ostensible nature.

Therefore, our aim, based on achievements of moral psychology, is to show the role of moral fundaments in formulating moral judgments and explain why judges' moral reasoning cannot be characterised as fully rational. In other words, we would like to answer the question: why are there so many imitative *ratio legis*?

Due to the aims and scope of this study, we will not broach the classic controversy of whether the law is inextricably linked to morality or not. We will not focus on the intrinsic impact of philosophy, religion, lifestyles, values, moral standards, legal culture on the moral reasoning of judges. Without a doubt, philosophy, religion, lifestyles, values and moral standards all influence our moral choices, particularly when it comes to issues that evoke social and political controversy, such as the freedom of speech, violations of privacy or the legalisation of abortion. Furthermore, if we agree that judges have to function as moral arbitrators, it should be borne in mind that the judges' role may be affected by whether a given social practice is generally accepted by the political community or whether it is rejected by the majority of the community. If there is widespread agreement in a given political community, such as the consensus view that capital punishment is unacceptable, then the court's decision may be justified by appeal to general social approval for the constitutional values in question. However, we should mention that the appeal to social consensus is not always authoritative. It is possible to imagine a situation in which there is a broad consensus in a political community on the acceptability of the death penalty and yet, for example, a constitutional court decides that the penal law containing the death penalty is incompatible with the constitution. It is a very different situation when there is no general approval in the community, for example when we agree on the social or political importance of the abstract principle of the value of freedom of speech but we disagree over the practice of exercising that freedom.[9]

Bearing the aforementioned situations in mind, let us recall here the famous syllogism of J. Waldron:

1. Any decision concerning constitutional rights requires reference to moral arguments.
2. When justifying decisions on the basis of moral arguments, judges should have special moral competences.
3. Judges therefore have a special responsibility when making decisions in which they refer to constitutional rights.[10]

We challenge the second premise of the syllogism given above. If judges refer to constitutional rights when making their decisions, we assume that they do not have any special moral competence to resolve dilemmas that would distinguish them from legislators, for example. Of course, a proper understanding of constitutional rights and an ability to justify them are connected with moral reasoning, but the reasoning of judges is not necessarily morally superior to that of other actors in the public sphere. Nor is their reasoning morally superior to reasoning that is not devoted to the articulation of constitutional rights. And neither do we agree with the view that judges have acquired special moral powers as a result of their judicial practice, i.e. from the continuous resolution of moral problems, which has thereby supposedly equipped them with a special ability to empathise with or perceive real human problems. There is no empirical basis to the claim that judges possess unique moral competences due to their experience.[11] There are also no grounds for believing that moral thought experiments, which are an inextricable component of a judge's work when making decisions on factual disputes, are particularly privileged in relation to abstract moral reasoning based on principles or values. Let us now present some arguments in favour of that view.

According to philosophers, reasoning allows the human mind to transcend perception, customary habits and intuition and enables us to develop knowledge and make better decisions. In rationalism, pride of place is taken by the mind, which draws on the support of knowledge, information and experience, but also the emotions, in the pursuit of truth (rationalism treats the emotions as an important component of human nature and as a complement of the intellect). People can thereby evaluate and select accepted moral norms to guide their behaviour and, thanks to the arguments against certain behaviour, to condemn people who have behaved inappropriately. According to many philosophers (such as St. Thomas Aquinas or Kant), whether an act is ethically good or bad depends on whether it is consistent with reason, whereas the philosophers of the Enlightenment (e.g., Hume, Smith) argued that our moral judgments are not the result

[9]See e.g. Mancini and Rosenfeld (2010).

[10]Waldron (2009), pp. 2–4.

[11]Sadurski (2009), pp. 26–45.

of rational deduction or logical reasoning. Instead, they credited the emotions, or moral feelings, with bringing about the emergence of moral norms. In psychology, one can also find proponents of the view that reasoning is the best way to raise ethical awareness. Examples of this are provided by the views of Piaget, who held that morality is acquired with maturity, just like rationality, or the views of Kohlberg, who developed the theory of moral development and, following Piaget, argued that as they go through successive phases of development, children begin to better understand the reasons for observing moral norms, and they form their own, coherent moral system based on a deepening understanding of harm.[12] However, studies conducted in recent years have undermined this theory by showing, for example, that children react to violations of principles even at the age of three, before language and thought develop.[13]

Utilitarianism defines moral actions as those that maximise utility for a group and suggests that all actions should aim to maximise the general good, even if some individuals would suffer harm as a consequence. In this regard, utilitarianism shares similarities with more contemporary theories, such as the expected utility theory, from economics, or the theory of input-output analysis, from management psychology (which focuses on motivational concepts, such as the balance between effort and reward theory or the theory of equity). Utilitarianism requires us to make judgments on the basis of calculations, but does the human mind act like a computer? Psychology has demonstrated the weakness of economic theory when it is used to analyse moral decisions, based on the assumptions that the decision-maker makes optimal decisions and that the process can be described by means of a mathematical formula (optimisation concerns how to improve the fate of individuals in such a way that no one suffers). Numerous studies in the field of decision-making psychology (including studies where the decisions did not address moral issues) have shown that our decisions diverge significantly from optimal, rational processes and that we rely on heuristics and are prone to illusions.[14] The best example of this is perhaps the work of Kahneman and Tversky, due to their many years of experimental research and critique, which undermined the rationality model of human judgment. It's worth to notice, that in 2002, Kahneman was awarded the Nobel Prize in Economics.

As Tyszka observed, the term 'decision' is often accompanied by the term 'rational' or 'irrational'. We would of course prefer our decisions to be rational, and we are inclined to consider them as such. We tend to judge the quality of a decision in terms of its outcome, but while the positive consequences of a decision are associated with the rationality of the choice, the same consequences may in fact be the result of an irrational decision (and some decisions that are made with care and thought may have disastrous consequences). The rationality of decisions is determined by the decision-making strategy. Normative theories describe which decision-making strategies are best suited for which situations. For example, when dealing with a complex decision-making problem, a rational decision-making process would

[12]Kohlberg (1968), pp. 25–30.

[13]LoBue et al. (2011), pp. 154–170.

[14]Kahneman (2011), p. 11.

involve outlining the decision-making process and then carefully analysing the pros and cons. This could involve drawing a 'decision tree' that would make it easier to trace such a process. The alternative choices would have to be placed on the diagram, along with the consequences of these actions and the possible determinants of those consequences, and the rationale for the choice would be to decide on the action leading to the optimal outcome. The normative theory of decisions assumes that the choices made by decision-makers are generally rational, which allows us to build a utility function, which in practice enables decision-makers to make choices.[15]

However, we observe that people's preferences are not always consistent; they are also unstable, and therefore we should conclude that they violate the postulate of rationality. The question is: under what conditions does this happen? Knowledge of how people actually make decisions belongs to the descriptive theory of decision-making, which is generally accepted in contemporary psychology.

This is worth illustrating with the example of a study by Redelmeier and Kahneman on the ability to remember painful medical procedures. The memory of certain procedures may influence patients' future decisions—for example, it may result in them avoiding further examinations, even though they are necessary and recommended. Redelmeier and Kahneman observed that these memories are often inaccurate and prone to distortion. This was analysed in relation to procedures of the less invasive kind, but which are still painful, such as colonoscopy and lithotripsy (stone removal). While the procedures were taking place, patients provided information on the intensity of the pain and then afterwards retrospectively evaluated the painfulness of the whole experience. Comparisons revealed that the patients' memories were strongly influenced by two factors: the peak intensity of the pain and the intensity of the pain in the last stage of the experience (the last 3 min). However, the length of the experience did not have a significant effect on the evaluation of the painful memories, even though the duration of the procedures varied greatly among the individual patients (from a few minutes to over an hour). The patients' judgments turned out to be the average of the two pain evaluations, namely the peak intensity of the pain and the pain experienced in the final stage, which means that the judgments of pain were higher when the unpleasant experience increased during the procedure. This contrasted with situations when the peak intensity of pain was similar and the duration of the unpleasant experience was even longer, but the pain intensity decreased during the course of the procedure, so that it ended with less discomfort. In this case, the duration of the treatment (and suffering) was not significant.[16]

The results of numerous experimental studies conducted by psychologists defy explanation by means of the classical concept of utility; therefore, the theory of experienced utility was proposed. This theory takes into account the subjective perceptions of the individual, and this eventually led to the emergence of behavioural decision theory. The results of these studies, which have now been running for decades, show that decision-makers are generally far from rational. For example, we rarely entertain the idea that there are different perspectives other than the one that

[15]Tyszka (2010), p. 17.

[16]Redelmeier and Kahneman (1996), pp. 3–8.

we see the world from, and once we have identified a problem requiring a decision, only a few possible choices occur to us (and then we are prone to reducing these). When it comes to making decisions that are supposed to be classed as rational, we often lack information (about the situation, the cost associated with choosing each alternative, the potential consequences of the actions taken, etc.), and this is not only because this information is inaccessible but above all because we do not go out of our way to search for it. And even if this information were readily available, we still have a limited capacity for information, and so we limit the excess. Do judges have all the necessary information at their disposal in order for their decisions to be considered rational (assuming all the other conditions are fulfilled)?[17]

In this process, we also use internal information—we have information stored in our memories and even comprehensive evaluations of individual alternatives, but access to this information varies (e.g., it is easier for us to access information that is more frequently repeated or when information is fresh or more important). Not only do people have difficulty with extracting this information from their memory, but also—because the information is subject to different distortions, e.g. we only remember general outlines and simplified summaries—we do not remember the details. In fact, we can even remember events that never took place (so-called false memory) because our memory is constructive in nature, and recollection does not involve simply extracting previously memorised information but also involves the processes of reasoning and problem solving. Since we only remember the general idea, we reconstruct the details ourselves, and we can make inferences concerning events we did not participate in. Bearing this in mind, lawyers involved in court proceedings during which witness testimony is used should be aware that caution needs to be exercised in relation to what people disclose to the public.

Furthermore, the fact that people do not make full use of information, and in particular incorrectly estimate the likelihood of events, is further proof that the decision-making process is not entirely rational. Classic research by Tversky and Kahneman has shown that people are guided by heuristics when making judgments, which may indeed be useful, but at the same time these are simplistic inference methods that do not provide any assurance of certainty. In some situations, they may lead to an overestimation or underestimation of probability and to systematic errors.

In one study, Tversky and Kahneman presented their research on how people estimate the probability of a particular sequence of heads or tails occurring when a coin is tossed six times in a row. People regarded the most likely result to be H-T-T-H-H-T, while H-H-H-T-T-T was judged to be less likely, and the least likely sequence was felt to be H-H-H-H-T-H, which apparently does not reflect the 'fairness' of the coin. The probability of each of these sequences is, of course, the same because each time the probability of a head or a tail is 0.5, the tosses are independent and the coin, as Tyszka once noted, 'has no memory'. This error results from people's tendency to use heuristics, in this case the heuristics of representativeness, by means of which probability is assessed on the basis of the extent to which the event is similar to the population from which it is derived. In this way we ignore general patterns of regularity, our

[17]Kahneman (2000), pp. 673–674.

thinking fails to follow the laws of formal logic and we estimate the probability of an event's occurrence through the prism of conformity with our imagination.[18]

Consider, for example, the problem that judges have with the *in dubio pro reo* principle (which states that the defendant cannot be convicted if there is any reasonable doubt of their guilt). For a judge to establish the exact meaning of 'beyond reasonable doubt', it would require the judge to make a complex calculation of the probability of the defendant's guilt, taking into account the four consequences of the decision: the utility of convicting the defendant, the (negative) utility of convicting an innocent person, the (negative) utility of acquitting a guilty person and the utility of acquitting an innocent person. Whether the judge ultimately decides to convict or acquit the defendant depends on how the judge evaluates these four consequences (their utility).[19]

The rationality of the decision-making process (or the absence thereof) also reveals a great deal about how inferences are made. The consequences of actions that could be taken are not available to us; thus, inference allows us to form convictions concerning these inaccessible alternatives. We form such convictions on the basis of our experience or accepted theories. For instance, we observe the coexistence of phenomena (correlation), and then the appearance of one phenomenon leads us to assume that the second will also appear (e.g., we associate a high price with quality, so when something is expensive, we conclude that it must be good). When we rely on a small number of observations, the causal relationship between two events can be even more unreliable. Similarly, belief in naive, common sense theories is based on the tendency to perceive relationships between phenomena when there are no such relationships (apparent correlation). Therefore, a committee that makes decisions on the conditional release of a convicted person should not rely on decontextualised, isolated information concerning prematurely released offenders, i.e. instead of drawing on media reports on recent events, the commission should take into account the frequency with which those on conditional release offend (and better still, should take socio-demographic data into account, i.e. the frequency of crimes committed by those who have been released on a conditional basis, such as homeless men over the age of 50).[20]

What remains to us if we reject the assumption that moral judgments are fully rational? Some philosophers have focused on intuition. The intuitionist approach to morality, which takes into account the social context, is adopted by Haidt, for example. Haidt asserts that the cult of reason is an illusion—our conscious reasoning (the stream of words and images that we are aware of) makes up a miniscule part of our mental processes. Other processes operate beyond consciousness and determine most of our behaviour. Haidt's model is in line with Hume's idea that intuition is the most important source of moral judgment. Moral intuitions are fast and effortless, lying behind the assessments that we make every day, with most of them not even reaching the level of moral emotion. And since violations of social conventions may be treated more seriously in other cultures, i.e. as moral offences, Haidt added that people learn to apply moral intuition within

[18]Kahneman and Tversky (1972), pp. 430–454.

[19]Tyszka (2010), p. 238.

[20]Tyszka (1999), p. 145.

their culture (although he also pointed out that the effect of the social class can be greater than the effect of culture).

Haidt has been conducting research for many years, inspiring many psychologists. His research has involved presenting participants with stories related to, for example, violations of moral principles (or 'moral foundations'); among these stories were examples of violations of norms that did not result in any harm being caused to anyone. The participants were then asked to rate them and justify their judgments. The situations described were intended to elicit the participants' disgust, without indicating the victim who suffered as a result of the offender's behaviour, so that the participants did not have grounds for moral condemnation. The stories dealt with people doing something disgusting or disgraceful (such as adult siblings engaging in sexual intercourse) or disrespectful (for example, cleaning a toilet with the cut-up pieces of a national flag). The people presented in the stories carried out their acts in private, and thus they could not have offended the feelings of others. In addition, Haidt asked whether anyone suffered as a result of what the protagonists of the stories did, in order to mitigate the influence of perceived injustice. The results showed that the participants often made moral judgments quickly and emotionally but were unable to explain their moral intentions with ease. Haidt called this inability to provide verbal explanations for intuitive judgments 'moral dumbfounding'. In other studies, the experimenters attempted to influence and change the participants' ratings, by arguing that the story merely involved a violation of a convention, since no one had suffered, or by showing the logical errors in their explanations. However, the participants remained confident in their judgments, even though they could not identify the rationale behind them and often referred to the emotions they felt (e.g., disgust). This may indicate that moral judgments are created automatically, without the participation of supervisory cognition.[21]

Moral reasoning, according to Haidt, is 'a servant of moral emotion'. One of his essays is entitled 'The Emotional Dog and Its Rational Tail'—this metaphor illustrates that the primary purpose of moral reasoning is to find arguments that can justify a previously formulated opinion, thereby confirming the emotional responses of the participants. In Haidt's view, this concocting of reasons serves to provide a rational justification of instinctive feelings. This issue had been previously raised by Margolis, who argued that our mind is not computer-like, that ready-made judgments are formed by 'unconscious brain machinery' and that justifications were only formulated in after-the-fact rationalisations.[22]

Moral judgments are not ordinary opinions because they assert that someone else has done something wrong—something that has to be identified as going against our personal preferences. In such cases, we have to resort to moral reasoning. However, as Haidt argues, moral reasoning is not really about reconstructing the real reasons why a person has formulated one moral judgment rather than another but rather to find reasons that will encourage others to agree with our opinion.

Mercier and Sperber argue that we need to rethink what functions moral reasoning fulfils. They suggest that the argumentative function predominates as reasoning

[21]Haidt (2014), p. 69.

[22]Margolis (1990), pp. 13 et seq.

usually follows the formulation of a judgment, its purpose being to justify and thus influence others. Reasoning has an evolutionary basis—we provide post hoc arguments because we have to maintain our reputation; we want to make alliances and win favour among other members of the group. Therefore, Haidt adds that we should not expect people to produce correct and impartial reasoning that strives for the truth, especially in situations where their interest is involved: moral reasoning is an evolving skill that serves social ends.[23]

Concepts that attempt to explain how people make moral decisions emphasise either the influence of reason or emotion. As the above considerations show, recent decades have provided a great deal of evidence that has prompted psychologists to liberate themselves from the dominance of rationalism and to adopt the other philosophical position, i.e. the intuitionist approach. It is increasingly evident that moral judgments derive primarily from the emotions we experience, which compel us to view behaviour as being in conflict with the norms (of a given culture). Research in this area has been additionally inspired and supported by neurobiological analyses, which have been helpful in resolving the 'heart or mind' dispute (i.e., affect or cognition). It has also reanimated normative ethical debates concerning our obligations to others and ourselves.

Moral psychology is dominated by two main approaches: utilitarianism and deontologism. The philosophical debate over what principles our moral judgments should be based on has inspired many psychologists to conduct research on the process of moral judgment. The normative approaches of utilitarianism and deontology now form the basis for evaluating the quality of moral judgments and decisions. It is also possible to find results of psychological research showing that people adopt a utilitarian or deontological attitude in response to various factors. Do judgments based on utilitarian principles differ qualitatively from those made on the basis of deontological principles? And does research on cognitive biases or the use of heuristics in the decision-making process help in answering this above question?

Moral dilemmas are often used in research on how people make moral judgments. Neuroscientists have shown that while people grapple with these problems, different parts of the brain are activated, involving both cognitive and emotional processes. The most well-known dilemmas are the 'Trolley Problem' and 'the Footbridge' (which is a variant of the former). Although these dilemmas have been modified in various ways, they all boil down to whether it is acceptable to sacrifice one life in order to save five others. In the trolley problem, the participant is supposed to imagine that a runaway tram coming down the track will hit five strangers working on the track and kill them all if the participant does nothing. However, the five people can be saved if the participant redirects the tram to a sidetrack on which another man is working, also a stranger and also unaware of any danger. If the tram is redirected to save five people, this man will die. What to do in this situation? The footbridge dilemma presents a similar situation to the trolley problem, with the difference that the track runs under a bridge on which the participant is standing. Next to the participant on the bridge is another stranger, similar to those on the track. If the man is pushed from the bridge onto the track, his body will stop

[23]Mercier and Sperber (2011), pp. 57–111.

the tram and save the lives of five people, but the man will surely die. What should the participant do? The results of these dilemmas have shown that in the first case, most people choose to redirect the trolley. This is a utilitarian solution because sacrificing one person to save five others serves the 'greater good' as maximising utility basically entails minimising inevitable loss. In the footbridge scenario, most people say that they would not push the person onto the track and thereby kill him. So they opt for the deontological solution, meaning that they would not break a basic moral principle even in the name of the greater good. In both cases, the decision is related to breaking the moral prohibition on harming others (in this case, even killing another person), but the difference between the dilemmas hinges on whether it is a personal or an impersonal violation of norms.[24]

Greene used functional magnetic resonance imaging (fMRI) to investigate the brain at work and see what lies behind different solutions to moral dilemmas. Together with his co-workers, he came up with a series of stories that featured direct personal harm, usually inflicted for some legitimate reason, while other situations involved harm caused due to impersonal reasons, as in the trolley problem. Greene's aim here was to see whether the participants would make utilitarian or deontological choices and analyse the brain's involvement in each case. He observed that when formulating deontological judgments, people are guided by instinctive feelings (he also observed the participants' initial shock when imagining situations in which they inflict harm on someone else). At these times, the brain areas associated with emotion and social recognition (e.g., the medial prefrontal cortex) were activated. In contrast, the dilemmas relating to impersonal harm were more carefully thought out as they did not involve such emotions, and these deliberations increased the activity in the brain areas associated with abstract reasoning and problem solving (the anterior dorsolateral prefrontal cortex and inferior parietal lobes), and consequently the participants were free to explore different options and arrive at a utilitarian solution. On this basis, Greene and his colleagues proposed the dual-process theory of moral judgment. The first process is automatic, intuitive, sensitive to emotions and fast. It triggers rapid reactions to emerging emotions and leads to judgments based on simple moral principles. The other process is reflexive, slower and more sensitive to consequences.[25]

Thus, psychologists of morality are becoming increasingly convinced that utilitarian moral judgments are based on rational moral reasoning, whereas deontological decisions are emotional judgments, which are just accompanied by moral rationalisation—a justification of a decision previously made.[26] Consequently, when moral judgments deviate from utilitarian ones, some psychologists of morality, such as Sunstein, argue that they are based on heuristics, which leads to distortions and errors of judgment. Baron and Ritov even stated directly: 'Decisions based on deontological principles usually do not lead to the best results.'[27]

---

[24]Greene et al. (2004), pp. 389–400.

[25]Greene et al. (2004), pp. 395–400.

[26]Baron and Ritov (1994), pp. 133–167.

[27]Sunstein (2005), pp. 531–573.

If the utilitarian approach is adopted as the normative standard, this may entail that the majority of people make morally wrong decisions since, according to Mikhail's study, 90% of people reject the utilitarian solution to the footbridge dilemma. This would mean that moral decisions are even more susceptible to cognitive errors than other forms of judgment. Are people who choose utilitarian solutions the best judges of morality? What are the characteristics of this 10% of people who choose the utilitarian solution to the footbridge dilemma? On the one hand, these are clearly people who prefer rational deliberation when making moral judgments. On the other hand, it is evident that the same deliberative reasoning involved in the adoption of utilitarian solutions is hindered when decisions are taken when there is time pressure or increased cognitive load, e.g. when the participants simultaneously make a moral judgment and do a task in which they have to memorise a longer string of numbers.[28]

Bartels also observed that people differ in the degree to which they experience strong intuitions, in their ability to justify their reasoning and in their arguments (including their openness to the arguments of others).[29] Bartels' findings show that people who opt for utilitarian solutions tend to be more rational individuals—they have a better working memory, and their thinking is more rigorous when solving problems. But does this mean that these people are able to control the emotions that prevent us from hurting another person, or, as Bartels and Pizarro suggest, maybe they are unable to feel these emotions? Bartels and Pizarro noted that people with utilitarian preferences have the characteristics typical of psychopaths: low empathy, callousness (lack of emotional experience), an inability to relinquish the pursuit of short-term pleasure, impulsivity and aggressiveness without remorse.[30] To a certain extent, this is consistent with the results of studies of people with brain lesions in areas primarily responsible for emotions, who are more likely to use utilitarian solutions than healthy people (i.e., those who have not suffered such damage).[31]

During the last decade, largely influenced by Greene's numerous studies, the dual process theory of moral judgment has become increasingly popular. This approach is based on the hypothesis that the dichotomy between cognition and emotion is a false one because information processing involves both the higher cognitive processes, i.e. conscious reasoning, and the lower cognitive processes, such as memorisation, perception and emotion. In the footbridge dilemma, the primary, intuitive response is a refusal to push the stranger onto the track, although some people weigh up the consequences and change their minds. However, such an intuition may not occur (or occur in favour of a utilitarian solution) when it comes to solving the trolley problem, which demands less emotional involvement.[32] As was previously

[28]Mikhail (2007), pp. 143–152. Also: Greene et al. (2008), pp. 1144–1154; Cummins and Cummins (2012), pp. 1–16.

[29]Bartels (2008), pp. 381–417. See also: Koenigs et al. (2007), pp. 908–911.

[30]Bartels and Pizarro (2011), pp. 154–161.

[31]Moore et al. (2008), pp. 549–557.

[32]Greene et al. (2008), pp. 1144–1154.

mentioned, with strong affective reactions, other areas of the brain are involved than those activated by deliberate decision-making. When there is no initial strong affective reaction, deliberative reasoning prevails. When there is conflict between these areas, the brain recognises this and signals the need for cognitive control—everything depends on whether the area responsible for reasoning reacts to the signal: if it does, the result is that the judgment comes from the deliberate system; if not, the judgment is determined by the initial emotional response.

As Haidt wrote, the process of formulating moral judgments is a cognitive one, so in this sense it is like making any other judgment. There are two types of cognition: intuitions (quick, automatic moral judgments) and reasoning, which is based on language. Therefore, intuitions are a form of cognition, but they are not forms of reasoning. The research of neurobiologists presents a wealth of evidence that during the process of forming the kind of moral judgments that we make on a day-to-day basis, both reason and emotion play their roles, in an integrated way, while engaging in a variety of interactions. One example of this is Paxton and Greene's research, which presented participants with a number of moral dilemmas for judgment—dilemmas known from other studies, such as one-off incestuous sex between consenting adult siblings, which nobody would ever find out about. The authors then presented arguments in an attempt to change the participants' decisions (utilitarian—deontological). These arguments were either weak or strong (requiring more serious reflection). The neuroimaging study (fMRI) showed that the effects of emotional affects lasted for less than 2 min, so when the participants had time to think about the solutions (or were forced to think for a long time about the strong argument), they became much more tolerant. The participants who were presented with weak arguments continued to condemn the violation of moral principles, while those who had time for self-reflection often formulated a judgment that was contrary to their initial intuition. So there are grounds for optimism because this research shows that there are some 'switches' that allow for greater engagement of reasoning, particularly in the kind of situations where we would hope to see rational deliberation.[33]

The achievements of contemporary moral psychology inform us that when making moral judgments, we also make many mistakes, not only in using heuristics but especially when we base our judgments on intuitions. The role of emotions in making moral judgments is beyond doubt, thanks to the results of recent research, which highlights our limited cognitive ability when it comes to solving moral problems. The only question remaining is how important a role these abilities (and especially intuitions) play in the process of decision-making. This would be one of the explanations why judges have often a different point of view about inadmissibility of *ratio legis*, why they differ in recognising that a given *ratio legis* is inadmissible, why efficiency and cohesion have so many meanings. Moral psychology, using the results of neuroscientists, may be helpful in this regard, at least to a certain extent.

[33]Greene et al. (2001), pp. 2105–2108.

4 Idea of Public Reason

If we assume that contemporary findings of moral psychology as to the role of intuitions in the moral judgments are correct, one arrives at an obvious and 'classic' question about which manner of argumentation should be adopted in order to convince the so-called doubtful. Regardless of the numerous difficulties, it seems that the most expedient solution is to invoke the public nature of those reasons. In this respect, the best alternative is the idea of public reason conceived by Rawls.[34] Two arguments are vital here. First, Rawls clearly delineates the boundary between public and non-public reasons. Second, one of the traits of public reason is the presumption that citizens of a liberal-democratic society are reasonable.

Obviously, public reason is not necessarily shared by the entire community, not even a majority. Many other circumstances need to be allowed for; therefore, it cannot constitute a common standard. On the other hand, there are such public reasons that are adopted almost universally.[35] It is also true that the latter include some that tend to be adopted less than reasonably and rationally, for instance when such reasons are based on prejudice. Moreover, if the sources of knowledge about the moral convictions of the community's members lack credibility (being based on astrological signs, for example), then the consensus on invoking particular public reasons is exceedingly difficult to achieve.[36]

How should one appeal to a public reason in order to persuade the doubtful about the inadmissible nature of imitative *ratio legis*? Den Otter put forward an interesting solution to the problem: public reasons are such reasons that a reasonable sceptic could recognise as sufficiently convincing in a given argumentation.[37] These reasons would not stand the test in an ideal circumstance of deliberation. Nor are they the kind of reasons that every reasonable person in specific conditions could find particularly strong or that would be suitable as a rationale. These are reasons that such reasonable individuals could deem at least not unreasonable. To approach it from a different angle, argumentation relying on public reason should be conducted in such a fashion that a reasonable sceptic would be convinced. Hence, the standard in invoking public reason would be as follows: public reason may constitute a fundament of argumentation when it is a reason that could not be rationally questioned or challenged by any reasonable sceptic, in which the latter would bear witness to their own responsibility for the community of citizens. Regardless of the objections they may have, the sceptic could accept that public reason as sufficiently convincing or, at least, not unreasonable.[38]

Such a structure of public reason appears to be in line with the principles of liberal democracy since it calls for providing reasons that no reasonable sceptic would challenge (who, let us add, is a member of a democratic-liberal community characterised by reasonable pluralism), nor could they question a decision based

---

[34] Rawls (2001) pp. 1–19.

[35] Smolak (2015), pp. 89–96.

[36] Rawls (1999), pp. 133–134.

[37] den Otter (2005), p. 336.

[38] See above, p. 356.

on such reasons. In other words, no reasonable sceptic could impugn the imitative and thus inadmissible nature of imitative *ratio legis*. A reasonable sceptic may of course prefer decisions whose substance is different, but they have to be prepared to recognise the decision irrespective of their dissent to its substance.

Since people tend to be unaware of the factors that influence their moral judgments, so it can be expected that judges may be similarly unaware of the influences on their moral judgments—judgments that lead to formalised decisions, mistakenly believing that their ex post explanations were in fact the cause of the decisions. Therefore, appealing to public reasons enables each citizen, including those who strongly contest the adopted decision, to accept it as theirs, in the sense that it represents a product of a certain decision-making process whereby reasons are stated with respect to which one cannot reasonably raise reservations or doubts.[39]

References

Baron J, Ritov I (1994) Protected values and omission bias as deontological judgments. Psychol Learn Motiv 50:133–167

Bartels D (2008) Principled moral sentiment and the flexibility of moral judgment in decision making. Cognition 108:381–417

Bartels D, Pizarro D (2011) The mismeasure of morals: antisocial personality traits predict utilitarian responses to moral dilemmas. Cognition 121:154–161

Cummins D, Cummins R (2012) Emotion and deliberative reasoning in moral judgment. Front Psychol 3:1–16

den Otter R (2005) Can a liberal take his own side in an argument? The case for John Rawls's idea of political liberalism. Saint Louis Law J 49:336

den Otter R (2009) Judicial review in the age of moral pluralism. Cambridge University Press, New York, pp 15–21

Dworkin R (1986) Law's empire. Harvard University Press, Cambridge

Fuller L (1964) The morality of law. Yale University Press, New Haven

Gizbert-Studnicki T, Dyrda A, Grabowski A (2016) Metodologiczne dychotomie. Krytyka pozytywistycznych teorii prawa (Methodological dychotomies. Critics of positivistic legal theories). Wolters Kluwer, Warsaw

Greene J, Sommerville R, Nystrom L, Darley J, Cohen J (2001) An fMRI investigation of emotional engagement in moral judgment. Science 293:2105–2108

Greene J, Nystrom L, Engell A, Darley A, Cohen L (2004) The neural bases of cognitive conflict and control in moral judgment. Neuron 44(2):389–400

Greene J, Morelli S, Lowenberg K, Nystrom L, Cohen J (2008) Cognitive load selectivity interferes with utilitarian moral judgment. Cognition 107:144–1154

Haidt J (2014) Prawy umysł. Dlaczego dobrych ludzi dzieli religia i polityka? (The righteous mind: why good people divided by politics and religion?). Smak Slowa, Sopot

Kahneman D (2000) Experienced utility and objective happiness: a moment-based approach. In: Kahneman D, Tversky A (eds) Choices, values and frames. Cambridge University Press, New York

Kahneman D (2011) Thinking, fast and slow. Farrar, Straus and Giroux, New York

Kahneman D, Tversky A (1972) A subjective probability: a judgment of representativeness. Cogn Psychol 3:430–454

[39]den Otter (2009), pp. 18–22.

Koenigs M, Young L, Adolphs R, Tranel D, Cushman F, Hauser M, Damasio A (2007) A damage to prefrontal cortex increases utilitarian moral judgments. Nature 446:908–911
Kohlberg L (1968) The child as a moral philosopher. Psychol Today 2(4):25–30
LoBue V, Nishida T, Chiong C, DeLoache JS, Haidt J (2011) When getting something good is bad: even three-year-olds react to inequality. Soc Dev 20:154–170
MacCormick N (2007) Institutions of law. An essay in legal theory. Oxford University Press, Oxford
Mancini S, Rosenfeld M (2010) The judge as moral arbiter? The case of abortion. In: Sajó A, Uitz R (eds) Constitutional topography: values and constitutions. https://ssrn.com/abstract=1721644
Margolis H (1990) Patterns, thinking and cognition. A theory of judgment. University of Chicago Press, Chicago
Mercier H, Sperber D (2011) Why do humans reason? Arguments for an argumentative theory. Behav Brain Sci 34:57–111
Mikhail J (2007) Universal moral grammar: theory, evidence and the future. Trends Cogn Sci 11:143–152
Moore A, Clark B, Kane M (2008) Who shalt not kill? Individual difference in working memory capacity, executive control, and moral judgment. Psychol Sci 8:549–557
Raban O (2015) The rationalization of policy: on the relation between democracy and the rule of law. N Y Univ J Legislation Public Policy. https://ssrn.com/abstract=2564548 or https://doi.org/10.2139/ssrn.2564548, p 52
Rawls J (1999) The idea of public reason revisited in: the law of peoples. Harvard University Press, Cambridge
Rawls J (2001) Collected papers. In: Freeman S (ed) Harvard University Press, Cambridge
Redelmeier DA, Kahneman D (1996) Patient's memories of painful medical treatments: real-time and retrospective evaluations of two minimally invasive procedures. Pain 66(1):3–8
Sadurski W (2009) Rights and moral reasoning: an unstated assumption – a comment on Jeremy Waldron's "Judges as moral reasoners". Int J Const L 1(7):26–45
Smolak M (2015) The method of reflective equilibrium in moral reasoning. Arch Philos Law Soc Philos 1:89–96
Sunstein C (2005) Moral heuristics. Behav Brain Sci 28:531–573
Tyszka T (1999) Psychologiczne pułapki oceniania i podejmowania decyzji (Psychological traps of judgement and decision). GWP, Gdańsk
Tyszka T (2010) Decyzje. Perspektywa psychologiczna i ekonomiczna (Decisions-psychological and economic perspective). Scholar, Warsaw
Waldron J (2009) Judges as moral reasoners. Int J Const L 1(7):2–24

Teresa Chirkowska-Smolak is a professor at Adam Mickiewicz University, Faculty of Social Sciences, Institute of Psychology, and Head of Work and Organizational Psychology Department. Her main research areas are organisational behaviour, work engagement, moral psychology. The article is the extended version of a speech "Moral Reasoning and Imitative Ratio Legis Institutional and Psychological Perspective" given during the XXVIII World Congress of IVR—Peace Based on Human Rights, 16–21 July 2017, University of Lisbon, Portugal, in the Special Workshop "Is There a *Ratio Legis* and if So, How Many Are There? – The Most Powerful Method of Legal Reasoning Uncovered".

Marek Smolak is a professor at Adam Mickiewicz University, Faculty of Law and Administration in Poznań and Head of Theory and Philosophy of Law Chamber. His main research areas are jurisprudence, constitutional law, legal interpretation, human rights law and moral and political philosophy. The article is the extended version of a speech "Moral Reasoning and Imitative Ratio Legis Institutional and Psychological Perspective" given during the XXVIII World Congress of IVR—Peace Based on Human Rights, 16–21 July 2017, University of Lisbon, Portugal, in the Special Workshop "Is There a *Ratio Legis* and if So, How Many Are There? – The Most Powerful Method of Legal Reasoning Uncovered".

Part III
What Practical Implications Can *Ratio Legis* Have?

Immanent *Ratio Legis*? Legal Forms and Statutory Interpretation

Konstanze von Schütz

Abstract The chapter explores the idea of an "immanent" *ratio legis* and assesses possible impacts of this conception for statutory interpretation. It asks if and how it is possible to extend a view of law as immanently rational to the understanding of *ratio legis* in the context of statutory interpretation, and tries to establish the outline of a method of interpretation responding to the specific requirements and challenges presented by an "immanent" *ratio legis*.

I begin by an exploration of the notion of *ratio legis* as it can be commonly encountered in statutory interpretation. I retrace the grounding of the prevalent interpretive methodology and show how it is based on a view of purpose and rationality as (necessarily) extrinsic to law.

I then introduce the idea of law as immanently rational as it is put forward by the Formalist theory developed in the work of Ernest J. Weinrib. An account of his Formalist approach to law focusing on legal forms, coherence, law's immanent rationality, and immanent intelligibility will provide the necessary basis for further assessment of the impact of an "immanent" *ratio legis* on interpreting posited norms.

In a final step, I then try to apply this account of Legal Formalism to the interpretation of positive law, and tentatively sketch out an interpretive methodology in line with the theory. I will highlight its potential but equally point out some of the challenges that such an approach might face.

1 What Is *Ratio Legis*? The Need to Uncover a Powerful Argumentative Move

The German lawyer most frequently encounters the idea of *ratio legis* in the context of statutory interpretation. More precisely, it is associated with the "teleological" method of interpretation that asks for the *ratio legis* of a (specific) provision in order

K. von Schütz (✉)
University of Toronto, Faculty of Law, Toronto, ON, Canada
e-mail: konstanze.vonschuetz@mail.utoronto.ca

V. Klappstein, M. Dybowski (eds.), *Ratio Legis*,
https://doi.org/10.1007/978-3-319-74271-7_8

to reveal this provision's meaning. This "teleological" branch of the interpretive *canones* (the four main methodological approaches to statutory interpretation used in the German-speaking context) asks for the *telos*, the purpose of a legal rule, and in order to do so, it refers to the *ratio legis* as indicating what this purpose is.[1]

This will resonate with colleagues from many other jurisdictions, familiar with interpretive approaches looking for the purpose of a provision in order to identify its meaning.[2]

Invoking the *ratio legis* in support of a specific way of understanding an unclear provision, so it is frequently viewed, counts among the most powerful argumentative moves, as among the strongest "tools" at a lawyer's disposal. The underlying assumption seems to be that an understanding in line with the *ratio legis* of a given legal rule deploys particularly compelling force. Even if a number of other arguments might be put forward, relying on a specific interpretation corresponding to a provision's *ratio* often takes "pride of place."[3]

In light of all this, it seems to be all the more surprising that, as has also been observed elsewhere,[4] what exactly the *ratio legis* is, where it comes from, and where it can be found is far from self-evident and obvious. Already upon first sight, several competing manners of defining and understanding *ratio legis* are conceivable. We could start by thinking of *ratio legis* as "reason". But is the *ratio legis* necessarily the reason for, or behind law, or could it not also refer to the reason of law?

Does *ratio legis* perhaps point to "rationality"? What, then, is the exact nature of this relation between rationality and law? Is the *ratio legis* the expression of a different rationality into law, or is law—and also every specific provision—to be seen as rational on its own, and the *ratio legis* as designating this specific rationality?

---

[1]See for example Larenz (1979), p. 336; Bydlinski (1982), p. 454.

[2]For instance under the label of "purposive interpretation", see only compilation offered by Barak (2005), pp. 87–89 mapping the connection between telos, purpose and *ratio*. I do not intend to neglect the existing differences between what the German lawyer refers to as "teleological" and what her Anglo-American colleague will mean by "purposive" interpretation [see for a more detailed depiction of purposive interpretation in Anglo-American law: Fikentscher (1975)], notably when it comes to the possible existence of an "objective" telos (see further: below at 6) and the impacts of an "originalist" understanding in the context of constitutional interpretation. However, I consider it to be sufficient here to point out that both share their orientation to some "purpose" the law serves to achieve and pursues (be this identified from an objective or from a subjective standpoint) and that this purpose—once identified—indicates how to best understand the provision. I therefore view it as permissible to leave it open for another occasion to further explore the exact relation of "purposive" and "teleological" interpretation.

[3]I do not ignore the vivid discussion about the relation of different methods of interpretation (i.e. how the approach looking at the provision's wording relates to the ones looking at its legislative history, the provision's systematic context or: its *telos* etc.; see only for the different positions defended in German-speaking context: Zippelius (2005), p. 62; Larenz (1979), pp. 334 seq.). Nevertheless, it should be noted that all too often, the way in which arguments based on the *ratio legis* are *de facto* treated lets them appear as superior indicators of an unclear provision's correct understanding.

[4]Larenz (1979), p. 157; Reimer (2016), p. 173.

In addition to fostering a better understanding of what *ratio legis* is, answers to these questions can ultimately also enlighten us on the very conception of legal interpretation that is presupposed, respectively entailed. Being able to provide answers provides further guidance on what the theoretical assumptions are that seemingly allow to understand posited law by looking at its *telos*/purpose, how this is exactly connected to the notion of *ratio legis*, and so ultimately from where an argument referring to *ratio legis* draws its particular force.

As with many other things, closer scrutiny of the seemingly familiar, instead of revealing more details, often first creates more blurriness and confusion. But it also opens up new angles of view and can point to aspects worth exploring. I set out to start by, perhaps, creating some "blurriness" in the first place, but will hopefully ultimately offer a clearer picture, detecting and uncovering the operation of interpretive arguments based on *ratio legis*, as well as their conceptual background, so as to then proceed with the development of an alternative view.

I will therefore start by carving out the understanding of *ratio legis* in the prevalent interpretive approaches and only in a subsequent step examine the possible impact of a conception of *ratio legis* as expressing law's immanent rationality on the method of legal interpretation.

In what follows, I will take the notion of *ratio legis* as encountered in the context of prevalent methods of statutory interpretation as my point of departure, and my analysis will mainly focus on statutory interpretation, too. I am neither going to look at contractual interpretation, nor will I sound out particular aspects of constitutional interpretation.

2 *Ratio Legis* Only as Extrinsic Purpose and Rationality?

Starting from the foregoing observations regarding the open questions on how to understand *ratio legis*, I do not intend to say that the long-established method of teleological interpretation in law is operating on shaky ground or even in a vacuum. Instead, my intention is to unfold the conceptual framework in which it inscribes, and to uncover the conception of *ratio legis* as understood by the prevalent approach, in order to generate the platform from where to begin the developing of a potentially viable alternative approach.

In doing so, I will focus on a notion of *ratio legis* against the background of the interpretive methodology developed and used in the German-speaking context. The theoretical underpinnings of the related debates appear to be paradigmatic examples of the connection between *ratio legis* and legal interpretation according to a view fairly widespread in other jurisdictions, too. For this reason, the analysis I will conduct allows to gain insight into the intricate connection between rationality, purposiveness and interpretation also applicable on a larger scale.

2.1 Interpretation and the Voluntarist Conception of Law

Before exploring one particular method of interpretation, it should in the first place, be reminded when it is necessary to have recourse to statutory interpretation. Broadly speaking, this is the case when the meaning of posited law is unclear.[5] This is in particular so where there is insecurity as to whether a specific provision applies to the dispute at hand, or, when the provision's application is beyond doubt, there are uncertainties with respect to the legal consequences it prescribes.[6]

What is more, the discussion about *ratio legis* and interpretive methodology has, as any discussion about legal interpretation, inevitably to be seen in to be seen against the background of debates about the overall view of law and the legislative process. Any theoretical conception of law is reflected in a corresponding position about its "correct" interpretation. To the same extent that any broader perspective on law devises an image of what a set of posited norms should look like, it suggests how they are to be best understood.[7]

The prevalent understanding of interpretation referred to in my introductory remarks has, for instance, been described as the result of a move from idealism to voluntarism in the overall conception of law.[8] This notably results in the fact that positive law is conceived of as based upon a specific, often: legislative[9] will and not as following any innate principles of ordering.[10]

This view has significant consequences for the corresponding interpretive methodology: when trying to understand what a posited law means, to which situations it applies and which consequences it prescribes, regard is to be had to the (legislative) "will" it translates. In line with this, the teleological *canon* of interpretation then informs the interpreter about the "meaning" of a law via the identification of the

---

[5]See for example: Wank (1997), p. 29: identification of "meaning" as the overall goal of interpretation.

[6]Cf. Larenz (1979), p. 298. For the present purposes, an analysis of one particular method of interpretation, I hold it defensible not to turn in further detail to the question if the very determination of a situation of unclarity is not itself already the result of a first interpretive step. This question pertains to a discussion about interpretation on a more general level. In addition, sometimes matters of "gap-filling" are equally discussed under the heading of interpretation. However, as the question how to deal with scenarios that are seemingly not covered by existing legal rules indisputably calls for a further development of the law (often referred to as "construction"), I will not examine this issue here.

[7]See for example Marmor (1992), in particular pp. 155-184 on the role of intent for legal interpretation. For the fundamental character of the connection between legal theory and a theory of interpretation, see only: Barak (2005), pp. 54 seqq.; MacCormick (1978), in particular pp. 229–264.

[8]For a more detailed description of the history of ideas underlying methodological considerations of legal interpretations, see notably: Schröder (2012), pp. 62, 64, 145–146, 236 highlighting important aspects of the development of the idea of *ratio legis* and legal interpretation.

[9]For a more moderate position developed in the German-speaking context that refers to an "objectified" will rather than only to a legislator's subjective will, see below at 6.

[10]See only Schröder (2012), p. 365.

"willed" purpose it is meant to achieve. It is viewed as one of the possible ways of identifying the "will" animating a yet unclear provision.[11] And in doing so, the teleological method seems also to be based on a view of *ratio legis* as by and large synonymous with this purpose. It has even been suggested that, due to this proximity of will and purpose, under the voluntarist conception, the very idea of *ratio legis* essentially collapses with the notion of will.[12]

This equalization might also explain why it is that the argument invoking *ratio legis*/purpose is considered to be so compelling. When trying to understand a will, identifying what it aims at, what it "wills" seems to be a particularly promising attitude.

In sum, according to the prevalent understanding, the search for law's goal is thus viewed as generating a possible way of gaining access to law's meaning, understood as the "will" animating it. In this spirit, one refers to the *ratio legis* to describe the goal, the purpose, or the *telos*, of the legal rule, that, once identified, indicates its meaning.

2.2 Locating "Will" and Purposiveness

But where exactly is the interpreter to look for this "will" that determines not only the meaning of the statute more generally but also its particular purpose, identified as its *ratio legis* in the "voluntarist" conception?

We could start by saying that the will embodied in positive law designates uniquely the legislative will at the moment when the law was enacted.[13] Purpose is thus "inserted" into positive law through the legislative process only and by a legislative body motivated and animated by its own specific concerns, including those stemming from the genuinely political context. Understanding the meaning of any posited law thus necessarily has to pass via this specific legislative body as an intermediary. Only by retracing this legislator's purposive action will the interpreter gain access to the "meaning" and provide clarification of a provision's ambiguous aspects.

Following this line of thought under which all posited law expresses a (subjective) legislative will, the interpreters consequently have to look outside the realm of Law and identify these externally defined purposes in order to have access to a law's meaning when they adopt the teleological approach. Positive law reflects the legislator's rationality which is, to the same extent as the purpose this rational legislator

[11]See for example Zippelius (2005), p. 41.

[12]Cf. notably Schröder (2012), p. 366. This position likening the "will" to the overall goal of interpretation: the meaning of law is particularly present in German methodology.

[13]This view falls together with what the German debate labels as the—overall—"subjective" view of interpretation. For a more detailed analysis of the relation of the respective *canones* in the German-speaking tradition to the overall aim of legal interpretation, see Larenz (1979), pp. 302–305; Zippelius (2005), pp. 21–24; Reimer (2016), pp. 123–124. In other traditions, the idea of identifying a subjective will is referred to as "purposive" interpretation and we encounter it rather as a specific method than as a statement about the overall goal of interpretation.

pursues necessarily located entirely "outside" the law itself. The rational[14] legislators—on this view—use positive law to pursue a goal they determine. Purpose (and *ratio legis*) are to be understood as the expression of these legislators' rationality only and it follows that the *ratio legis* in any interpretive exercise is necessarily external to law, too.

Pursuing another line of thought, we could suggest a more objectified conception of the "will", occasionally even completely detached from the subjective will of a particular legislative body at a particular moment in time, and argue that a provision's purpose can be determined with some degree of independence, referring not to the legislative but to the law's will.[15] The purpose indicating the meaning of law would thus not be the purpose pursued by a particular legislative body at a particular moment in time but a more "objectified" one.

It is essential to note, however, that those objectified aims do not differ in nature and substance from those aims which a specific legislative body could pursue. But in contrast to the view just outlined, they can be said to be woven into the fabric of all positive law, creating and underlying their own momentum.[16] They can animate positive law without a legislator specifically aiming at this.

While this view thus suggests a (possibly far-reaching) detachment from a legislator, it nevertheless adheres to the notion of purpose as external to law itself. Even in this understanding, positive law always wills something else but never wills "Law" itself. Consequently, even an objectified goal is something that uses posited law as a means to be realized and—in turn—is indispensable for understanding the "instrument's" meaning. As in the first line of thought, positive law is not expressing its own rationality but serves as a vehicle for a differently located rationality. So, again, in order to seek "understanding" of the specific provision at hand, regard is necessarily to be had outside the Law. An external orientation is required in order to identify the provision's purpose, and consequently also the *ratio legis* is a moment external to law itself.

---

[14]By "rational" in this context, I do not necessarily mean "reasonable", but merely as "disposing of reason".

[15]See Schröder (2012), p. 368 for a compilation of different conceptions of the "objective" understanding. For example: Larenz (1979), pp. 336–337 argues that law's objective-teleological dimension can even result in a *ratio legis* carved out from systemic considerations ex post facto and thus is impossible to make for the legislator. In the same vein, Bydlinski (1982), p. 454 suggests to look at objective-teleological elements for interpretation in cases when the legislative will is obscure. This understanding of teleological interpretation corresponds to an objectively conceived "will of the law" interpretation aims at identifying. The currently predominant view on the role of legislative will in interpretation shared by most academics and German courts is to resort to an "objectified" legislative will. It is acknowledged that the subjective will of the particular historical legislator is decisive as a starting point but that—especially over time—law's purpose gains some degree of independence, see for example Federal Court BGH (decision rendered 30.06.1966), BGHZ vol. 46, p. 76, Wank (1997), p. 32.

[16]Such as "efficiency", "wellbeing", or more generally: "the attainment of the social good", see Larenz (1979), p. 322.

This external determination of law's purposes in both lines of thought explains their characterization as "instrumentalist".[17] By this, I mean that law's objective, its purpose, necessarily lies in the realization of something beyond—be it a goal as defined by a specific legislative body or a goal that is somehow "objectified" over time. Positive law is always an instrument serving other ends than law but can never be understood as connected with an idea of law as an end in itself. The assumption that a "will" needs to be identified in order to understand its "product" automatically creates a distinction between the two. And insofar as the teleological *canon* sets out to inquire into this *telos*, it is premised on the idea of a distinction of law and the will/ the idea animating and guiding it.

So, for all possible manners to think about *telos*/purpose under the prevalent approach (centered around the notion of "will"), law pursues "something," but this "something" is always to be found elsewhere than in law itself—just as the *locus* of rationality giving rise to the determination of the purpose to be pursued. What is more, the prevalent position must readily accept that purposes can change over time, either by a change in the decision of the legislator or by shifts and modifications in the "social realities" they govern.[18] And as those purposes change, so does the correct understanding of positive law in line with them. The teleological method helps to identify the one—among a possibly infinite variety of purposes—that the respective provision is meant to achieve.[19]

From this, it also becomes clear that, following the prevalent approach, law cannot be self-sufficiently understandable, it always refers to something else. The purpose that the teleological/purposive approach to legal interpretation aims to identify can only be defined externally. Only by identifying this (external) purpose to the attainment of which this law is the intermediary can we, in the process of (teleological) interpretation, obtain access to its meaning.

In sum, none of the approaches just outlined would stop their interpretive undertaking at the stage of "the law itself" but instead look for and to some goal lying beyond that is to be realized. There is the indispensable necessity for something external in order to determine what the positive law should achieve. And when we look at law's purpose in the context of interpretation, we must necessarily look beyond law itself to find it.

The prevalent approach to statutory interpretation thus conceives of *ratio legis* as something necessarily external to law, for it is understood as synonymous with externally determined purposes that posited norms seek to achieve. These purposes being necessarily external, posited law can clearly never serve to realize Law itself. Instead, in order to find the appropriate *telos*, we have to identify it among a possibly infinite multitude of extra- and non-legal considerations.

---

[17]Cf. Weinrib (2012) pp. 49–50.

[18]See only: Zippelius (2005), pp. 24– 27.

[19]See for example Bydlinski ((1982), p. 473) who speaks of "rationes legis" and so presumes the possibility of a multiplication and variance.

This approach would most likely disqualify any interpretive enterprise looking solely to Law itself to learn about the latter's purpose as self-referential, circular, and therefore no fertile ground in the search for access to the meaning of the provision at hand. In fact, such positions, lacking the mediating external moment, might from the prevalent vantage point, simply be holding a view of law that does not bespeak any rationality at all.

2.3 Immanent Rationality and a Noninstrumental Conception of Law? Introducing an Alternative Conception

But does this have to be the case? Does the connection between purposiveness and rationality automatically imply an outwardly directed view when we seek to find law's meaning? Is there necessarily only room for conceiving of *ratio legis* in statutory interpretation as expressing a rationality external to law?

As I have pointed out earlier, a different view of Law might call for a different approach to legal interpretation and its associated methodology. The ideas outlined in the previous sections have been developed against the background of a "voluntarist" view of posited law, but how would a different view affect them?

In order to turn to these issues in more detail, I will introduce the idea of immanently rational Law that has been presented and developed in the Formalist theory of Ernest J. Weinrib.[20] For reasons of definitional clarity, in this chapter, reference to Formalism shall thus be understood to refer to his ideas only.[21] My choice of Weinrib's Formalism is motivated by my effort to ask if a view of law as immanently rational can be used to develop the idea of an immanent *ratio legis* and to assess the possible impact that such an immanently conceived *ratio legis* in the

---

[20]Weinrib's basic claim that there can be a level of law lying beyond the posited law makes very transparent that his Formalist position is grounded in a view of law closer to "Idealism" than to "Voluntarism" as described above (see *supra* note 8).

[21]As it has been pointed out elsewhere, the exact meaning of "Formalism" is not unequivocally clear, resulting in a too large variety of approaches to law being grouped together as "Formalist". (See only the overview provided by Schauer (1988), pp. 509–520, Stone (2012), pp. 170–171, Weinrib (1993a), p. 583 with further references; but also discussion of "positivist" and "natural law" definitions of Formalism, Weinrib (1988), p. 954 fn. 14). However, not all of those approaches explore the dimension of Law's immanent rationality to the same extent. What is more, in the attempt to draw out the "major common denominator" of the set of Formalist theories, they have often been boiled down, sometimes oversimplified and on a few occasions simply derided, as exemplified in the labeling as theories of "mechanical jurisprudence" by Roscoe Pound. This is not to deny that there are features clearly distinguishing all "Formalist" approaches to law from other lines of thought, in particular the idea that law is an autonomous discipline (see below at 11). I do however not intend to provide an exhaustive account of Formalism, but am interested in the connection between immanent rationality and legal interpretation and it is in this respect that Weinrib's Formalism provides a suitable starting point for my inquiry.

context of statutory interpretation can have on interpretive methodology.[22] Weinrib's version of Formalism is particularly well suited to do so as it refuses to consider any external, "instrumental" purposes in the process of understanding law. For him, "Nothing is more senseless than to try to understand law from a vantage point entirely extrinsic to it"[23] and the only possible way to render law "intelligible" is by means of adopting an extreme internal standpoint.[24]

This strict refusal to consider external, instrumental aspects in the process of understanding appears to refuse the implied equalization of *ratio legis* and external purpose. Especially the too ready look to the sphere of politics in the search for purpose is viewed with significant scepticism.

This is not to say that the Formalist view advocates for a complete detachment of law from all other disciplines—quite the contrary is true.[25] But it is the idea of locating all possible sources of rationality and purposiveness necessarily outside in order to inquire into law and its purpose that the Formalist view opposes.

Weinrib's ideas have generated much thought, appreciation, and criticism since they were first presented. This concerns especially the part of the theory identifying corrective justice as the underlying form of and for Private Law and its subsequent application to tort law. A dimension that, however, remains relatively underexplored to present day are the precise implications of his views about law's immanent rationality on legal interpretation.[26]

Clearly, it has to be borne in mind that the main focus of Weinrib's thoughts are centered on law "as a mode of ordering, not as a set of posited norms."[27]

But even though Weinrib's theory essentially encompasses Law in its most abstract dimensions, the possibility of an immanent intelligibility and its repercussions on the possibility to "understand" also provide valuable insights for an interpretive methodology of positive law. The issue of law's immanent rationality undeniably percolates into the questions about what positive law should look like

---

[22]In this paper, I want to concentrate on the "Formalist" side of Weinrib's theory and leave further considerations with respect to the appropriate forms of justice and the implication of Kantian Right aside. Especially against the background that it is suggested that legal formalism is one of the three theses constituting "The Idea of Private Law" (see Weinrib 2012, p. 18), separating the theory in this way seems to be defensible.

[23]Weinrib (1988), p. 952.

[24]Weinrib (1988), p. 952.

[25]See only Weinrib (1988), pp. 1002–1008 and Weinrib (2012), pp. 214–222 with a focus on the perspective of Private Law.

[26]Superposing a theory of law developed in a common law context and against the background of tort law as an area of Private Law (still strongly permeated by case-law-oriented reasoning, focusing on underlying ideas), with a methodological canon developed in a civil law context (expressing the "civilian", more "textual" mode of reasoning) presents an acknowledged challenge to my undertaking. I will still attempt to establish dialogue where there seems to have been much "talk at cross purposes" in the past. The observations I will make are of overarching pertinence, encompassing both the common law, as well as the civilian tradition.

[27]Weinrib (1988), p. 957 fn. 27.

and how to best understand and interpret it. This is especially true as Weinrib's Formalism self-identifies as an "evaluative theory". It is considered to bear in itself the critical potential to assess if the posited norms live up to the ideal that the theory stipulates.[28] Its ideal conception then also posits a benchmark for the appropriate interpretation of these posited norms.[29]

When we consult Weinrib's writings for details related to the methodology of interpreting positive law, we can find a few hints, for instance in the following description:

> The Formalist construes the doctrines, institutions and concepts of a sophisticated legal system as embodying the intelligible structures of external interaction and therefore as expressing in positive law the forms through which judicial coherence can be achieved.[30]

I set out to unbundle this statement, in particular: what is meant and implicated by "forms" and "coherence" in the context of Formalism and to develop an outline of what an interpretive methodology for positive law grounded in the idea of law's immanent rationality and in line with the formalist understanding of what law could look like.

3 Formalism and Law's Immanent Intelligibility

My inquiry will begin with a description of Formalism in which I will further flesh out the idea of law's immanent rationality and examine how it plays out in the process of understanding positive law. In order to do so, I will make the idea of law's autonomy my starting point and then turn to the notions of legal forms and coherence.

3.1 Law's Autonomous Rationality: From Legislative Intent to Law's Immanent Purposiveness

In the Formalist view, Law is autonomous. It is and has to be conceived of as a discipline distinct from, notably, politics[31] and also from all other disciplines and areas of thought.[32] This position has manifold implications and

---

[28]See Weinrib (1993a), p. 593; Weinrib (1993b), p. 697.

[29]See below at 13–14 on how the critical, evaluative character of the formalist view plays out in the interpretive practice.

[30]Weinrib (1988), p. 1013.

[31]See for example: Weinrib (1988), pp. 950 and 952.

[32]I will refrain, for the purpose of this analysis, from entering into a discussion about the exact definition of a "discipline"—it will presently suffice to say that by characterizing law as an autonomous discipline, the Formalist wants to put forward the idea that there is a clear and impermeable line delimiting legal from non-legal considerations.

> extend[s] to every aspect of reflection about law. It affects one's view of the nature of legal justification, the limits of the judicial role and judicial competence, the meaning of legal mistake, the relevance of instrumentalism, the relation of law and society, the viability of contemporary legal scholarship, and the place of law among the intellectual disciplines.[33]

Two aspects are of particular interest when asking for the Formalist approach to *ratio legis* and legal interpretation: the call for a reconsideration of the "location" of rationality as well as for a modified view of law's purposiveness.

The Formalist conceives of Law as an abstract mode of ordering juridical relationships. Factual relationships, such as the causal link between an act and a harm that it causes, are approached from the specifically legal vantage point, held to illuminate the specifically juridical significance of a given event.[34] The systematization and unification of all these legal elements into a single, integrated whole result from a specific rationality at work, a rationality that is specific to and immanent in law.[35] For the Formalist, the idea of rationality and its relation to law is therefore inseparable from the idea of immanence.[36] There is no need to seek for an external purpose to the attainment of which law is a means—it is an "end in itself."[37] From this, it follows from this that the only "purpose" that law can be said to pursue is to realize itself, to maintain its unity and internal structuring—a "goal" that looks to law itself instead of to something external.

This understanding challenges the "prevalent" view about law's "provenance, nature, and characteristic process."[38] It diametrically opposes to accept the legislative process as "the distinctive vehicle of legality,"[39] especially insofar as it assumes as a necessary condition that "aims" originate in a rational body external to law. To presume that the very notion of legislative purpose can "depend on the metamorphosis into law of material that is originally non-legal"[40] goes against the notion of law's immanent rationality and makes clear why the Formalist has to advocate for a strict separation of law from, especially, politics: the latter being "the domain of collective instrumentalist purposes."[41] To look to politics in order to identify law's purpose would be at odds with the Formalist view of law's autonomy.

[33]Weinrib (1988), pp. 951–952.

[34]See Weinrib (1988), p. 957 fn. 28. The Formalists make the juridical relationship the basic unit of their analysis. This idea can be retraced to the the influence of Kantian Legal Philosophy, according to which governing a person's external relationships is the very domain of law (cf. Kant (transl. Gregor (1996), pp. 20–21: "Duties in accordance with rightful lawgiving can only be external duties."), see further for this idea: Weinrib (1987), p. 487. For a criticism of the relationship as the basic unit of analysis in Weinrib's theory of Private Law, see: Menke (2015) questioning its apolitical character, p. 37: (translation by KvS): "The normativity of the private law relationship is . . . not, as claimed by the correlational theory, autonomous, but made – an effect of the [posited] law. Consequently, the normativity of the private law relationship has a political basis."

[35]See Weinrib (1987), p. 480 on the systematizing function of reason.

[36]Weinrib (1988), p. 954 referring to a formulation offered by Roberto Unger.

[37]Weinrib (1988), p. 956.

[38]Weinrib (1988), p. 956.

[39]Weinrib (1988), p. 956.

[40]Weinrib (1988), p. 956.

[41]Weinrib (1988), p. 965.

In the Formalist view, law's immanent rationality defines its purpose. Law sets its own goals and aims to realize itself. The legislative process is then restricted to expressing this internal purpose into positive law, instead of introducing and incorporating multiple other aspects. All posited law shall respond to the requirements of Law's immanent rationality so that there can be no choice between a multiplicity of possible purposes. The notion of *ratio legis* then points to this internal, immanent rationality.

The most abstract embodiment of law's immanent rationality, the structures guiding and shaping juridical thought and which hold it together as a coherent whole, are the legal forms. In the next part, I am going to lay out what the Formalist understands by its eponymous idea, the theoretical "bedrock"[42] on which it rests, and examine how it could help us to interpret positive law in line with the Formalist theory.

3.2 Legal Forms

According to the Formalist account, a form is

> the ensemble of characteristics that constitute the matter in question as a unity identical to that of other matters of the same kind and distinguishable from matters of a different kind.[43]

It incorporates three interrelated aspects: character, genericity (which is later referred to as kind[44]), and unity.

By "character," Weinrib understands the essential features of a thing, those elements allowing to identify it as what it is—and to distinguish it from other things that do not share this same set of essential features.[45] Every element constituting a thing's character could not be left out without resulting in a loss or change of this very character.

"Genericity," or "kind," refers to a form's ability to constitute a general class of all things sharing the same character.[46] It requires a level of abstraction that allows for comparison and distinction, enabling us to situate each particular thing within the overall order of things in the world. In doing so, genericity/kind prevents overfragmentation and contingency. It helps to identify what belongs together in the same "group" of things.

Finally, the way in which the different essential features constituting character are connected and structured is described by "unity." Unity ensures that the essential features are not simply accumulated and arbitrarily assembled but that their assembling reflects an internal ordering, attributing to each feature its place in the whole.[47]

[42] Weinrib (1988), p. 957.
[43] Weinrib (1988), p. 958.
[44] See for example Weinrib (2012), pp. 22 and 27.
[45] Weinrib (1988), p. 959; Weinrib (2012), p. 27.
[46] Weinrib (1988), p. 959; Weinrib (2012), p. 27.
[47] See Weinrib (1988), p. 960.

In sum, a thing's form will tell us what its essential features are (cf. "character"), how they relate to one another (cf. "unity"), and how the thing can be classified (cf. "kind"). In other words: forms tell us what a thing "is".

The notion of a "legal form" takes up these features and applies them to the set of juridical relationships. The various juridical relationships making up a legal system are not just amassed like pebbles in a pile,[48] but each part has its position in relation to every other part and to the overall structure. Different legal forms represent different possible modes of their ordering.

For instance, in the case of Private Law, Weinrib has identified corrective justice as the appropriate legal form. He describes the way in which this legal form can be identified as follows:

> We discover the concept of corrective justice ... by reflecting on the legal institutions we have and on the forms of order they presuppose. We see that particular legal holdings fit into a certain conceptual framework that makes salient the apparently fixed points of legal reasoning in a sophisticated legal culture ... We can then examine the presuppositions about interaction evidenced in the components of this framework, all the while preserving the tendency toward coherence that characterizes both thought in general and sophisticated legal systems in particular.[49]

As legal forms, from the Formalist viewpoint, describe what Law, at the most abstract level, "is," they deploy normative force for positive law: it has to express law's immanent rationality because the expression of legal forms in positive law must strive to achieve "judicial coherence". Consequently, positive law has to retrace and conform to the structuring prescribed by the respective legal form describing the juridical relationship to which the provision applies/shall apply.[50] Legal forms then become the already mentioned "benchmark" against which any precise posited norm has to be assessed—every posited norm has to "vindicate" the underlying form that describes the set of juridical relationships to which this specific rule applies.[51]

3.3 Coherence

We have just seen that legal forms play a central role for coherence, the very possibility of which stems in turn from law's immanent rationality.[52] In this sense,

---

[48]Weinrib (2012), p. 29.

[49]Weinrib (1988), p. 1000 fn. 106.

[50]See for the exposition of the normative dimension of forms: Weinrib (1988), pp. 995–999.

[51]It is clear that the requirements of the Formalist theory equally apply to judge-made law. Within the realms of a court's authority, any decision equally has to ensure the proper expression of the underlying legal forms, see below at 19.

[52]Weinrib (1988), p. 952.

coherence "signifies the intrinsic unity of [their] features."[53] Legal forms describe coherent internal structuring of juridical relationships.[54]

But what is more, in order for there to be a single integrated whole of (all of) law, not only the respective structures but also the structuring of the different juridical relationships in relation to one another needs to be coherent. Law's doctrines and institutions, so the Formalist holds, articulate its unity, encompassing the entirety of juridical relationships within its purview.[55] The requirement to prevent arbitrariness relates not only to the abstract level of legal forms but ultimately extends to their expression in the overall legal system through each and every posited rule. Striving for an overall integrated legal system entails that also all of positive law must express these structures and their structuring in a coherent fashion. It is the function of positive law to make explicit the already implicit connection between the different essential features of a juridical relationship.[56]

At the level of positive law, this implies that all sophisticated legal systems (must) aspire to coherence in the overall adherence to and implementation of legal forms. They should aim to realize the integration of all their elements into a coherent whole. In this context, coherence thus becomes a regulative ideal. This is because only insofar as a system's doctrines, principles, and its institutions coherently express the appropriate form is it possible to speak of it as an overall coherent system. And the system constituted, in turn, by these doctrines, principles, and institutions becomes the guideline for (further) positive law.[57]

Weinrib acknowledges that this conception of coherence is an "extremely ambitious" one.[58] It does not only intend to avoid contradictions and smooth out inconsistencies, but furthermore strives "to realize a self-adjusting harmony of principles, rules and standards".[59]

---

[53]Weinrib (2012), p. 35.

[54]The idea of coherence is intricately intertwined with justification. "Law is a justificatory enterprise" (Weinrib 2012, p. 12), among other things because it ultimately allows, authorities to enforce decisions. Consequently, all considerations justifying a particular decision must cohere (in their entirety)—otherwise they do not provide the justification they claim to. See for the constitutional dimension of this aspect below note 94.

[55]Weinrib (1987), p. 478.

[56]Weinrib (2012), p. 35.

[57]Despite some parallels with the "systematic" method of interpretation, the notion of coherence in this context extends beyond the sphere of posited norms. It aims to harmonize those posited norms with the structure of the juridical relationship to which they apply and moreover looks for coherence, not mere consistency.

[58]Weinrib (1988), p. 970. For possible challenges presented by this fact, see below at 23.

[59]Weinrib (2012), p. 12. Contrary to the externally oriented conception of a possible *telos* held by the views presented above, the aim for a coherent expression of the underlying legal form is an internal one. It looks (only) to itself, refers to itself, and hereby implements the position of law as an end in itself.

At the same time, it is essential to underline that the Formalist theory does not argue that complete coherence has ever been achieved by any system of positive law.[60] Repeatedly, the (purely) aspirational nature of the concept of coherence is stressed.[61] Coherence is possible, but Formalism equally acknowledges the possibility of its defective implementation.[62] Nevertheless, positive law not corresponding to the appropriate legal forms is considered a "juridical mistake."[63]

Other than maintaining law's unity, coherence operates at a further dimension of particular interest for my undertaking: for the Formalist, it is the very idea of coherence that can render law immanently intelligible.

3.4 *Implications of the Formalist Position for "Understanding" and Interpretation*

As pointed out earlier, Formalism urges us to look (only) to law itself in the process of understanding it. For the Formalist, the immanent intelligibility of any thing presupposes its coherence, made possible by immanent rationality. Coherence results from immanent rationality and is at the same time required for immanent intelligibility. Weinrib therefore argues that it is only possible to understand something in and of itself—as is the case with law understood as autonomous and self-sufficient in the Formalist perspective—when it is coherent in the way just outlined. It follows that anything that is incoherent is (immanently) unintelligible.[64] When setting out to inquire into what something is, we need to know what its essential features are but even more importantly how they relate to one another. It can thus be said that in the process of understanding law, coherence serves as a criterion for the truthful understanding of juridical relationships, grounded in the notion of law's autonomous rationality.[65]

As law's immanent rationality pervades the legal material,[66] through its doctrines, concepts, principles, and institutions, it renders law self-sufficient and also allows seeing any posited law as potentially expressing this rationality. Consequently, in order to comprehend this immanent ordering the adoption of an "extreme"[67] internal standpoint is indispensable and enlightens on why, for Weinrib, trying to understand law by adopting a standpoint entirely extrinsic to it is senseless. The central task of all legal activity is therefore not the implementation of extrinsic considerations but to

[60] See for example Weinrib (1993b), p. 697.

[61] See for example Weinrib (2012), p. 13.

[62] See Weinrib (1988), p. 972.

[63] Weinrib (1988), p. 985.

[64] See for example Weinrib (2012), p. 38.

[65] Weinrib (1988), p. 972; Weinrib (2012), p. 45.

[66] Weinrib (1988), p. 955.

[67] Weinrib (1988), p. 952.

"understand what is intimated by juridical relationships and arrangements",[68] and so to retrace and bring to expression law's immanent rationality.

This idea must be reflected in the process of understanding posited norms. In order to identify the content of a norm, its scope of application, and the legal consequences it prescribes to a particular situation, Formalism must equally call upon the interpreter to look (only) to law itself.[69] When law is to be viewed as intelligible on its own, the task of statutory interpretation can only be to "make sense of law on its own terms."[70]

It must equally follow that, in order to understand posited law, it is not simply unnecessary but detrimental to take into consideration aspects not encompassed by the purely internal standpoint. There is neither need nor room for additional, i.e. external, goal setting. An external *ratio* falls outside the scope of the conceptual framework of Formalism since posited law shall only aim at making explicit the underlying legal forms.

These legal forms making "salient the nature of unity and coherence both within and among legal relationships"[71] then become indispensable for the understanding of law, both in the abstract and as posited rules.[72] Forms provide us with the necessary "lens" to see and "grasp" the juridical element in a given factual relationship and to identify the "benchmark" applicable to positive law. This makes them, so Weinrib holds, "universal": independent of specific social or historical circumstances and external goal setting responding to these specific circumstances.[73]

At the same time, they are, as law itself, constituted by thoughts[74] and "concepts"[75] so that their "application" does not amount to the imposition of something external to the process of understanding law on its own terms. As legal forms describe the way we think of juridical relationships, their content can be elaborated from within.[76]

In the context of statutory interpretation, I therefore argue that we encounter "legal forms" as what might be called "epistemological tools." Due to their "concern

[68]Weinrib (1988), p. 956.

[69]At least as a starting point. On the need to supplement this perspective with further elements and ensuing challenges, see below at 20–22.

[70]Weinrib (1993a), p. 592.

[71]Weinrib (1988), p.963.

[72]Weinrib (1988), p. 957.

[73]Weinrib (1988), p. 1000 and below at 23 for a critical assessment of forms' universal character.

[74]Weinrib (1988), p. 962.

[75]Weinrib (1988), p. 962. The examples for such concepts that provided (cause, remoteness, duty, consideration, offer and acceptance) raise doubts concerning the universality of legal forms. Can we really say that the lawyer from a tradition that does not know the concept of consideration is not "doing" law? Respectively: What are possible consequences of differing sets of fundamental concepts for the Formalist view? See further on this issue below at 22–23.

[76]Weinrib (2012), pp. 23–24.

... with the understanding of juridical relationships,"[77] they make immanently intelligent ordering visible.

And as they provide the indispensable access to understanding law out of itself, legal forms refer back to law's immanence, which makes of them a set of "epistemological tools" truly in line with law's immanent intelligibility.

These observations will guide the following section, in which I will turn more specifically to a possible formalist approach to legal interpretation. My reflections about the need to develop a specifically Formalist method originate in the observation that the understanding of *ratio legis* as held by the teleological *canon* under the prevalent approach to statutory interpretation appears to be failing to respond to this immanent conception of rationality and purposiveness. Immanently rational law does not express a, yet to be determined, (legislative) purpose. On the contrary, the vindication of the underlying legal form is the only acceptable purpose so that a method of interpretation aiming to single out one among a possible infinite variety of purposes appears to be "beside the point".

In what follows, I will not only point to (theoretical) prerequisites, implied assumptions and potential limits, but also try to provide some practically oriented guidelines for carrying out interpretation in line with the Formalist understanding of law.

4 Formalism and Interpretation: Immanent *Ratio Legis* and a Formalist Method of Statutory Interpretation?

In this part, I will outline the general conception of statutory interpretation that can be derived from the Formalist theory of law as described above. I will suggest how the interpretation of an "unclear" provision can be based on the Formalist theoretical framework. I will in particular look at consequences resulting from the notion on an immanent *ratio legis*. This will be followed by a critical evaluation of a "Formalist" method of statutory interpretation in which I will highlight its strengths but equally point to possible difficulties and challenges it might face.

4.1 Redefining Statutory Interpretation

In the second section of this chapter, I have said that, under the prevalent approach the overall aim of statutory interpretation is to identify the will animating and translated into a specific provision. The *ratio* of a given *lex* points to the purpose that this "will" seeks to achieve with the specific provision. As a result, there is a potentially infinite variety of purposes. The teleological *canon* as a method of

[77] Weinrib (1988), p. 957.

statutory interpretation then assists in identifying the "correct" one and makes it the basis for understanding the meaning of the unclear provision.

For the Formalist, there can be no such ambiguity. Instead, the only "purpose" of positive law is to be the adequate and coherent expression of an underlying legal form, which in turn coherently expresses the structure of the juridical relationship to which it applies.

As we have seen, the reason for this is that, for the Formalist, law is an immanently intelligible mode of ordering juridical relationships. Law does thus never serve any "collective pursuit of a desirable purpose."[78] The Formalist approach to law cannot embrace open-ended discussions about desirable goals[79] since there can be no plurality of purposes within the same legal system other than the coherent expression of the underlying legal forms.[80] It aspires to coherence, an internal goal, reflecting its immanent rationality. Only by the adoption of an internal standpoint that "grasps" law as an immanently intelligible phenomenon can we understand law, both in its abstract form and as posited rules. Working out law's meaning therefore lies in the identification of this internal structuring and the vindication of the underlying legal forms, regardless of any other considerations.

Consequently, the interpreters have to ensure that their suggested understanding of a posited norm fits into the coherent whole of the preexisting body of law. And as the Formalist view holds that it is law's immanent rationality that pervades and structures this "whole," the interpreter is called upon to give expression, also in positive law, to the essential features of the juridical relationship it governs. Overall, the interpretive process in the Formalist view thus has to be characterized as discovery, as making explicit the form of the juridical relationship that is immanent, in other words, already "present" in the integrated web of law. The interpreter shall consequently make explicit the intrinsic unity in the suggested understanding of positive law as applied to a juridical relationship.[81]

This is equally of particular importance in the context of court adjudication and discussions about the delimitation of interpretation and construction, respectively the limitations for lawmaking by judges.[82] In deciding, courts shall give effect to the

---

[78]Weinrib (1988), p. 964.

[79]Weinrib (2012), p. 23.

[80]For difficulties resulting from an understanding of "legal system" as synonymous with "jurisdiction", see below at 23–24.

[81]See Weinrib (2012), p. 35.

[82]See Weinrib (1988), p. 956. Operating as a court of law, non-legal considerations are out of reach. The court is bound to "discover", respectively, "give expression" to legal forms. Interestingly, this idea of a discovery of what the law is resonates with the formula German courts use to introduce their judgments: "für Recht erkannt" (literally translated as: "As recognized for right"). Furthermore, the lawmaking court faces its own institutional boundaries—the institutional arrangements of a given legal system are part of what constitutes the abstract legal form. The court has to give expression to law's immanent rationality—not only as its interpreter, but also in its legislative function: any "gap-filling", or "innovation" can equally only look to the preexisting body of legal material that it must coherently develop. This point touches upon fundamental questions of the separation of powers, and reflects a particular concern: the "retrospectivity-problem". It describes the puzzle arising from a court potentially seen as "making" law by adjudicating a particular

elements of positive law as expressing and specifying aspects of the legal forms in a coherent manner and equally proceed restrictively when "developing" law.[83]

In addition, the Formalist view about law's immanent rationality and its autonomous conception must result in a specifically "legal" approach to interpretation. The transfer of interpretive methodologies from other disciplines insofar as they integrate an outlook to external sources for law's purpose counteracts the approach premised on immanent intelligibility and the opposition against a conception of law as a purely interpretive practice, subjecting law's truth to the views of particular interpretive communities,[84] is its immediate consequence.

4.2 *Coherently Expressing Legal Forms in Positive Law: Steps of a Formalist Method of Interpretation*

In order to understand any "unclear" provision, the interpreter thus has to identify the appropriate legal form as a coherent expression of which it must be understood to operate.

As has been described in the citation I have referred to earlier,[85] the interpreter—in a first movement of abstraction—has to identify the legal concepts, doctrines, principles, and institutional arrangements describing the underlying juridical relationship and then, in a second movement of abstraction, to determine the most abstract legal form under which they can be subsumed.

The Formalist conception of statutory interpretation might therefore be described as shifting the interpretive moment to this carving out of the underlying legal form in a twofold movement of abstraction, or: regression.

Since law—in the Formalist view—is immanently intelligible, the identification of the relevant legal material has to be done from an internal standpoint, too. It is constituted by those legal concepts, doctrines, principles, and institutional arrangements considered to be the essential basics, the fundamental features viewed as indispensable for the participation in juristic activity by the jurists operating in the respective system.[86] The interpreters therefore have to identify the "systemic

---

dispute—but without the rule as later declared by the judge being known to the parties beforehand in a way that would have allowed them to adjust their conduct accordingly (Weinrib 1988, p. 999). The Formalist view of law tries to prevent such scenarios: as any positive law, so equally any rule established in what will later become a precedent, has to express law's preexisting immanent rationality, the task also of the lawmaking judge is to "discover", not to "create" (see also Weinrib 1988, p. 956).

[83]See Weinrib (2012), p. 209.

[84]Weinrib (1988), p. 1014 with reference in particular to R. Dworkin.

[85]See above at 13.

[86]Weinrib (2012), p. 13. This idea might at first sight be perceived as in tension with the conception of the "internal to law"-view. As, however, legal forms are considered to be universal, the Formalist position does not leave it to the interpretive community to design the basic modes of ordering, for a criticism see below at 23.

context" into which the respective provision belongs and then to select the corresponding "legal material". They then have to carve out the most abstract legal form that describes the juridical relationships in this system or subsystem. Ultimately, the interpreters must adopt the understanding of the provision that best vindicates this form.

For example:[87] a provision of tort law dealing with the compensation of losses incurred after a wrong was inflicted is unclear as to whether it covers all or only a part of the victim's losses. The Formalist would first ask what system of subsystem of law this rule belongs to (here: tort law as a subsystem of private law). It would then ask for the fundamental features considered indispensable by jurists to participate in private law juristic activity (here: action by plaintiff against defendant leading to an adjudicative procedure that terminates in a judgment that retroactively affirms the correlative rights and duties of the parties and rules on the corresponding relief/compensation[88]). These fundamental elements are then subjected to a further movement of abstraction, aiming at identifying the legal form describing them at the highest possible degree of abstraction—for Weinrib, in the case of private law, this most abstract legal form is corrective justice.[89] Finally, the interpreter would have to opt for the understanding of the unclear provision that corresponds to corrective justice, here: one that reflects in particular the bipolar relationship between victim and wrongdoer. The understanding of the provision in line with corrective justice is the appropriate one and should determine the amount of damages, which the provision properly expressing the juridical relationship having given rise to the dispute can only result for the plaintiff.

This outline hints to an important consequence of the Formalist approach, but at the same time points to a first, crucial challenge to Formalism's potential as a self-sufficient way of understanding (also) posited law: the Formalist method's open-endedness.

I have pointed out that the Formalist view requires coherence but does not necessarily prescribe any particular outcome.[90] On the legislative level, it does not prescribe the choice between different legal forms but requires (only) that whatever mode of ordering is chosen, the system of positive law has to correspond to the immanent rationality of this chosen ordering.[91] Applied to the level of legal

[87]Here, I adapt an example provided by Weinrib (2012), pp. 36–38 to the context of statutory interpretation.

[88]Cf. Weinrib's layout of the essential institutional and conceptual features of Private Law in Weinrib (2012), pp. 9–10.

[89]Cf. Weinrib (2012), p. 63; Weinrib (1988), p. 978.

[90]This idea is closely interconnected with—in particular—Kantian Right as the second theoretical pillar of Weinrib's theory. Furthermore, the identification of corrective justice as the underlying legal form of private law enables to think about this area of law in the absence of a decision about a particular "good", see notably Weinrib (1988), p. 988; Weinrib (2012), p. 210. Both these aspects can only be hinted at for present purposes. With respect to the possibility of the universal application of a method of interpretation grounded in the Formalist understanding, see below at 24.

[91]Cf. Weinrib (2012), p. 22 fn. 37 with the example of different possibilities of legislative design for employer liability.

interpretation, this seems to indicate that, as long as the result of the interpretation is coherent, the Formalist can accept all possibly conceivable ways of understanding a norm, too. To the same extent that the legal forms do not impose a specific rule to be adopted, they do not prescribe only one specific outcome of interpretation, as long as this outcome vindicates the underlying form.

It is thus conceivable that the Formalist method fails to deliver clear results in ambiguous cases, when two or more possible ways of understanding an unclear provision would fulfill the requirements of the governing legal form, but nevertheless have different results for the outcome in the particular case, for example a different amount of compensation. Other than at the legislative level, at the level of interpretation of particular provisions to be applied to particular situations, clear and definite results are needed. It seems, however, as if a Formalist approach to positive law alone cannot always fulfil these requirements. Whereas the Formalist analysis of law on the abstract level can, without great difficulty, accommodate the idea of open-endedness, an interpretive methodology based uniquely on this theory might be inconclusive for the concrete case. Other *canones*, notably the one looking more closely for wording might be a necessary supplement. The interpreter must however maintain the internal perspective that Formalism requires, even when resorting to other methods of interpretation.[92]

When thinking about other ways and approaches to interpreting an unclear provision, a further question arises: how does the Formalist method I am outlining react to explicit legislative decisions not coherently expressing the underlying legal form? In other words: how to interpret clearly incoherent positive law? I have introduced Formalism as an evaluative theory that would consider positive law deviating from the underlying forms as "legal mistake."[93] I have equally pointed out that the conception of interpretation I am looking at seeks to clarify ambiguous provisions. At the same time, the Formalist requirements do not automatically authorize the interpreter to discard a clear legislative decision, even if this legislative decision is flawed from the normative standpoint of the theory. This has the consequence that a clear and unambiguous provision, even if "mistaken", is, for instance, nevertheless to be applied by courts, which are in principle bound by legislative supremacy. Legal interpretation serves to clarify, not to correct or reform.[94]

[92]This raises the question if and how the other interpretive methods can have a place in the Formalist interpretive framework. A clear answer in the positive seems particularly difficult as the further methodological *canones* (wording, legislative history, systematic context) are all looking to the identification of "will" (see above). A detailed analysis of their respective compatibility with the Formalist theory of law would however go beyond the scope of my inquiry in this chapter. I will therefore refer it to another occasion.

[93]See above at 15.

[94]At the same time, there is strong reason to assume that the very requirement of internal coherence is grounded in the respective constitutional orders that bind the legislative authorities, be it as a manifestation of "Rechtsstaat", "rule of law" or in any other way. Incoherent, and unintelligible legislation violates these fundamental constitutional principles of the highest order and can in exceptional scenarios entitle interpreting courts to give expression to fundamental constitutional principles in their dealing with "incoherent" positive law. I am highly indebted to Ernest J. Weinrib for bringing this utterly important point to my attention.

However, in the case of an unclear provision, the Formalist's view of an internal purposiveness that is: to realize the respective legal form's immanent rationality establishes what might be called a "rebuttable presumption" in favor of the form's coherent expression. The Formalist conception of law I have outlined above imposes an understanding of each provision at hand as coherently expressing law's immanent rationality as the starting point of the interpretive process. Only when this interpretive "presumption" is rebutted by an unequivocal expression of legislative intent pointing in a different direction can the interpreter deviate from the requirements of coherence.[95] In all other cases, as the Formalist view of law refuses to consider externally determined purposes, the legislative body is to be presumed to have acted in accordance with the requirements imposed by the only admissible goal: the coherent expression of law's immanent *ratio*.

From this, it must also follow that even if of several possible ways of understanding a posited rule none is fully in line with the underlying form, the interpreter must opt for the one that best vindicates this form.

4.3 Further Limits and Challenges

In the previous section, I have already pointed to Formalism's open-endedness as a potential problem when its conceptual framework is applied to the interpretation of posited law.

A few more limits and challenges, mainly concerning the choice of legal materials and the system's delimitations, shall be highlighted in this section.

Following the steps of the Formalist approach to interpretation outlined above, the interpreter will eventually face the issue of how to determine the appropriate legal materials used and consulted to identify forms. This can be difficult since, on the one hand, Formalism holds that a system's immanent rationality is expressed in the ensemble of authoritative legal materials constituting it[96] while at the same time conceding that this expression in positive law might be imperfect and flawed.[97] But as the legal concepts, doctrines, principles, and institutional arrangements are also (at least partially) derived from posited rules, there is the possibility that a "legal mistake" could find its way into the authoritative legal materials. Only when the mistaken rule can clearly be identified as incoherent (as "mistaken") is it possible for the interpreter to disregard a particular element. The strategy to assess which parts of the "material" at hand might be deficient expressions of the underlying legal form thus presupposes that the system overall maintains its coherence and that it is possible to identify both a "flawed" posited rule as well as an incoherent principle, doctrine, or even institution. The Formalist method can therefore only result in a

[95]In these scenarios it is in fact even questionable if there is need for interpretation at all.

[96]See Weinrib (1988), p. 953.

[97]Weinrib (1988), p. 962.

successful abstraction within the framework of an already predominantly coherent system—mere aspiration without any implementation will hardly suffice. While the aspiration for coherence has been introduced as a normative ideal in the context of abstract reflections about law, we have to assert that—as far as statutory interpretation is concerned—it becomes an empirical claim, too.[98] And obviously, once the "flawed" expressions of form become prevalent and cannot be said to be of exceptional character anymore, leading maybe even to a modification of the set of legal materials, a Formalist method of interpretation will face further difficult problems.

In addition, proceeding in the way I have outlined raises questions as to which, respectively whose internal viewpoint is to be taken into consideration. Are all jurists relevant for its determination? And more importantly: can the "Formalist" interpreter only rely on undisputed basic legal materials or exceptionally also include elements the acknowledgment of which is disputed? And if yes, is it sufficient that a majority of jurists recognize the disputed legal concept, doctrine, principle, or institutional arrangement?

Next, the "systemic" perspective that the Formalist approach adopts constitutes a further important implicit prerequisite: even if the forms of (corrective and distributive) justice are, according to Weinrib, universal,[99] we have to bear in mind that, first, they have been reached as the result of a regression process within a specific legal system or subsystem[100] and that, second, the principles, doctrines (for instance, the doctrine of consideration), and institutional settings at their outset are specific to this system, too. There is the possibility that the same method applied to different systems, in different jurisdictions, generates diverging results.

In addition, the aspiration for coherence as prerequisite for immanent intelligibility, as well as the description of the abstraction process are equally anchored in a system-oriented perspective. It will be the respective system's borders that inform the interpreter about which elements are to be considered and which fall outside of the set of eligible "legal materials." Pointing to the elements' convergence,[101] their working themselves and the system into which they inscribe pure[102] in order to find these borderlines provides only limited guidance. In default of any more precise elaboration on what constitutes a "system" in the Formalist perspective, the latter can easily be subject to the reproach of an arbitrary drawing of systemic borders, allegedly aiming to make a certain interpretive result appear as the sole correct vindication of a legal form, even if differently drawn systemic borders might point into another direction. This lack of substantive criteria for the delimitation of systems

[98]Insofar as the Formalist approach argues that the forms of corrective and distributive justice are universal, it would be possible to identify the correct "benchmark" even in an entirely incoherent system. It nevertheless matters to point out the presumption for the Formalist "pillar" of the theory as such.

[99]See for example Weinrib (1988), p. 983: "Corrective and distributive justice are the most abstract forms that render juridical relationships intelligible."

[100]Anglo-Canadian Common Law, Private Law, in particular tort law.

[101]Weinrib (1988), p. 969.

[102]See only: Weinrib (2012), pp. 13 and 206–207.

makes it even more difficult to accommodate cases, which at first sight might fall under different (sub)systemic categories.[103] And while it is conceivable that the Formalist view would refer the interpreter to the structuring operated by law's immanent rationality as indicating the systemic delimitations, the question of how to deal with the theoretical oxymoron of—(however arguably) empirically possible—overwhelmingly "incoherent systems" remains.[104]

What is more, these reflections point to the question of the possibility of dynamic evolution of a legal system. To the extent that—over time—the set of principles, doctrines, and the institutional framework are subject to change, when can such a change or modification be said to affect the potential outcome of the abstraction process? There is a certain openness for dynamism built into the Formalist model; we are informed that, for example, doctrinal innovations "are reserved for special occasions and require special justification."[105]

However, the ideal of coherence with the universal legal forms might ultimately reflect back on the development of positive law and generate some kind of *stasis* since the dynamism of the law in Formalist terms is inwardly directed, law's immanent rationality has a regulative character working inwardly; it "works itself pure."[106] It remains unanswered when "new" developments can be integrated into what is otherwise a self-sufficient and self-reinforcing process.

Ultimately, it remains an open question if the Formalist theory and the interpretive method developed out of its main claim: an immanently rational law that is to be realized in posited norms and consequently sets Law as its own goal can be extended beyond private law, governed by corrective justice and with the primordial role that Kantian Right plays in it.[107]

[103]For instance: consumer protection laws and/or rules on contractual Terms and Conditions—Do they belong to Private Law or Public Law ordering? Does it—consequently—belong to the realms of the legal form of corrective of rather of distributive justice?

[104]While we can learn that complete loss of coherence might lead to the loss of the legal character of the system (cf. Weinrib 2012, p. 31), it is not as clear to which extent the system needs coherence to stay as such, nor to which degree a loss of coherence is acceptable for a "legal" system.

[105]Weinrib (1988), p. 968.

[106]See Weinrib (2012), pp. 13 and 206–207.

[107]See only Weinrib (1988), pp. 988–992 on the conceptual necessity for an "external" consideration under distributive justice governing public law. An interpretation of positive law in systems of distributive justice appears to require the indispensable "look to the outside aim" that the Formalist Theory refused in the context of private law.

5 Conclusion: Immanent *Ratio Legis* and Legal Interpretation

I began by carving out that the conception of *ratio legis* under the prevalent approach is grounded in the idea of an externally determined purpose that paves the way for access to law's meaning when a provision needs to be interpreted.

In contrast, the Formalist understanding is based on the view that law is immanently rational and strives for its coherence which—ultimately—also makes it immanently intelligible.

The *ratio* we encounter in the Formalist approach to interpretation approximates a *ratio iure*, a *ratio* that pervades the entire statutory system and that extends to any single posited law, too.

This different conception of law and *ratio legis* gives rise to a different conception of statutory interpretation, centered around "legal forms."

As I could show, they are a valuable tool in the enterprise of trying to "make sense of law on its own terms." However, an interpretive method based on the Formalist view of law might only have a limited applicability—due to important prerequisites and questions that are still unanswered.

My analysis of the view of *ratio legis* in the prevalent conception of interpretation and the elaboration of a different view of an immanent *ratio legis* should draw our attention to the extent to which any methodology is loaded with underlying theoretical considerations.

The knowledge of these background positions and assumptions is essential to any lawyer who shall not just use methodological "tools" but use them responsibly. We are reminded to always strive to be aware of our own underlying assumptions when we claim that one type of argument is "stronger" than another.

Acknowledgements I thank the participants and guests of the Special Workshop at the XXVIII IVR World Congress in Lisbon for their most helpful questions and comments. I equally thank E. J. Weinrib for introducing me to the fascinating world of his Legal Formalism and discussing my thoughts and ideas about it, as well as J.-C. Bédard Rubin for providing valuable hints and advise at different stages during the development of this chapter. Notwithstanding, all remaining errors and omissions are obviously mine only.

References

Barak A (2005) Purposive interpretation. Princeton University Press, Princeton

Bydlinski F (1982) Juristische Methodenlehre und Rechtsbegriff. Springer, Wien

Fikentscher W (1975) Methoden des Rechts in vergleichender Darstellung, Anglo-Amerikanischer Rechtskreis, vol 2. Mohr Siebeck, Tübingen

Kant I (1996) The metaphysics of morals (trans: Gregor M). Cambridge University Press, Cambridge

Larenz K (1979) Methodenlehre der Rechtswissenschaft, 4th edn. Springer, Berlin

MacCormick N (1978) Legal reasoning and legal theory. Oxford University Press, Oxford

Menke C (2015) Kritik der Rechte. Suhrkamp, Berlin
Reimer F (2016) Juristische Methodenlehre. Nomos, Baden-Baden
Schauer F (1988) Formalism. Yale Law J 97:509–548
Schröder J (2012) Recht als Wissenschaft, 2nd edn. C.H. Beck, München
Stone M (2012) Formalism. In: Coleman JL, Himma KE, Shapiro SJ (eds) The Oxford handbook of jurisprudence and philosophy of law. Oxford Handbooks Online, Oxford
Wank R (1997) Die Auslegung von Gesetzen. C.H. Beck, München
Weinrib EJ (1987) Law as a Kantian idea of reason. Columbia Law Rev 87:472–508
Weinrib EJ (1988) Legal formalism: on the immanent rationality of law. Yale Law J 97:949–1016
Weinrib EJ (1993a) The jurisprudence of legal formalism. Harv J Law Public Policy 16:583–595
Weinrib EJ (1993b) Formalism and practical reason. Harv J Law Public Policy 16:683–699
Weinrib EJ (2012) The idea of private law. Oxford University Press, Oxford
Zippelius R (2005) Juristische Methodenlehre, 9th edn. C.H. Beck, München

Konstanze von Schütz is a Doctor of Juridical Science Candidate at the University of Toronto's Faculty of Law. Her doctoral thesis examines the *numerus clausus* of property rights. Her main areas of research are Private Law and Private Law Theory (especially Property Law and Property Theory), and Comparative Private Law.

This chapter is the extended version of a presentation given at the Special Workshop "Is There a *Ratio Legis* and if So, How Many Are There?—The Most Powerful Method of Legal Reasoning Uncovered" during the XXVIII World Congress of the International Association for the Philosophy of Law and Social Philosophy (IVR), July 16–21, 2017, University of Lisbon, Portugal.

How Can *Ratio Legis* Help a Lawyer to Interpret a Legal Text? Employing the Purpose of a Regulation for Legal Interpretation

Mikołaj Hermann

Abstract Legislative activity is undoubtedly purposive. By enacting the law, the lawgiver means to achieve set goals that refer to the organisation of a society and its functioning. This fact must be considered in the interpretation of legal provisions, and, consequently, an interpreter is obliged to reconstruct legal norms that allow the aim of a given regulation to be attained.

Ratio legis, conceived of as the lawmaker's purpose of establishing a specific regulation, i.e. a legal provision, a set of provisions or an entire normative act, can be understood instrumentally—as the certain configuration of social relations that should be achieved through such a regulation—or axiologically—as the value that a given regulation serves to protect or actualise.

The objective of this article is to discuss possible ways that *ratio legis* influences the result of the interpretation process and to determine the relation of the purposive (teleological) rules of interpretation to those that are linguistic or systemic. It should be noted that the mere fact that such issues can be raised is based on the premise that the wording of legal provisions does not always adequately reflect the intent of the law-creating body, which means that there may be a conflict between a legal text and the lawmaker's intention.

1 Introduction

Legislative activity is undoubtedly purposive. By enacting the law, the lawgiver means to achieve set goals that refer to the organisation of a society and its functioning. This fact must be considered in the interpretation of legal provisions, and, consequently, an interpreter is obliged to reconstruct legal norms that allow the aim of a given regulation to be attained.

The objective of this article is to discuss possible ways that *ratio legis* influences the result of the interpretation process and to determine the relation of the purposive (teleological) rules of interpretation to those that are linguistic or systemic. It should

M. Hermann (✉)
Adam Mickiewicz University, Faculty of Law and Administration, Poznań, Poland

V. Klappstein, M. Dybowski (eds.), *Ratio Legis*,
https://doi.org/10.1007/978-3-319-74271-7_9

be noted that the mere fact that such issues can be raised is based on the premise that the wording of legal provisions does not always adequately reflect the intent of the law-creating body, which means that there may be a conflict between a legal text and the lawmaker's intention (on the concept of the legislator's intention, see Raz 2009, pp. 265–298; Tobor 2013; Gizbert-Studnicki 2014, pp. 116–117).

When illustrating different variants of the impact of *ratio legis* on the interpretation of legal regulations, I employ examples drawn from or inspired by Polish law (on the functioning of the teleological directives in the Polish legal practice, including the jurisprudence of the highest courts, see Gizbert-Studnicki 1985–1986; Bielska-Brodziak 2010; Bogucki 2011; Smolak 2012, pp. 25–42). However, I believe that they are of universal value, provided that the rules constituting a legal system allow the application of the purposive directives of interpretation at least to a similar degree.

2 Adopted Conception of Legal Interpretation

To elaborate on the impact of *ratio legis* on the interpretation of legal provisions, one can accept assumptions of various theoretical trends, and within them—different conceptions of legal interpretation. I believe, however, that the best analytical tools in this regard are provided by the derivational conception of legal interpretation (Zieliński 1972, 2012). Foremost, this conception is currently the basis for the development of the integrated approach to legal interpretation in Poland (Zieliński 2006; Zieliński et al. 2009; Zieliński and Zirk-Sadowski 2011). Furthermore, its formulation has been based on findings relating to actual characteristics of legal texts. Finally, within its framework, a precise conceptual apparatus has been proposed.

The fundament of the derivational conception of interpretation is a distinction between a legal provision and a legal norm (Ziembiński 1960; see also Hermann 2013a). It can be presumed that a legal provision constitutes a basic editorial unit of a normative act, covering a grammatical sentence and graphically distinguished by means of an individual name, with the proviso that the last of such criteria is not definitional because multi-sentence graphic units can also be encountered (Zieliński in: Wronkowska and Zieliński 1993, p. 20; Zieliński 2012, pp. 14–15). In turn, a legal norm is a norm of conduct—understood as an unambiguously formulated utterance that either orders certain entities, referred to as addressees, to perform specific actions under given circumstances or prohibits them from performing it—which has been enacted or recognised principally by the state authority (Ziembiński 1980, pp. 119 and 149; Zieliński 2012, p. 14). By issuing a legal provision, changes are introduced to the legal system, which involve the addition of new norms or the elimination of existing ones. The changes in question, unlike a provision itself, are not directly articulated by the legislator but require reconstruction by interpreting a regulation contained in a normative act.

The findings of the derivational conception are based on the premise that legal texts possess specific properties that include the *quasi*-idiomaticity of provisions, the fragmentation (dismemberment) of norms in provisions and the condensation (concentration) of norms in provisions.

The *quasi*-idiomaticity consists in the fact that legal provisions, formulated in a descriptive way, should be regarded as expressing normative utterances (Zieliński in: Ziembiński and Zieliński 1992, pp. 107–108; Zieliński in: Wronkowska and Zieliński 1993, pp. 18–20; Zieliński 2012, pp. 99–107 and 223; see also Sarkowicz 1995).

The fragmentation of legal norms in legal provisions means that a single norm is usually reconstructed based on many provisions that express various elements of a normative utterance or that allow their specification (Zieliński in: Ziembiński and Zieliński 1992, pp. 110–119; Zieliński in: Wronkowska and Zieliński 1993, pp. 23–25; Zieliński 2012, pp. 108–133 and 224). There are two kinds of fragmentation: one syntactic and the other semantic.

Due to the syntactic fragmentation of norms in provisions, one can distinguish between framework provisions, which contain at least an order or a prohibition of a certain conduct, and supplementary provisions, which contain addressees or circumstances (normatively supplementary provisions) or which enable the particular elements of a norm to be meaningfully defined in the situation where phrases indicating them are of relative character (logically supplementary provisions). If a given provision constitutes the basis for recreating all elements of a legal norm and does not include any phrase that would require relativisation (a complete framework provision in both normative and logical sense), the supplementary provisions do not occur.

In turn, due to their semantic fragmentation, legal provisions are divided into central provisions, which are complete or supplemented framework provisions, considered yet in terms of their content rather than syntax, and into modificatory provisions, which—together with the central provision—co-determine a legal norm, indicating limitations or extensions of its sphere of application, i.e. the class of situations to which the norm applies, or its sphere of realisation, i.e. the class of behaviours that are ordered or prohibited by the norm. If a given provision independently expresses an entire norm (a total central provision), the modificatory provisions do not occur.

Finally, the condensation of legal norms in legal provisions means that a specific provision serves to reconstruct many norms by fulfilling the same or different functions during the course of their recreation (Zieliński in: Ziembiński and Zieliński 1992, pp. 109–110; Zieliński in: Wronkowska and Zieliński 1993, pp. 22–23; Zieliński 2012, pp. 134–138 and 225). Consequently, one can distinguish singular provisions, expressing elements of a single legal norm, as well as plural provisions, containing elements of various norms. Interestingly, a legal provision may turn out to be both central in relation to a certain norm and modificatory for another (Zieliński 1972, pp. 76–77; Zieliński in: Ziembiński and Zieliński 1992, pp. 117–118; Zieliński 2012, p. 122). I believe that detecting such a possibility allows one to address the exceedingly complex issue of the competition (concurrence) of legal regulations (Hermann 2012, pp. 195–196; Hermann 2016).

If the arranging (preliminary) phase, aimed towards verifying legal provisions in terms of their validity and current wording (Kanarek and Zieliński 2001; Zieliński 2012, pp. 216–221, 224–225, 289–290, and 319–324), is omitted (see Hermann

2012, pp. 30–32 and 195–196; see also Wronkowska et al. 2017, pp. 32–38), the process of interpreting legal provisions can be divided into two main stages: the reconstructive phase and the perceptual phase.

The reconstructive phase comes down to recreating a norm-like expression, i.e. a bare structure of a legal norm, based on all legal provisions that are relevant to interpreting a specific legal norm (Zieliński 2012, pp. 253–254, 289, and 325–329). In this phase, one can distinguish two tasks: (1) determining a framework provision and searching appropriate supplementary provisions as well as (2) finding possible modificatory provisions and allowing for their impact on the content of a decoded normative utterance.

In turn, the perceptual phase leads to obtaining a legal norm from a norm-like expression, which is usually preceded by a number of clarificatory procedures that require the application of three sets of interpretative directives: (1) the linguistic rules, ordering to understand legal provisions in accordance with semantic and syntactical rules of a particular ethnic language, subject to priority of a specific meaning given to a certain expression in legal or juristic language; (2) the systemic rules, aimed at preserving coherence of the legal system; and (3) the functional rules, referring to the values or purposes attributed to the lawmaker (Zieliński 2012, pp. 235–244, 253–254, 289–293, 299–302, and 330–344; on the distinction of three kinds of interpretative directives, see Wróblewski 1959; for the proposals to remodel the derivational conception in respect of the functional interpretation, see Zajęcki 2008; Bogucki 2010, 2016a, b).

It must, however, be noted that distinguishing the reconstructive and the perceptual phase does not mean that the interpretation process is to be conducted in a linear manner. One deals here, necessarily, with the interweaving of interpretative tasks carried out within the mentioned phases, and the reconstruction is always accompanied by clarification to a greater or lesser extent (Zieliński 2012, pp. 253–254). It should be emphasised that even determining a singular or plural character of a legal provision or classifying it as a framework (central), supplementary or modificatory provision requires at least an introductory linguistic interpretation, and sometimes extra-linguistic rules are to be activated as well (Leszczyński 2002, pp. 119 and 245; Hermann 2016). Thus, in my opinion, it is the hermeneutic circle (spiral) rather than a sequential algorithm that seems to depict the process of interpretation in the most appropriate way.

3 *Ratio Legis* and the Functional Rules of Legal Interpretation

Ratio legis, conceived of as the lawmaker's purpose of establishing a specific regulation, i.e. a legal provision, a set of provisions or an entire normative act, can be understood instrumentally—as the certain configuration of social relations that should be achieved through such a regulation—or axiologically—as the value that a given regulation serves to protect or actualise (Bogucki 2010, 2016a, pp. 61–63; Zieliński 2012, pp. 305–306; Smolak 2014, pp. 10–11; in the field of transitional justice, see Krotoszyński 2017, pp. 204–301).

Although, from a philosophical perspective, one certainly deals with two fundamentally different categories, they are difficult to distinguish apart in the practice of interpretation. Let us note, for example, that a legal regulation setting a low rent for social housing can be treated either as a means of creating a state of affairs in which no person is deprived of a dwelling place or as a means of realising the value that consists in providing decent living conditions for everyone. It must be acknowledged that the identification of the lawmaker's purpose with the values it accepts is a consequence of adopting the assumption of its axiological rationality, according to which the legislator seeks solely to achieve objectives that it perceives as valuable (on the assumption of the lawmaker's axiological rationality, see Zieliński 2012, pp. 304–307; Potrzeszcz 2016).

The adoption of the presented concept of *ratio legis* makes it necessary to consider the relation of the purposive rules of interpretation to those that are functional. According to the traditional standpoint, the former constitute a subset of the latter (Gizbert-Studnicki 1985–1986, pp. 52–53; Smolak 2012, pp. 45–47 and 49; Zieliński 2012, pp. 237 and 305–306; cf. Leszczyński 2002, pp. 132–139). Such an approach seems to be fully justified since the teleological directives only refer to a concretised goal of enacting a given regulation, whereas the functional directives also allow for general objectives attributed to the legal system as a whole, irrespective of particular regulations contained therein, e.g. protection of human dignity, equitable arrangement of social relations, legal security for individuals or peaceful coexistence of people.

The purposive rules may affect the result of an interpretation in each of the distinguished phases. This is so because, as mentioned previously, the distinction between the reconstructive phase and the perceptual one does not mean that the process of interpretation runs linearly.

4 Employment of *Ratio Legis* in the Reconstructive Phase of Interpretation

In the reconstructive phase, aimed—let us recall—at recreating a norm-like expression from a legal text, *ratio legis* can influence the resolution of issues related to the condensation and the fragmentation of norms in provisions, including the settlement of various cases for the competition of legal regulations.

The considerations should begin with the analysis of the possible involvement of purposive rules in determining a singular or plural character of a legal provision and classifying it as a framework (central), supplementary or modificatory provision.

Let us commence with the issue of the fragmentation of norms in provisions. Establishing the function of a legal provision does not cause difficulties in most typical situations, for even an introductory linguistic interpretation often seems to be sufficient to that end. If the former provision defines entities covered by a normative act and the latter indicates obligations assigned to them, it will be easily recognised that one deals—respectively—with a supplementary and a framework (central) provision. Yet there are cases where a solution to this problem is much more complex, thus sometimes requiring an interpreter to ascertain the purpose of a given regulation.

To find out about this, we should consider an example. Let us suppose that the public property law provides that an immovable property of the State Treasury or the local government may be transferred to private entities only by way of a tender, with one of its provisions stipulating that a tender procedure is to be preceded by a public announcement of a list of the properties that are to be sold. The regulation does not, however, specify which consequences are entailed by omitting the notice.

The classification of the indicated provision is related to an intricate issue referring to defects of conventional acts (Wronkowska 2001; Hermann 2013b; Wronkowska and Hermann 2015, pp. 200–217 and 221–238; generally, for conventional acts, see Nowak et al. 1972; Gizbert-Studnicki 1975; Czepita 1996, 2006, 2008, 2016; Patryas 2001, pp. 130–146). It should be noted that such defects may have various consequences. Considerably simplifying the discussed problem, failure to comply with some requirements for a conventional act results in its nullity (non-existence), while a violation of others results in its being treated as valid (existing) but illicit.

In the former case, if a legal provision defines an additional requirement for a conventional act, it serves to co-determine the content of a competence norm, understood as a norm of conduct that sets forth obligations for addressees on the condition that the conventional act is performed by an empowered entity (Ziembiński 1969a, 1991; Zieliński 1997; Patryas 2005, pp. 87–89). The mentioned provision is thus a modificatory one that limits the sphere of application of the legal norm; since non-compliance with the requirement provided by such a provision entails nullity of the conventional act, carrying it out cannot then lead to the creation of the obligation envisaged by the norm. In the latter case, a legal provision turns out to be a framework (central) provision, for it expresses—separate from the competence norm—a legal norm forbidding an empowered entity from performing a conventional act if a prescribed requirement is ignored. The conventional act remains valid, yet breaching the ban usually involves the possibility of its nullification or of legal responsibility of its perpetrator.

Returning to interpreting the provision of the public property law, let us note that to classify it appropriately, one must determine whether forbearing a public announcement of a list of the properties that are to be sold results in nullity of the tender or merely makes it disallowed. Since this circumstance has not been clarified by the legislator, it is necessary to refer to the *ratio legis* of the regulation.

In this context, it must be emphasised that if transferring an immovable property to private entities can only take place through a tender, being a conventional act, the objective of the analysed regulation must be to ensure that this property could be purchased on equal terms by everyone concerned, which would, in turn, make it possible to obtain the best price, and thus protecting the public interest. This objective is unlikely to be reached if the public administration does not announce its intention to sell through a publicly available notice and limits itself to informing only selected subjects. In this case, the legislator's purpose is to maintain transparency in the disposition of public assets and to protect it from unjustified depletion, which clearly indicates that the tender without the required announcement would be in practice fictional and, consequently, should be considered invalid. Therefore, the interpreted legal provision is to be classified as a provision that modifies the content of a competence norm empowering a tender to be carried out, by restricting the sphere of application of this norm.

Proceeding to the issue of the condensation of norms in provisions, let us note that recognising a character of a legal provision does not cause difficulties in typical situations, for even an introductory linguistic interpretation often seems to be sufficient to that end. If one provision indicates a specific obligation and other provisions determine various entities on which such an obligation is imposed, the first turns out to be a plural framework provision, which serves to recreate many norms that envisage the same duty for different addressees. It may, however, happen that the solution to the problem is much more complex, thus sometimes requiring an interpreter to ascertain the purpose of a given regulation.

To find out about this, we should consider an example. Let us suppose that the agricultural law provides that farmers receiving increased subsidies to farming should annually carry out certain agrotechnical treatments on their lands within a specified period, for instance from 1 July to 31 August. Yet the provisions do not indicate whether the failure to fulfil such a duty within the required span implies its final infringement or, despite exceeding the set deadline, the farmer remains bound to conduct the mentioned treatments.

The resolution of the indicated problem is related to the very interesting issue of delay in performing an obligation, which has been largely ignored in legal theory. Let us note that if a subject does not comply with a duty within the span prescribed by a legal norm, such a norm has been violated, and, consequently, no subsequent behaviour of the subject can change this state of affairs. At times, however, despite the failure to meet an obligation within due time, it is maintained that such a duty is still to be fulfilled, yet the obliged entity is in delay with its execution. It is relatively easy to demonstrate that the presented approach is merely a useful mental shortcut. In fact, we deal here with a new obligation imposed by a legal norm, separate from the norm determining the original duty, provided that from a practical point of view both these obligations are undoubtedly treated as a functional whole since their implementation leads to the same substantive outcome. There are two significant arguments for this:

1. Taking the stance that the addressee of a legal norm that has already infringed a duty envisaged by the norm may still comply with the obligation is unacceptable as it leads to a manifest contradiction; furthermore, the original and the new duties are to be performed at different times, which excludes their formal identification.
2. It happens that the lawmaker orders in two separate provisions that a given obligation is to be fulfilled by a certain time and—in a situation where the term is exceeded by an obliged entity—to implement it immediately in the period of delay (as is the case in the area of civil law and tax law); it is worth pointing out

that sometimes, even without expressly establishing the latter of these prescriptions, the norm that determines it is reconstructed from the legal provision containing the norm imposing the original obligation if this is supported by appropriate teleological arguments (for example, if only one provision of the election ordinance regulates the calling of parliamentary elections, indicating that the president performs it no later than 6 months prior to the end of the term of the current parliament, it would be unacceptable to assume that if the set date has been ignored, the president is no longer bound to issue a proper decree, for it could mean that the elections would not take place at all).

Returning to interpreting the provision of the agricultural law, let us note that to determine its singular or plural character, one must settle whether the farmer remains bound to carry out the required agrotechnical treatments in the case of exceeding the appointed term. Since this circumstance has not been clarified by the legislator, it is necessary to resort to the *ratio legis* of the regulation.

In this context, it should be emphasised that establishing the period of performing the agrotechnical treatments has not been an accidental solution. Its determination by the legislator, who has acted based on scientific knowledge, is aimed at enabling soil regeneration and, in general, at protecting the natural environment, with the increased subsidies being a means of compensating farmers for their additional efforts and expenditures. In this case, the lawmaker's purpose is to maintain the standards of good agricultural practice, which clearly indicates that the treatments under consideration must be carried out precisely within the time frame set by the legal regulation and the failure to comply with the deadline implies a final infringement of the obligation, without the possibility or—even more so—the duty of its later realisation. Therefore, the interpreted legal provision is to be considered as being singular which—apart from the legal norm ordering the agrotechnical treatments to be conducted within a specified period—does not additionally express a legal norm which would require such actions after the appointed term has been exceeded.

There is also the competition of legal provisions, understood as a specific category of the interpretative problem, which must be settled in the reconstructive phase. The concurrence of legal regulations, as I assume, occurs when two or more central provisions remain in such a relation that considering them as expressing legal norms independently of each other could, at least potentially, seem contrary to the assumption of the lawmaker's rationality, especially from the point of view of *ratio legis* ascribed to the mentioned regulations (Hermann 2016; see also Ziemski 1978; Ziembiński 1979). Based on the cause of the competition, one can distinguish three types:

1. a non-collision concurrence, where competing central provisions determine identical legal consequences of the same facts or even different legal consequences of the same facts if they serve a similar purpose, and the question is whether this multitude (excess) of legal effects attached to given events—equal to the content or at least to the function—is intended by the legislator;
2. a collision concurrence, where competing central regulations express the norms of conduct that are inconsistent with each other in a formal sense, which occurs in

two cases: if one norm commands specific behaviour, while another norm prohibits it—the contradiction of norms—or if two or more norms command or prohibit various actions that can be jointly neither undertaken nor abandoned—the opposition of norms (Ziembiński 1969b, pp. 88–92; Piotrowski 1978, pp. 98–100);
3. a *quasi*-collision concurrence, where competing central provisions contain norms of conduct inconsistent with each other in a praxeological sense, which takes place if fulfilling one norm undoes a state of affairs caused by implementing another norm (Ziembiński 1969b, pp. 92–94; Piotrowski 1978, pp. 100–102), a special case of which is the co-called Sisyphean orders (von Wright 1963, pp. 145–147).

If the legislator has not directly resolved a given concurrence of legal provisions, its settlement is the task of an interpreter. This task consists in referring to *ratio legis* of competing regulations in order to establish (1) whether such regulations are to be applied independently of each other (an ideal concurrence) or (2) whether they should be combined in some way, in particular, conjunctionally or alternatively (a real concurrence), which would entail a mutual modification of both central provisions, or (3) whether one of them partly or entirely excludes the application of the other (an apparent concurrence), which would, in turn, mean that one of the central provisions is also a provision modifying the latter one—with the proviso that, depending on the type of the competition, the choice is sometimes limited to two variants or there remains only one possibility. A detailed discussion of this eminently interesting issue would, however, go far beyond the scope of my analysis (see Hermann 2016) (Fig. 1).

5 Employment of *Ratio Legis* in the Perceptual Phase of Interpretation

The way of using *ratio legis* in the perceptual phase, aimed—let us recall—at obtaining a fully developed and completely unequivocal legal norm from a reconstructed norm-like expression, depends primarily on one circumstance, namely whether an interpreted regulation is clear or, to the contrary, its wording raises some doubts that cannot be resolved according to the linguistic rules. One should consider both situations separately.

The first situation, where a legal provision turns out to be ambiguous, seems to be less complex. Since the wording of a legal regulation allows different ways of its understanding, the task of an interpreter is only to select one of the existing variants of the linguistic interpretation (Gizbert-Studnicki 1985–1986, pp. 60–63; Gizbert-Studnicki 2014, p. 131; Zieliński 2012, pp. 336–338 and 340–343). This choice, however, cannot be perceived as discretionary. According to the teleological rules, one is obliged to opt for a solution that enables an ascertained purpose of a specific regulation to be achieved to the highest degree.

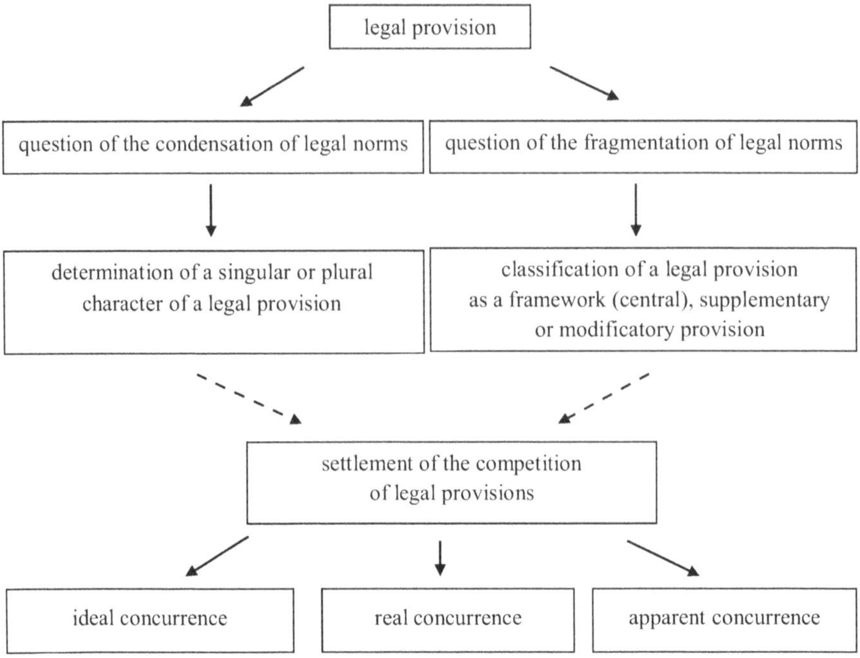

Fig. 1 Possible impact of *ratio legis* on the result of an interpretation in the reconstructive phase

To elucidate the matter, let us present an example. Supposing a legal provision of the wildlife law prohibits, under criminal penalty, individuals from keeping or raising greyhounds without proper consent of the public administration, there arises a doubt as to the number of dogs of this breed that one must own to breach the mentioned regulation. Since that circumstance has not been specified by the law-maker, two options of interpretation allowed by the linguistic rules should be particularly considered: is it sufficient to have one dog, or it is necessary to have at least two for the law to apply? When settling the controversy, it is indispensable to resort to the purpose of establishing the interpreted provision, which consists in limiting the scale of poaching and thus protecting the welfare of forest animals. Given that owning a single greyhound is enough to course effectively and its hiding justifies a suspicion of the involvement in illegal hunting, it seems reasonable to opt for a solution that having even one dog of this breed, without required permission, is illicit.

The second situation where a legal provision turns out to be unambiguous seems to be simple but is, in fact, much more complex than the other. In the mentioned case, a reference to *ratio legis* can confirm the result of an interpretation obtained according to the linguistic rules or, exceptionally, lead to a modification of this result (Gizbert-Studnicki 1985–1986, pp. 60 and 63; Gizbert-Studnicki 2014, pp. 131–136; Zieliński 2012, pp. 238–243 and 343–344). To explain the issue, one must distinguish three variants of the relation between a norm interpreted from a clear regulation and the purpose of its enactment by the law-making body:

1. The norm is entirely compatible with the purpose—in these circumstances, *ratio legis*, ascertained by an interpreter, serves for nothing else but to affirm the result of a linguistic interpretation.
2. The norm is slightly incompatible with the purpose—in this situation, the reference to teleological arguments does not support the result of a linguistic interpretation, but it may not, however, justify departing from the clear meaning of a legal provision either; adopting the assumption of the lawmaker's linguistic rationality makes it impossible to change unambiguously expressed content of legal norms due to a small discrepancy with the established legislative intent (such a solution corresponds with the need to protect the value of legal security).
3. The norm is extremely incompatible with the purpose—in the considered case, it seems permissible to correct the result of a linguistic interpretation, for a conspicuous discrepancy with *ratio legis* must be seen as a sufficient reason for modifying even an unequivocal meaning of a legal provision; under this unique condition, the assumption of the lawmaker's axiological rationality is to prevail over the assumption of its linguistic rationality since it would be unacceptable to approve of a solution plainly contrary to the legislative intent.

If it is necessary to adjust the normative content contained in a clear legal provision to the requirements implied by *ratio legis*, the application of teleological rules may result in the rejection of the literal meaning of such a provision (*interpretatio declarativa*) and, consequently, lead instead to the acceptance of either its extensive understanding (*interpretatio extensiva*) or its restrictive understanding (*interpretatio restrictiva*) (Zieliński 2012, pp. 238–243 and 343–344; Płeszka 2010).

The first mentioned variant of modification consists in extending the sphere of application or the sphere of realisation of an interpreted legal norm so that the regulation also covers those cases that are indispensable if the values or objectives attributed to the legislator are to be fulfilled; otherwise, the lawmaker's intent, at least in part, would be totally ignored. Let us suppose, for example, that the labour law orders an employer to give a day off to an employee who is a parent of a minor child in the event of their illness. Since the purpose of this provision is to provide necessary care for a sick child, one must consider extending the sphere of application of the legal norm expressed in the indicated regulation to include also situations such as where the ill child is an orphan reared by grandparents or other relatives. It seems preposterous to accept that children could remain unaccompanied in these cases, which means that the grandparents or other relatives should be entitled to exercise the same right.

In turn, the second distinguished variant of modification consists in narrowing the sphere of application or the sphere of realisation of an interpreted legal norm to exclude from the scope of the regulation any situations the inclusion of which would be clearly contrary to the values or objectives attributed to the legislator; otherwise—again—the aim of enacting such a regulation would be utterly undermined, at least in part. This time, let us suppose, for instance, that family law states that in the event of an adoption, the parental authority of natural parents expires. Bearing in mind that the purpose of the considered institution is to provide a child—after the death of biological parents or in the case where they cannot or do not want to rear their offspring—with proper care, it is necessary to exclude from the sphere of application of the recreated legal norm situations where the adoption of a child is made by a new spouse of their mother or father. Undoubtedly, in such cases, it would be completely incomprehensible to deprive a natural parent of parental authority.

Reference to *ratio legis* can also justify a decision for the use of statutory analogy (*analogia legis*). The considered measure can be undertaken when two legal provisions regulate substantially similar matters, with only one of them attaching certain legal consequences to the situations indicated by it. In such a case, if there are strong axiological arguments, including those referring to an identical or at least very close purpose of both regulations, these consequences may also be linked to the situations specified by the second provision (on various approaches to *analogia legis* and attempts to distinguish it from *analogia iuris* as one of the methods of legal inference, see Nowacki 1966; Ziembiński 1980, pp. 294–295 and 302–304; Leszczyński 2002, pp. 249–255; Walasik 2013; Ribeiro 2014).

To illustrate the issue of the interpretation *per analogiam*, let us consider a situation where, according to the public procurement law, a public contract is invalid under conditions defined in two provisions. The first details several serious infringements of the contract award procedure, while the other is limited to indicating a general premise concerning minor procedural misconduct if it may affect the selection of the contractor. Recognising that such a solution results in instability of contracts for public procurement since invalidity—at least formally—can be declared without time restrictions, the lawmaker decides to amend the regulation. Departing from the sanction of nullity, it instead empowers interested parties to petition the court for the annulment of such a contract, with a newly established provision specifying that the mentioned competence expires 4 years after the date on which a contract was concluded. However, the provision only refers to the regulation detailing the serious infringements of the procedure, thus omitting the regulation indicating the general premise concerning minor procedural misconduct. The literal interpretation would lead to the conclusion that in the latter situation, the possibility of demanding the annulment of contracts remains, in spite of everything, temporally unlimited. The teleological inconsistency of the lawmaker may be then removed, solely by adopting an analogous interpretation of the newly established provision, as a consequence of which, also in the case of minor procedural misconduct, interested parties could petition for an annulment only for a period of 4 years.

After all, it is not possible to exclude other forms of modification of the normative content expressed in an unambiguous legal provision if it is justified for the sake of *ratio legis*. In particular, it may consist in replacing one of the expressions contained in a given regulation with another one. Such an operation should be allowed only exceptionally. Thus, its application is limited to a situation where for various reasons it can be recognised that the legislative body has mistakenly used a given expression, as clearly indicated by axiological arguments, including those that are teleological.

In this context, let us take under consideration a legal provision that sets a requirement according to which—after each successive modification of a normative act—its consolidated text should be published within 2 weeks of the entry into force of

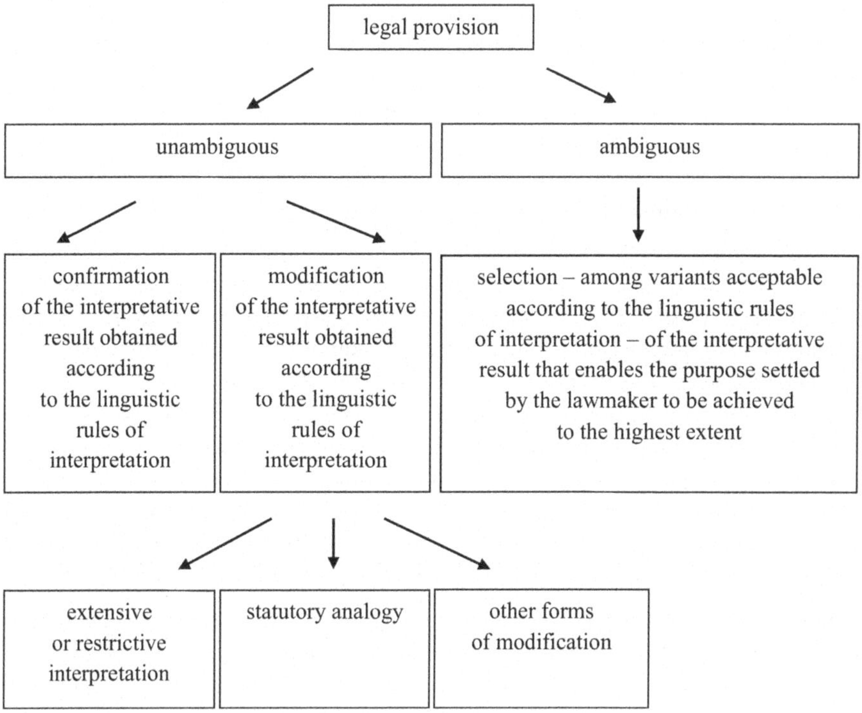

Fig. 2 Possible impact of *ratio legis* on the result of an interpretation in the perceptual phase

an act being amended. Indisputably, the purpose of such a solution is to provide all concerned with information about the current wording of the regulation. The literal interpretation of the legal provision leads, however, to absurdity. Regardless of the date on which amendments were introduced, a consolidated text is to be promulgated within 2 weeks of the entry into force of an act being changed, which—excepting a rather special situation where a given regulation is modified directly after its enactment—is simply infeasible. The only way to preserve the sense of the interpreted provision is obviously to accept that, in fact, the 2-week period should be counted not from the entry into force of an act being amended (Polish: 'akt nowelizowany') but from the entry into force of an amending act (Polish: 'akt nowelizujący') (Fig. 2).

6 *Ratio Legis* and the Systemic Rules of Legal Interpretation

A separate issue to be resolved relates to the importance of *ratio legis* in comparison to the requirements implied by the systemic rules of interpretation, which prescribe an interpreter to reject the result of an interpretation that is incompatible either with norms of the same legal force that perform a function of legal principles—a horizontal aspect—or with norms of higher legal force—a vertical aspect (Zieliński 2012, pp. 235–239, 244, and 338–340).

The application of systemic rules is limited to the case where a legal regulation turns out to be unclear, for these directives do not allow one to correct an unambiguous result of a linguistic interpretation. If a legal norm recreated from a legal provision, the wording of which is indisputable, collides

1. with a norm of a higher legal force, it should be recognised that one deals with an unconstitutional law, the removal of which—at least in continental legal systems—is not the task of an interpreter but the task of a constitutional court or another body performing a similar function, authorised to invalidate a defective legal regulation (Zieliński 2012, pp. 244, 299–300, and 338–339), with the proviso of the possibility of eliminating a hierarchical incompatibility—if it is a matter of the formal inconsistency—by means of a rule of collision, *lex superior derogat legi inferiori* (Wronkowska and Hermann 2015, pp. 211–217);
2. with a norm of the same legal force that is a legal principle, it must be assumed that one deals here with an exception to a generally adopted standard that has been intended by the lawmaker (Zieliński 2012, pp. 301–302 and 339–340).

Consequently, the issue of the competition between the systemic and the purposive rules arises only when an interpreted legal regulation is linguistically vague. The answer to the question of the primacy of one of these types of interpretative directives is still complex. Let us try to discuss this problem separately for the systemic rules in the vertical and in the horizontal aspect. In both cases, however, it should be emphasised that the directives of interpretation in question are aimed only at preserving the coherence of the legal system. Thus, their impact is solely negative since it is limited to rejecting—out of possible results of the linguistic interpretation—the results that violate the coherence. Their application, therefore, is not intended to ensure the selection of the understanding of a legal provision that meets requirements set by norms of higher legal force or standards envisaged by coequal legal principles to the maximum degree.

When analysing the functioning of the systemic rules in the vertical aspect, let us assume that a legal provision can be interpreted in several ways according to the linguistic rules, whereby—depending on the choice made—a legal norm expressed therein (1) infringes the requirements set forth by higher-ranking regulations, (2) satisfies the mentioned requirements or (3) implements them to a greater extent than prescribed.

Regardless of the *ratio legis* of the considered provision, established by an interpreter, the first option should be rejected (Czarny 2005, pp. 81–82; Gizbert-Studnicki 2014, p. 123; Hermann 2015, pp. 21–23; for a contrary view, see Tuleja 2003, pp. 214–215). Even if the arguments referring to the purpose attributed to the legislative body would justify its acceptance, the systemic rules in the vertical aspect have absolute priority. The requirement to preserve the hierarchical coherence of the legal system, i.e. compatibility of lower-ranking acts with higher-ranking ones, particularly with the constitution, is unquestionable. Recreating an unconstitutional legal norm from a legal text is, in fact, the last resort, which takes place only if the wording of an interpreted legal provision does not allow its different understanding.

Regarding the choice between the two other interpretative variants, it should be underlined that the systemic rules in the vertical aspect do not in this case play any role since both solutions are in conformity with higher-ranking regulations (Hermann 2015, pp. 24 and 28; cf. Tuleja 2003, pp. 330–331; Bator and Kozak 2005; Czarny 2005, pp. 82–85). The decision to adopt one of them depends, therefore, only on the *ratio legis* of the interpreted provision. Unless the purpose of its enactment is to provide a better level of protection for certain values than the one guaranteed by norms of a higher legal force, the second option should be selected. If, however, the lawmaker intends to increase the indicated level, it would be justified to accept the third one.

When analysing the functioning of the systemic rules in the horizontal aspect, let us assume again that a legal provision can be interpreted in several ways according to the linguistic rules, whereby—depending on the choice made—a legal norm expressed therein (1) introduces a departure from a standard set forth by a coequal legal principle, (2) indicates a solution satisfying the mentioned standard or (3) stipulates a solution that surpasses it.

Irrespective of the *ratio legis* of the considered provision, ascertained by an interpreter, the first option should be rejected. Even if the arguments referring to the purpose attributed to the legislative body would justify its acceptance, I believe that priority should be given to the systemic rules in the horizontal aspect. Compatibility of legal norms with a coequal legal principle is, in fact, not as significant as in the case of hierarchical relations, for it is admissible to regulate a given matter in a way that differs from a standard envisaged by a norm that is a legal principle; however, if the lawmaker intends to introduce such an exception, its design should be articulated unambiguously.

As for the choice between the two remaining interpretative variants, it should be noted that the systemic rules in the horizontal aspect are no longer relevant since both solutions are compatible with a standard established by a legal principle. Therefore, the decision to accept one of them depends solely on the *ratio legis* of the interpreted provision, namely whether its enactment is aimed at preserving the mentioned standard or implementing it to a higher degree.

References

Bator A, Kozak A (2005) Wykładnia prawa w zgodzie z Konstytucją [Interpretation of law in conformity with the constitution]. In: Wronkowska S (ed) Polska kultura prawna a proces integracji europejskiej [Polish legal culture and the process of the European integration]. Zakamycze, Kraków, pp 43–66

Bielska-Brodziak A (2010) O rodzajach argumentów interpretacyjnych [On the kinds of interpretative arguments]. In: Staśkiewicz W, Stawecki T (eds) Dyskrecjonalność w prawie. Materiały XVIII Ogólnopolskiego Zjazdu Katedr Teorii i Filozofii Prawa. Miedzeszyn k. Warszawy, 22–24 września 2008 r. [Discretionality in law. Materials of the XVIII Polish Nationwide

Convention of Chairs of the Theory and Philosophy of Law. Miedzeszyn near Warsaw, September 22–24, 2008]. LexisNexis, Warszawa, pp 326–335
Bogucki O (2010) Odtwarzanie celów i innych wartości z tekstu prawnego [Reconstruction of purposes and other values from the legal text]. In: Choduń A, Czepita S (eds) W poszukiwaniu dobra wspólnego. Księga jubileuszowa Profesora Macieja Zielińskiego [In search of the common good. Jubilee Book of Professor Maciej Zieliński]. Wydawnictwo Naukowe Uniwersytetu Szczecińskiego, Szczecin, pp 195–213
Bogucki O (2011) Wykładnia funkcjonalna w działalności najwyższych organów władzy sądowniczej [Functional interpretation in the practice of the highest judicial authorities]. Wydział Prawa i Administracji Uniwersytetu Szczecińskiego, Szczecin
Bogucki O (2016a) Model wykładni funkcjonalnej w derywacyjnej koncepcji wykładni [Model of the functional interpretation in the derivational conception of interpretation]. Polgres Multimedia, Szczecin
Bogucki O (2016b) Perspektywy rozwinięcia normatywnego ujęcia wykładni funkcjonalnej [Prospects for developing a normative approach to the functional interpretation]. In: Hermann M, Sykuna S (eds) Wykładnia prawa. Tradycja i perspektywy [Legal interpretation. Tradition and prospects]. Wydawnictwo C.H. Beck, Warszawa, pp 205–219
Czarny P (2005) Trybunał Konstytucyjny a wykładnia ustaw w zgodzie z Konstytucją [The Constitutional Tribunal and interpretation of statutes in conformity with the constitution]. In: Wronkowska S (ed) Polska kultura prawna a proces integracji europejskiej [Polish legal culture and the process of the European integration]. Zakamycze, Kraków, pp 67–91
Czepita S (1996) Reguły konstytutywne a zagadnienia prawoznawstwa [Constitutive rules and the issues of jurisprudence]. Wydawnictwo Naukowe Uniwersytetu Szczecińskiego, Szczecin
Czepita S (2006) Formalizacja a konwencjonalizacja działań w prawie [Formalisation and conventionalisation of activities in law]. In: Czepita S (ed) Konwencjonalne i formalne aspekty prawa [Conventional and formal aspects of law]. Wydawnictwo Naukowe Uniwersytetu Szczecińskiego, Szczecin, pp 9–28
Czepita S (2008) Formalizacja i konwencjonalizacja w systemie prawnym [Formalisation and conventionalisation in the legal system]. In: Bogucki O, Czepita S (eds) System prawny a porządek prawny [Legal system and legal order]. Wydawnictwo Naukowe Uniwersytetu Szczecińskiego, Szczecin, pp 109–116
Czepita S (2016) O koncepcji czynności konwencjonalnych w prawie [On the conception of conventional acts in law]. In: Smolak M (ed) Wykładnia konstytucji. Aktualne problemy i tendencje [Interpretation of constitution. Current problems and trends]. Wolters Kluwer, Warszawa, pp 109–147
Gizbert-Studnicki T (1975) O nieważnych czynnościach prawnych w świetle koncepcji czynności konwencjonalnych [On invalid legal acts in the light of the conception of conventional acts]. Państwo i Prawo [State Law] 4:70–82
Gizbert-Studnicki T (1985–1986) Wykładnia celowościowa [Purposive interpretation]. Studia Prawnicze [Legal Stud] 3–4:51–70
Gizbert-Studnicki T (2014) Wykładnia celowościowa z perspektywy normatywnej [Purposive interpretation from the normative perspective]. In: Budziło K (ed) Wykłady w Trybunale Konstytucyjnym z lat 2011–2012 [Lectures in the Constitutional Tribunal from the years 2011–2012]. Biuro Trybunału Konstytucyjnego, Warszawa, pp 111–138
Hermann M (2012) Derogacja w analizach teoretycznoprawnych [Derogation in theoretical analyses]. Ars boni et aequi, Poznań
Hermann M (2013a) Norma prawna: wyrażenie czy wypowiedź? [Legal norm: an expression or an utterance?]. Przegląd Sejmowy [Sejm Rev] 2:67–85
Hermann M (2013b) Stwierdzenie niekonstytucyjności jako czynność konwencjonalna unieważnienia aktu normatywnego [Declaration of unconstitutionality as the conventional act of annulling a normative act]. In: Bernatt M, Królikowski J, Ziółkowski M (eds) Skutki wyroków Trybunału Konstytucyjnego w sferze stosowania prawa [Effects of rulings of the Constitutional Tribunal for the application of law]. Biuro Trybunału Konstytucyjnego, Warszawa, pp 249–277

Hermann M (2015) Wyroki interpretacyjne Trybunału Konstytucyjnego z perspektywy teoretycznoprawnej. Instrument ochrony ładu konstytucyjnego czy środek zapewniania jednolitości orzecznictwa? [Interpretative rulings of the Constitutional Tribunal from the theoretical perspective. An instrument for the protection of constitutional order or a means of ensuring the uniformity of case law?]. Biuro Trybunału Konstytucyjnego, Warszawa

Hermann M (2016) Zbieg przepisów prawnych jako problem interpretacyjny [Concurrence of legal provisions as an interpretative problem]. In: Hermann M, Sykuna S (eds) Wykładnia prawa. Tradycja i perspektywy [Legal interpretation. Tradition and prospects]. Wydawnictwo C.H. Beck, Warszawa, pp 167–204

Kanarek B, Zieliński M (2001) Porządkująca faza wykładni prawa [The arranging phase of legal interpretation]. Ruch Prawniczy, Ekonomiczny i Socjologiczny [J Law Econ Sociol] 3:1–12

Krotoszyński M (2017) Modele sprawiedliwości tranzycyjnej [Models of transitional justice]. Wydawnictwo Naukowe UAM, Poznań

Leszczyński L (2002) Zagadnienia teorii stosowania prawa. Doktryna i tezy orzecznictwa [Problems of the theory of the application of law. Doctrine and theses of judicial practice]. Zakamycze, Kraków

Nowacki J (1966) Analogia legis. Państwowe Wydawnictwo Naukowe, Warszawa

Nowak L, Wronkowska S, Zieliński M, Ziembiński Z (1972) Czynności konwencjonalne w prawie [Conventional acts in law]. Studia Prawnicze [Legal Stud] 33:73–99

Patryas W (2001) Rozważania o normach prawnych [Considerations on legal norms]. Wydawnictwo Forum Naukowe, Poznań

Patryas W (2005) Performatywy w prawie [Performatives in law]. Wydawnictwo Forum Naukowe, Poznań

Piotrowski M (1978) O rodzajach i odmianach niezgodności norm [On the kinds and varieties of inconsistency of norms]. Studia Filozoficzne [Philos Stud] 11:93–103

Płeszka K (2010) Wykładnia rozszerzająca [Extensive interpretation]. Wolters Kluwer, Warszawa

Potrzeszcz J (2016) Racjonalność aksjologiczna prawodawcy jako założenie interpretacyjne [The lawmaker's axiological rationality as an interpretative assumption]. In: Hermann M, Sykuna S (eds) Wykładnia prawa. Tradycja i perspektywy [Legal interpretation. Tradition and prospects]. Wydawnictwo C.H. Beck, Warszawa, pp 53–72

Raz J (2009) Between authority and interpretation. On the theory of law and practical reason. Oxford University Press, New York

Ribeiro HJ (ed) (2014) Systematic approaches to argument by analogy. Springer, Amsterdam

Sarkowicz R (1995) Poziomowa interpretacja tekstu prawnego [Tiered interpretation of the legal text]. Uniwersytet Jagielloński, Kraków

Smolak M (2012) Wykładnia celowościowa z perspektywy pragmatycznej [Purposive interpretation from the pragmatic perspective]. Wolters Kluwer, Warszawa

Smolak M (2014) Aksjologiczne założenia stosowania dyrektyw wykładni celowościowej [Axiological assumptions of applying the directives of purposive interpretation]. Ruch Prawniczy, Ekonomiczny i Socjologiczny. J Law Econ Sociol 1:5–12

Tobor Z (2013) W poszukiwaniu intencji prawodawcy [In search of lawmaker's intention]. Wolters Kluwer, Warszawa

Tuleja P (2003) Stosowanie Konstytucji RP w świetle zasady jej nadrzędności (wybrane problemy) [Application of the constitution of the Republic of Poland in the light of the principle of its supremacy (selected issues)]. Zakamycze, Kraków

von Wright GH (1963) Norm and action. A logical enquiry. Routledge & Kegan Paul, London

Walasik M (2013) Analogia w prawie procesowym cywilnym [Analogy in the civil procedure law]. LexisNexis, Warszawa

Wróblewski J (1959) Zagadnienia teorii wykładni prawa ludowego [Problems of the theory of interpretation of the people's law]. Wydawnictwo Prawnicze, Warszawa

Wronkowska S (2001) O wadliwych aktach normatywnych w ujęciu wiedeńskiej szkoły teorii prawa [On defective normative acts from the perspective of the Vienna School of Legal Theory]. In: Stelmach J (ed) Studia z filozofii prawa [Studies in legal philosophy]. Wydawnictwo Uniwersytetu Jagiellońskiego, Kraków, pp 207–218

Wronkowska S, Hermann M (2015) Problematyka intertemporalna prawa konstytucyjnego. Zagadnienia wstępne [Intertemporal problems of the constitutional law. Basic issues]. In: Mikołajewicz J (ed) Problematyka intertemporalna w prawie. Zagadnienia podstawowe. Rozstrzygnięcia intertemporalne. Geneza i funkcje [Intertemporal problems in law. Basic issues. Intertemporal resolutions. Origin and functions]. Wydawnictwo C.H. Beck, Warszawa, pp 195–240

Wronkowska S, Zieliński M (1993) Problemy i zasady redagowania tekstów prawnych [Problems and principles of the technique of editing legal texts]. Urząd Rady Ministrów, Warszawa

Wronkowska S, Hermann M, Łyszkowska A (2017) Wpływ orzeczeń Trybunału Konstytucyjnego na tekst jednolity aktu normatywnego [Influence of rulings of the Constitutional Tribunal on the consolidated text of a normative act]. In: Laskowska M (ed) Znaczenie wyroków Trybunału Konstytucyjnego dla tekstu jednolitego ustawy [Significance of rulings of the Constitutional Tribunal for the consolidated text of a statute]. Wydawnictwo Sejmowe, Warszawa, pp 31–61

Zajęcki M (2008) Algorytm czy idealizacja? Dyrektywy wykładni funkcjonalnej opartej na założeniu o racjonalności aksjologicznej prawodawcy w derywacyjnej koncepcji wykładni [Algorithm or idealisation? The directives of functional interpretation based on the assumption of the lawmaker's axiological rationality in the derivational conception of interpretation]. In: Guzik B, Buchowska N, Wiliński P (eds) Prawo wobec wyzwań współczesności [The law towards contemporary challenges], vol V. Wydawnictwo i Drukarnia UNI-DRUK, Poznań, pp 53–65

Zieliński M (1972) Interpretacja jako proces dekodowania tekstu prawnego [Interpretation as the process of decoding the legal text]. Wydawnictwo Naukowe UAM, Poznań

Zieliński M (1997) Dwa nurty pojmowania "kompetencji" [Two trends of understanding 'competence']. In: Olszewski H, Popowska B (eds) Gospodarka. Administracja. Samorząd [Economy. Administration. Self-government]. Printer, Poznań, pp 581–607

Zieliński M (2006) Derywacyjna koncepcja wykładni jako koncepcja zintegrowana [The derivational conception of interpretation as an integrated conception]. Ruch Prawniczy, Ekonomiczny i Socjologiczny [J Law Econ Sociol] 3:93–102

Zieliński M (2012) Wykładnia prawa. Zasady. Reguły. Wskazówki [Legal interpretation. Principles. Rules. Hints], 6th edn. Wolters Kluwer, Warszawa

Zieliński M, Zirk-Sadowski M (2011) Klaryfikacyjność i derywacyjność w integrowaniu polskich teorii wykładni prawa [The clarifying and the derivational aspects in the integration of Polish theories of legal interpretation]. Ruch Prawniczy, Ekonomiczny i Socjologiczny [J Law Econ Sociol] 2:99–111

Zieliński M, Bogucki O, Choduń A, Czepita S, Kanarek B, Municzewski A (2009) Zintegrowanie polskich koncepcji wykładni prawa [The integration of Polish conceptions of legal interpretation]. Ruch Prawniczy, Ekonomiczny i Socjologiczny [J Law Econ Sociol] 4:23–39

Ziembiński Z (1960) Przepis prawny a norma prawna [Legal provision and legal norm]. Ruch Prawniczy i Ekonomiczny [J Law Econ] 1:105–122

Ziembiński Z (1969a) Kompetencja i norma kompetencyjna [Competence and the competence norm]. Ruch Prawniczy, Ekonomiczny i Socjologiczny [J Law Econ Sociol] 4:23–41

Ziembiński Z (1969b) O rodzajach niezgodności norm [On the kinds of inconsistency of norms]. Studia Filozoficzne [Philos Stud] 1:85–94

Ziembiński Z (1979) Problematyka ogólna zbiegu przepisów prawnych [General problems of the concurrence of legal provisions]. In: Radwański Z (ed) Studia z prawa zobowiązań [Studies in the law of obligations]. Państwowe Wydawnictwo Naukowe, Warszawa, pp 333–346

Ziembiński Z (1980) Problemy podstawowe prawoznawstwa [Basic problems of jurisprudence]. Państwowe Wydawnictwo Naukowe, Warszawa

Ziembiński Z (1991) O zawiłościach związanych z pojmowaniem kompetencji [On the intricacies related to the understanding of competence]. Państwo i Prawo [State Law] 4:14–24

Ziembiński Z, Zieliński M (1992) Dyrektywy i sposób ich wypowiadania [Directives and the method of uttering them]. Zakład Semiotyki Logicznej Uniwersytetu Warszawskiego, Warszawa

Ziemski K (1978) Rola i miejsce reguł kolizyjnych w procesie dekodowania tekstu prawnego [Role and place of the rules of collision in the process of decoding the legal text]. Ruch Prawniczy, Ekonomiczny i Socjologiczny [J Law Econ Sociol] 2:1–15

Mikołaj Hermann is an assistant professor at the Faculty of Law and Administration of Adam Mickiewicz University in Poznań, the Chair of Theory and Philosophy of Law, a law clerk at the Constitutional Tribunal and a lecturer for the legislation course run by the Governmental Legislation Center. His main research areas are legal theory, legislation and constitutional review. The article is the extended version of a speech 'How Can *Ratio Legis* Help a Lawyer to Interpret a Legal Text?' given during the XXVIII World Congress of IVR—Peace Based on Human Rights, 16–21 July 2017, University of Lisbon, Portugal, in the Special Workshop 'Is There a *Ratio Legis* and if So, How Many Are There? – The Most Powerful Method of Legal Reasoning Uncovered'.

The manufacturer's authorised representative in the EU is Springer Nature Customer Service Centre GmbH, Europaplatz 3, 69115 Heidelberg, Germany. If you have any concerns regarding our products, please contact ProductSafety@springernature.com

Printed and bound by CPI Group (UK) Ltd, Croydon, CR0 4YY
05/10/2026
02228141-0001